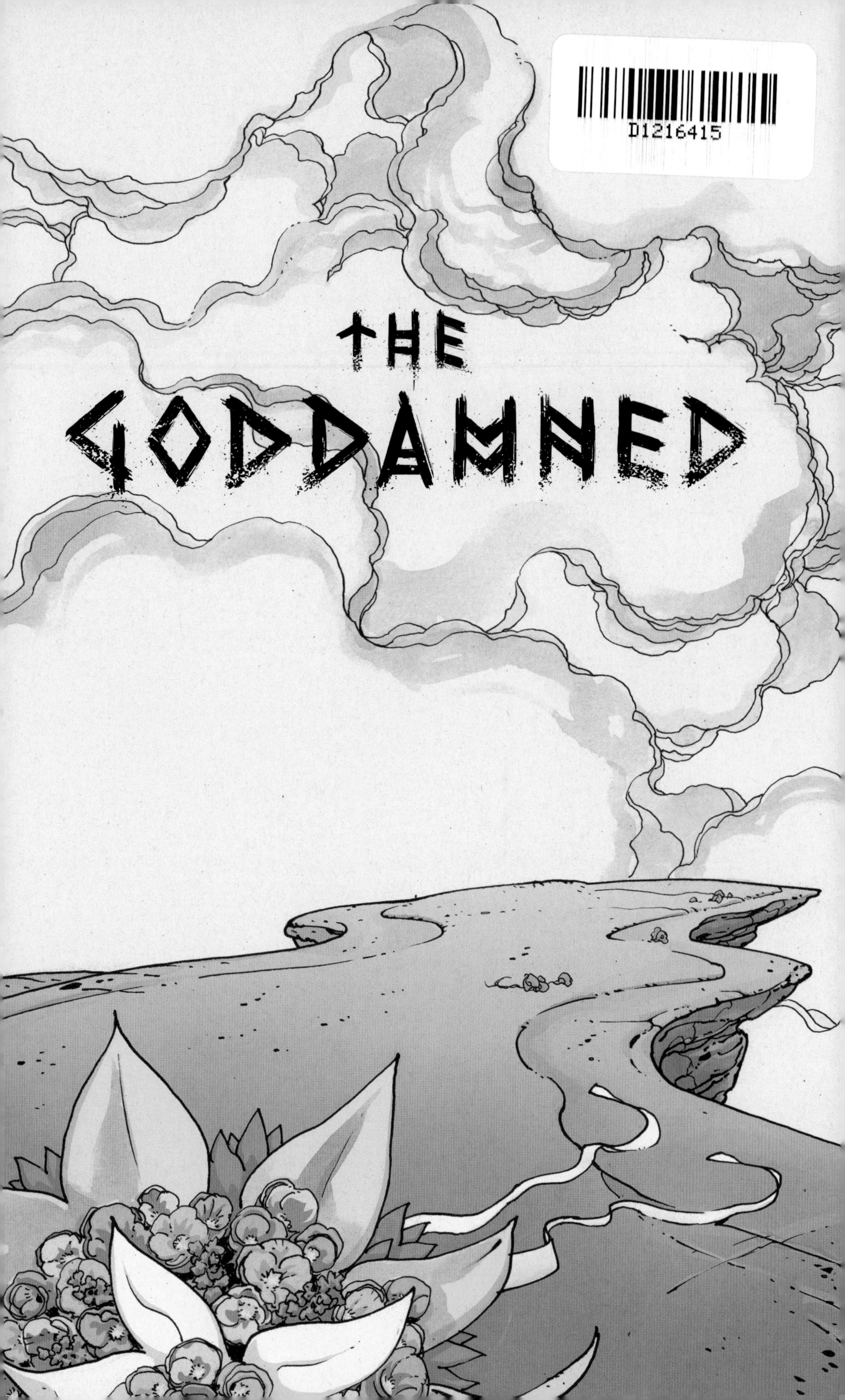
THE
GODDAMNED

THE GODDAMNED, VOL. 2: THE VIRGIN BRIDES. First printing. July 2021. Published by Image Comics Inc. Office of publication: PO BOX 14457, Portland, OR 97293.



ISBN: 978-1-5343-1720-8.

Representation: Law Offices of Harris M. Miller II, P.C. (rights.inquiries@gmail.com).

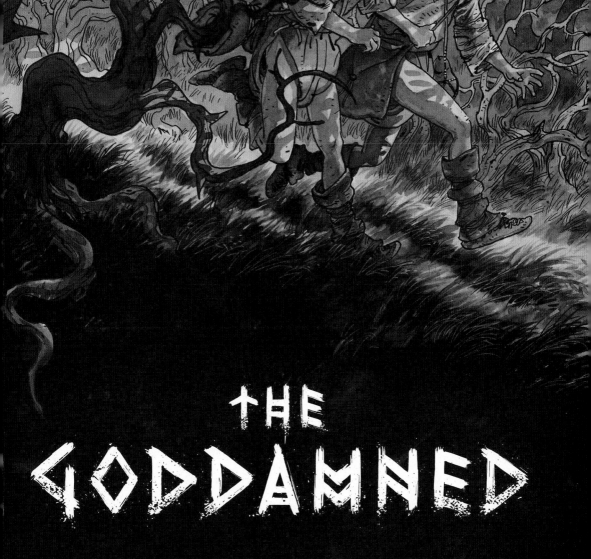

# THE GODDAMNED

## Book Two

## *The Virgin Brides*

*Written by* Jason Aaron
*Art by* r.m. Guéra

*Colors by* Giulia Brusco
*Letters & Design by* Jared K. Fletcher
*Editor* Sebastian Girner

The Goddamned *created by* Aaron & Guéra

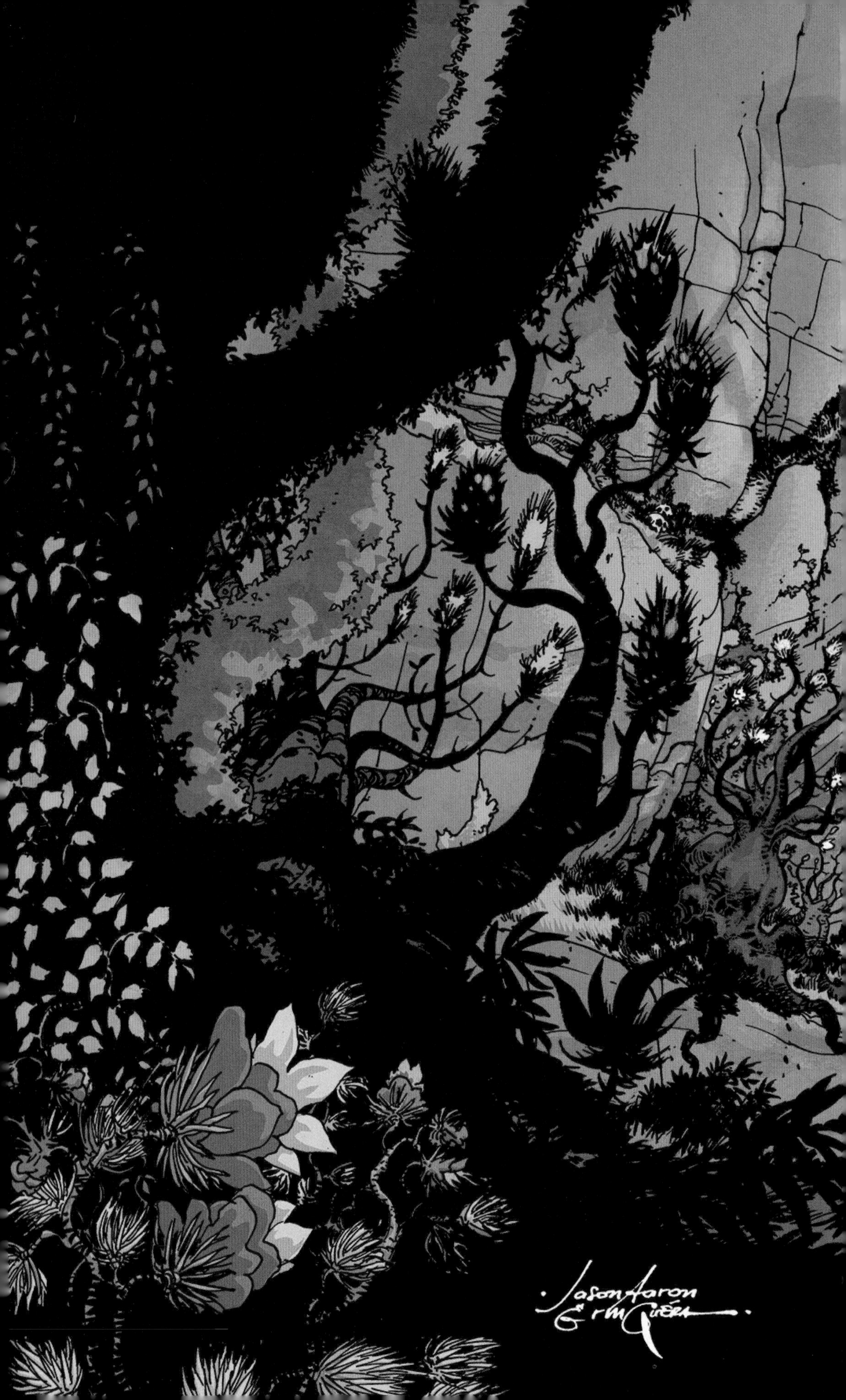
Jason Aaron

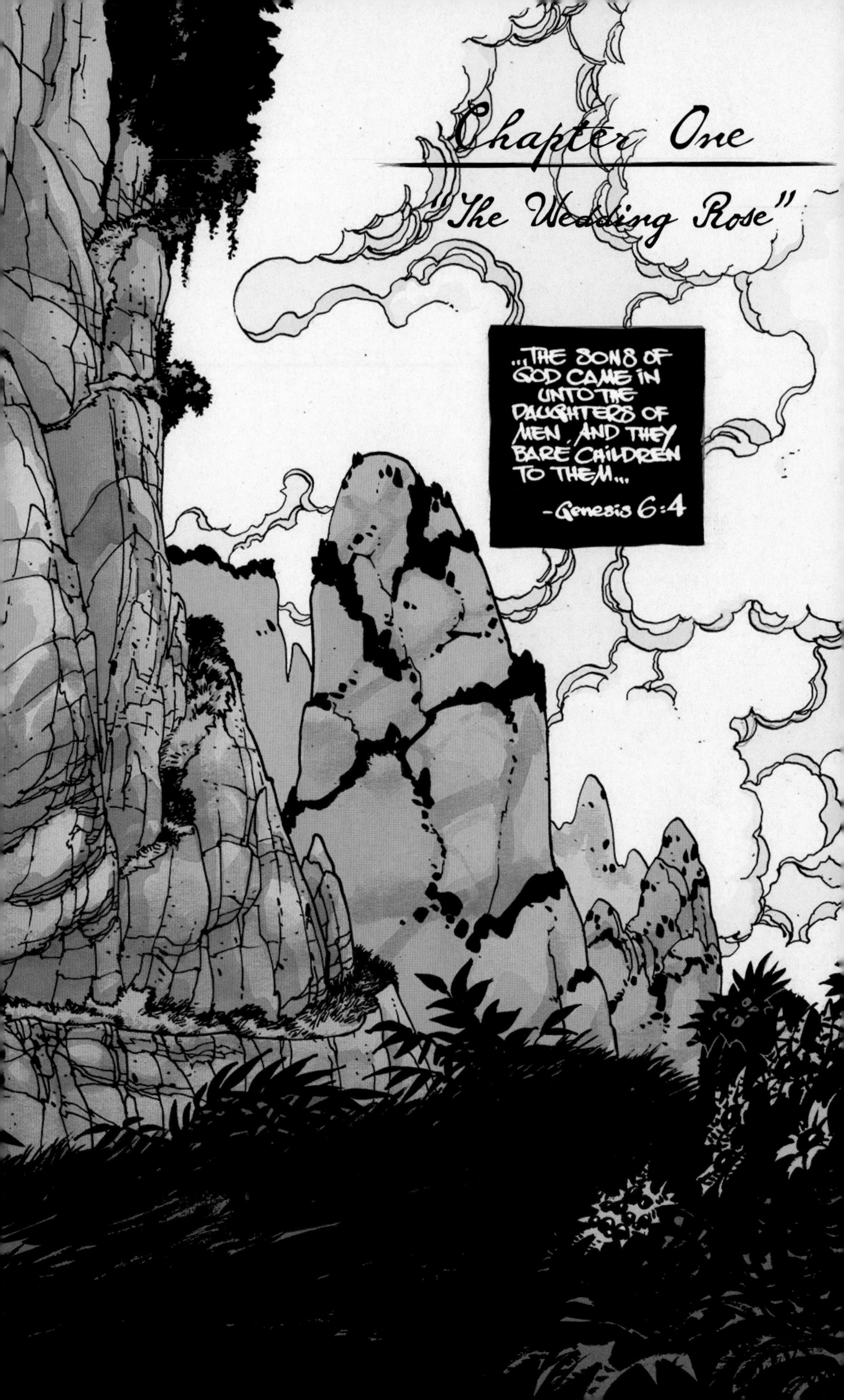
Chapter One
"The Wedding Rose"
...THE SONS OF GOD CAME IN UNTO THE DAUGHTERS OF MEN, AND THEY BARE CHILDREN TO THEM...
-Genesis 6:4

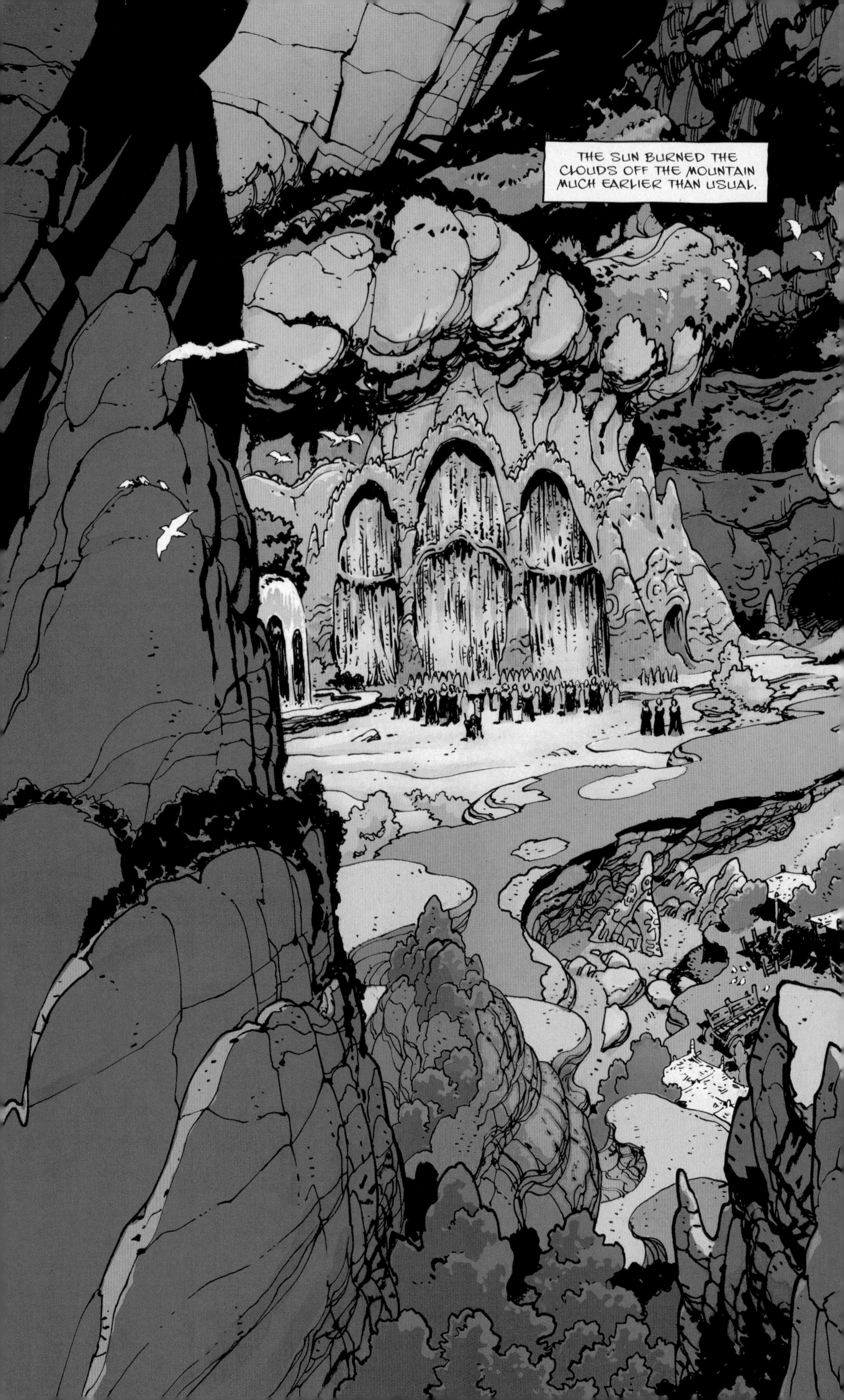
THE SUN BURNED THE CLOUDS OFF THE MOUNTAIN MUCH EARLIER THAN USUAL.

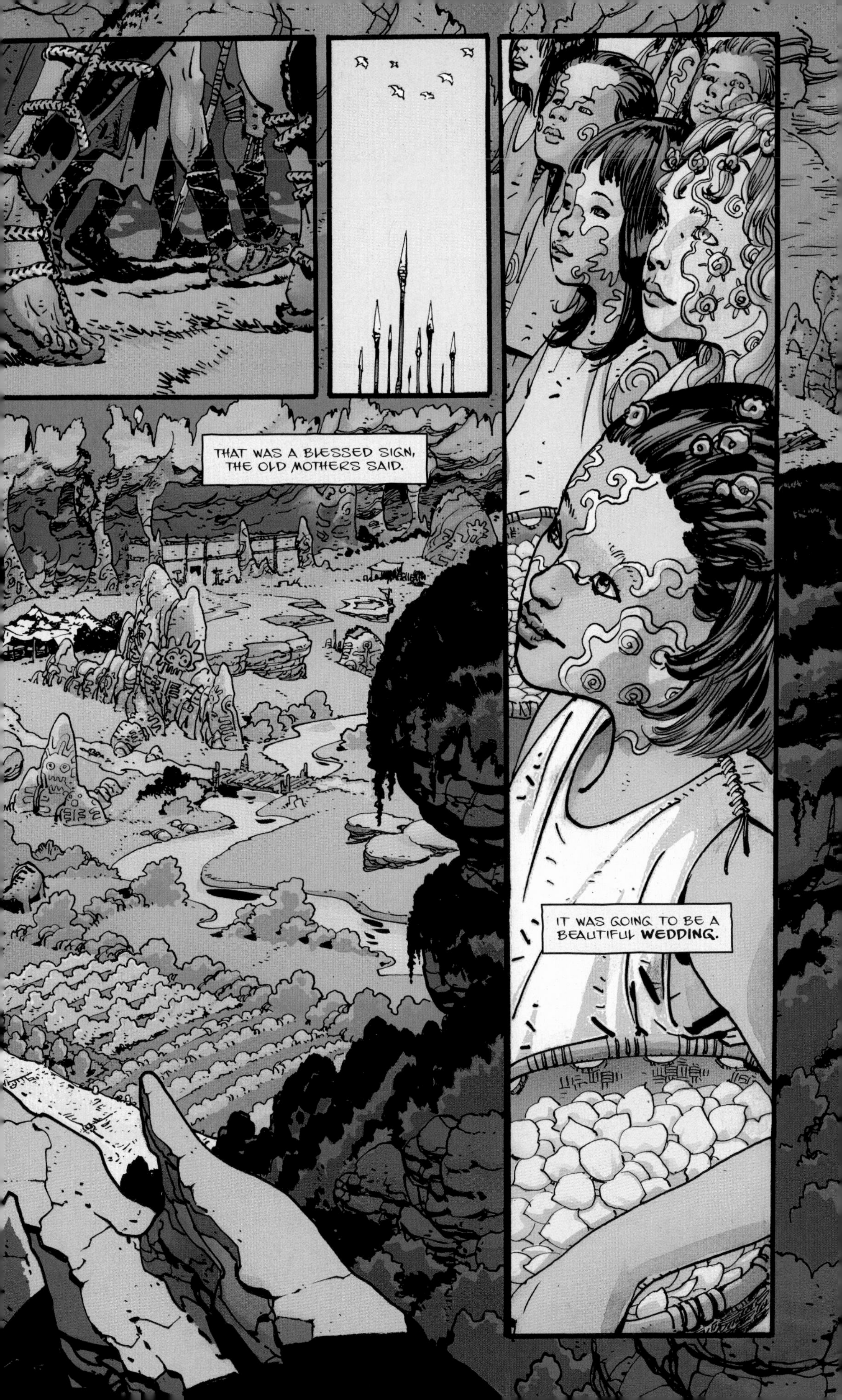
THAT WAS A BLESSED SIGN, THE OLD MOTHERS SAID.
IT WAS GOING TO BE A BEAUTIFUL WEDDING.

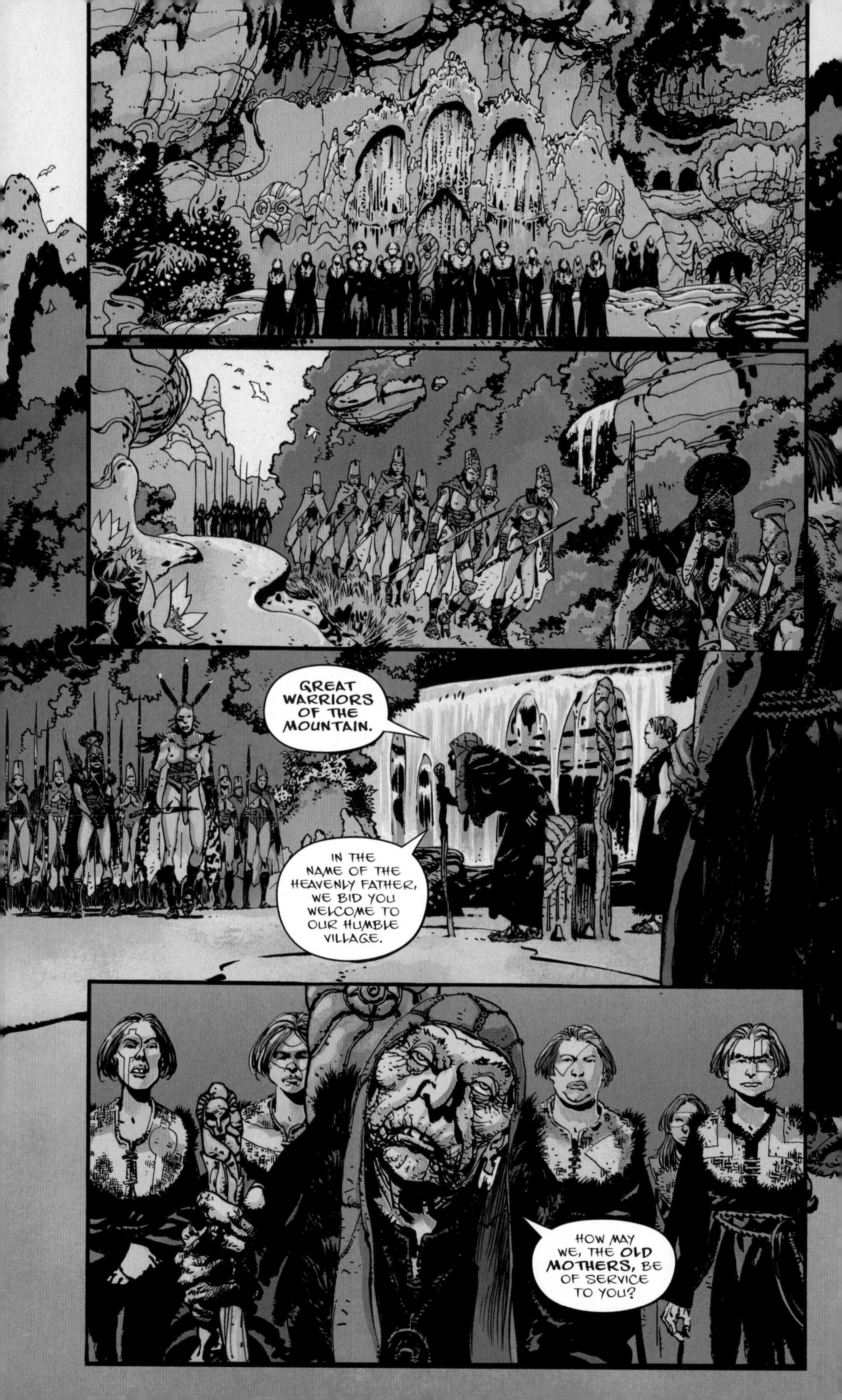

GREAT WARRIORS OF THE MOUNTAIN.
IN THE NAME OF THE HEAVENLY FATHER, WE BID YOU WELCOME TO OUR HUMBLE VILLAGE.
HOW MAY WE, THE **OLD MOTHERS,** BE OF SERVICE TO YOU?

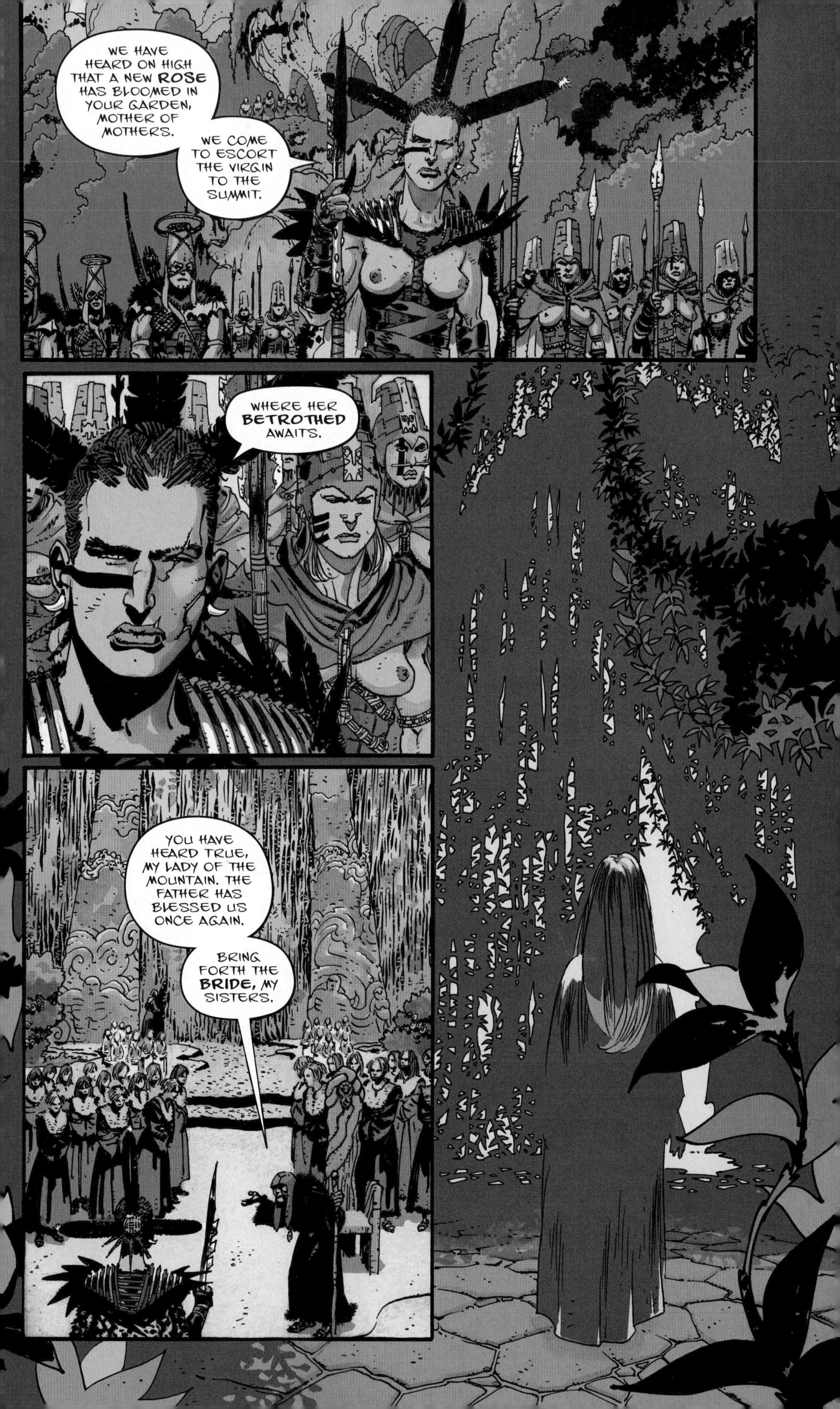
WE HAVE HEARD ON HIGH THAT A NEW ROSE HAS BLOOMED IN YOUR GARDEN, MOTHER OF MOTHERS.
WE COME TO ESCORT THE VIRGIN TO THE SUMMIT.
WHERE HER BETROTHED AWAITS.
YOU HAVE HEARD TRUE, MY LADY OF THE MOUNTAIN. THE FATHER HAS BLESSED US ONCE AGAIN.
BRING FORTH THE BRIDE, MY SISTERS.

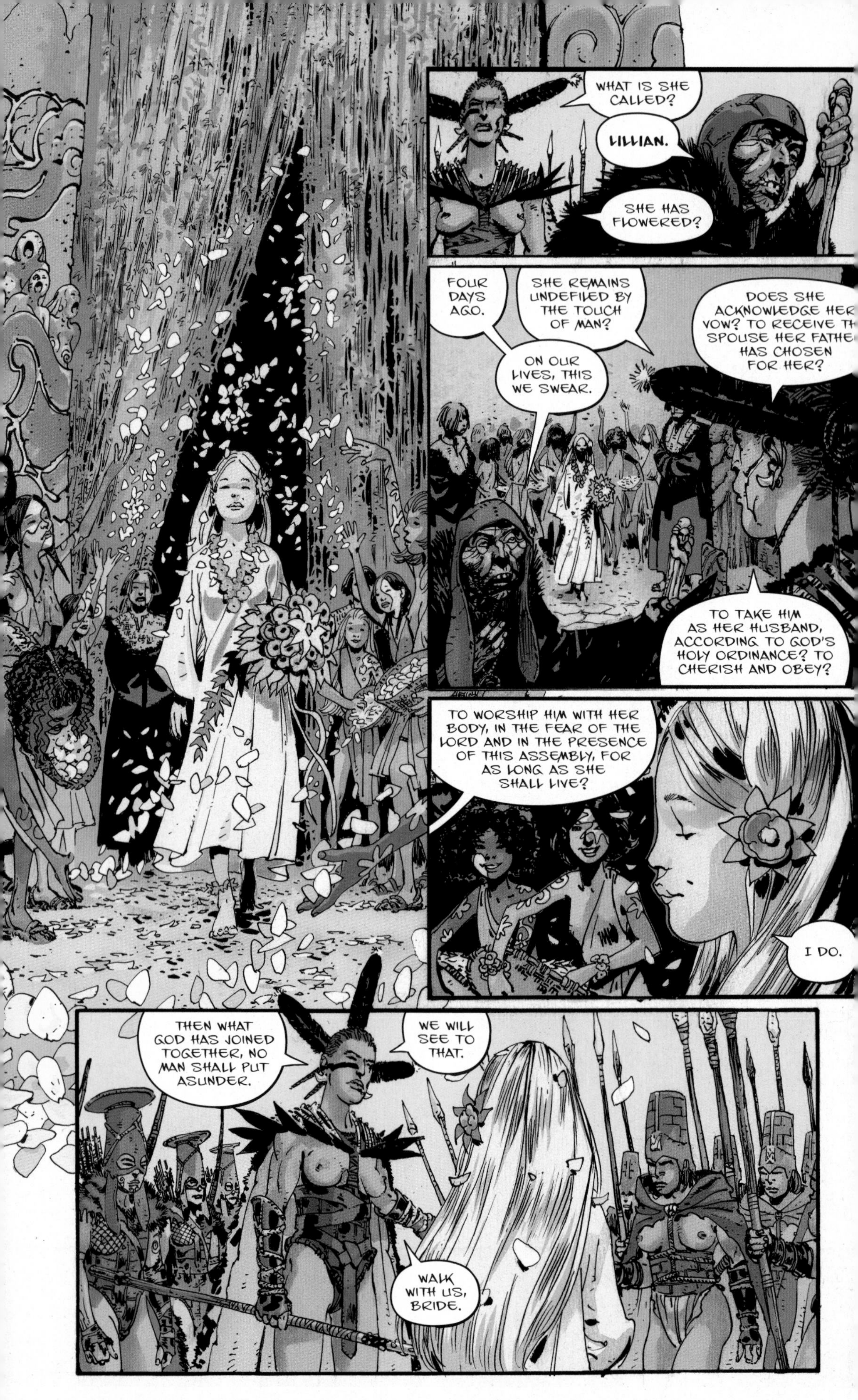
WHAT IS SHE CALLED?
LILLIAN.
SHE HAS FLOWERED?
FOUR DAYS AGO.
SHE REMAINS UNDEFILED BY THE TOUCH OF MAN?
ON OUR LIVES, THIS WE SWEAR.
DOES SHE ACKNOWLEDGE HER VOW? TO RECEIVE TH SPOUSE HER FATHE HAS CHOSEN FOR HER?
TO TAKE HIM AS HER HUSBAND, ACCORDING TO GOD'S HOLY ORDINANCE? TO CHERISH AND OBEY?
TO WORSHIP HIM WITH HER BODY, IN THE FEAR OF THE LORD AND IN THE PRESENCE OF THIS ASSEMBLY, FOR AS LONG AS SHE SHALL LIVE?
I DO.
THEN WHAT GOD HAS JOINED TOGETHER, NO MAN SHALL PUT ASUNDER.
WE WILL SEE TO THAT.
WALK WITH US, BRIDE.

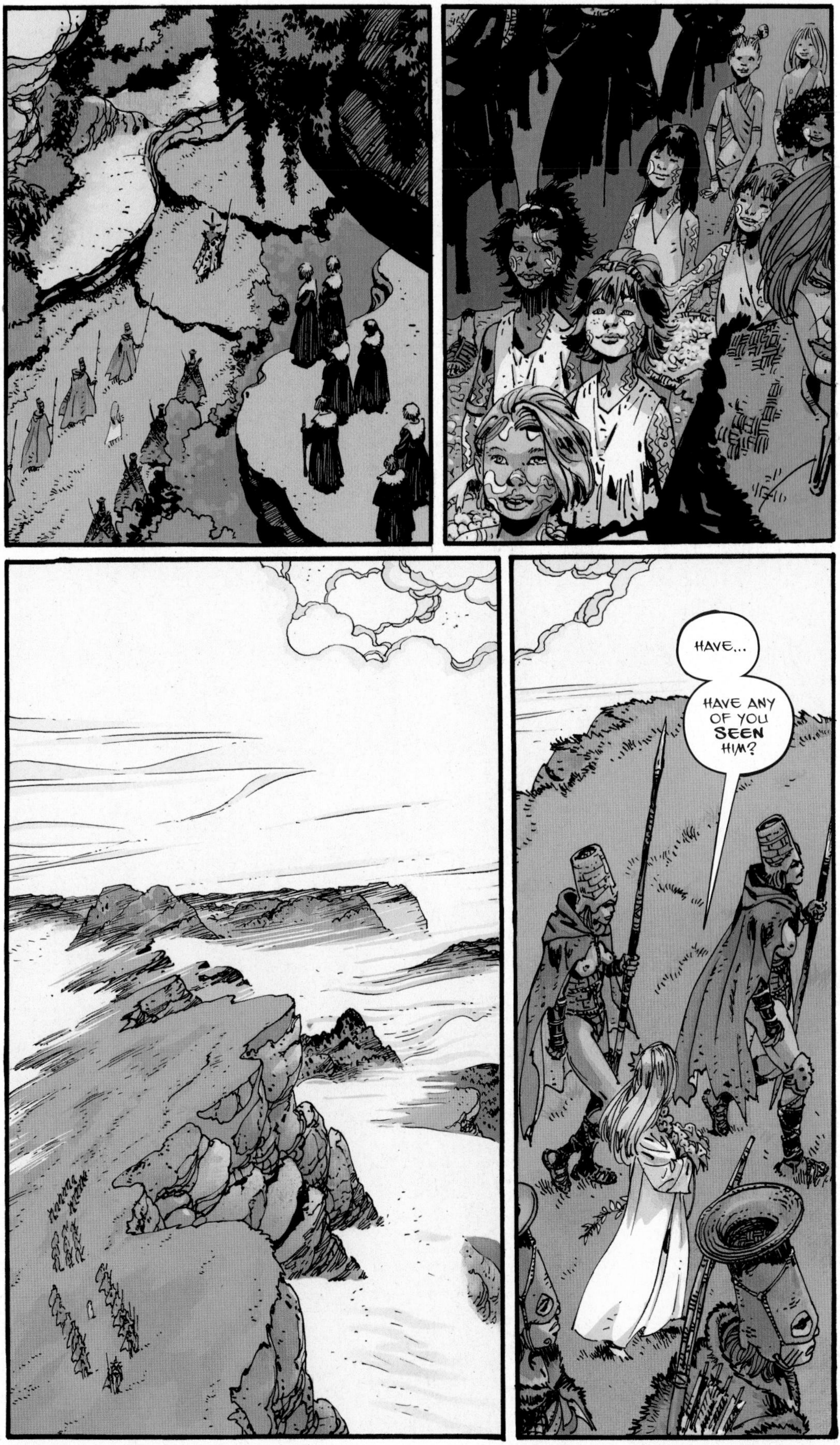
HAVE...
HAVE ANY OF YOU SEEN HIM?

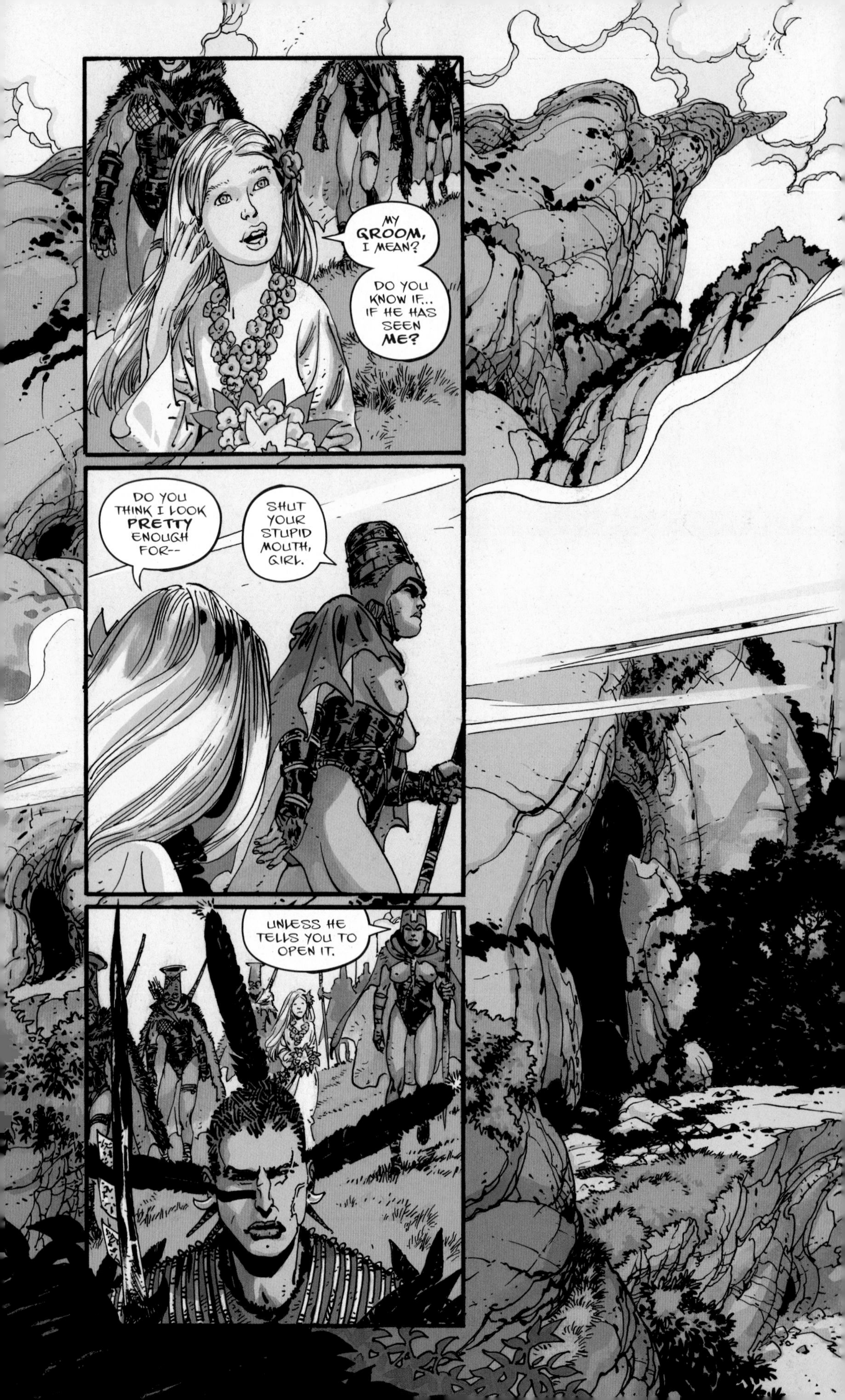
MY GROOM, I MEAN?
DO YOU KNOW IF... IF HE HAS SEEN ME?
DO YOU THINK I LOOK PRETTY ENOUGH FOR--
SHUT YOUR STUPID MOUTH, GIRL.
UNLESS HE TELLS YOU TO OPEN IT.

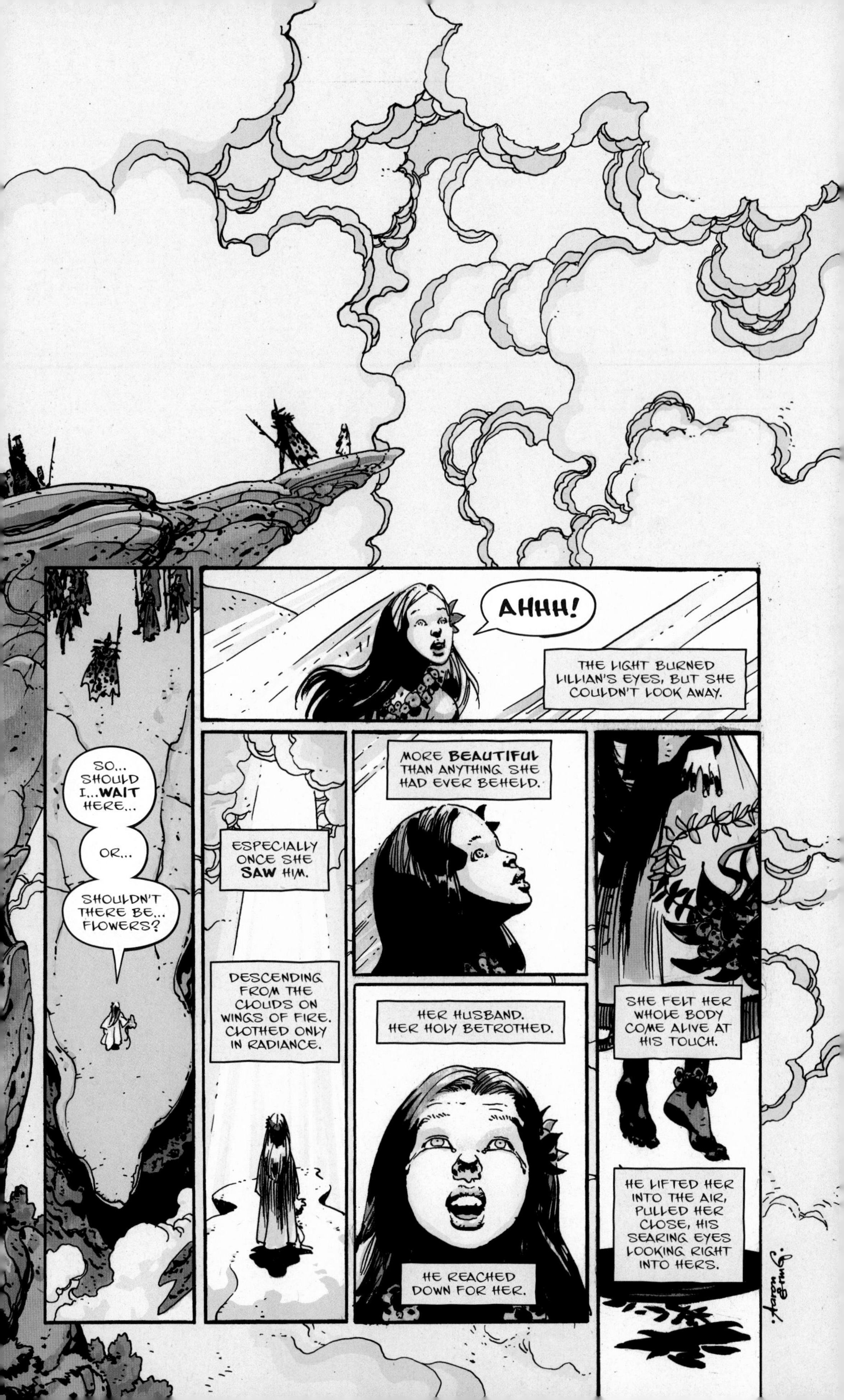
AHHH!
THE LIGHT BURNED LILLIAN'S EYES, BUT SHE COULDN'T LOOK AWAY.
SO... SHOULD I...**WAIT** HERE...
OR...
SHOULDN'T THERE BE... FLOWERS?
ESPECIALLY ONCE SHE **SAW** HIM.
DESCENDING FROM THE CLOUDS ON WINGS OF FIRE. CLOTHED ONLY IN RADIANCE.
MORE **BEAUTIFUL** THAN ANYTHING SHE HAD EVER BEHELD.
HER HUSBAND. HER HOLY BETROTHED.
HE REACHED DOWN FOR HER.
SHE FELT HER WHOLE BODY COME ALIVE AT HIS TOUCH.
HE LIFTED HER INTO THE AIR, PULLED HER CLOSE, HIS SEARING EYES LOOKING RIGHT INTO HERS.

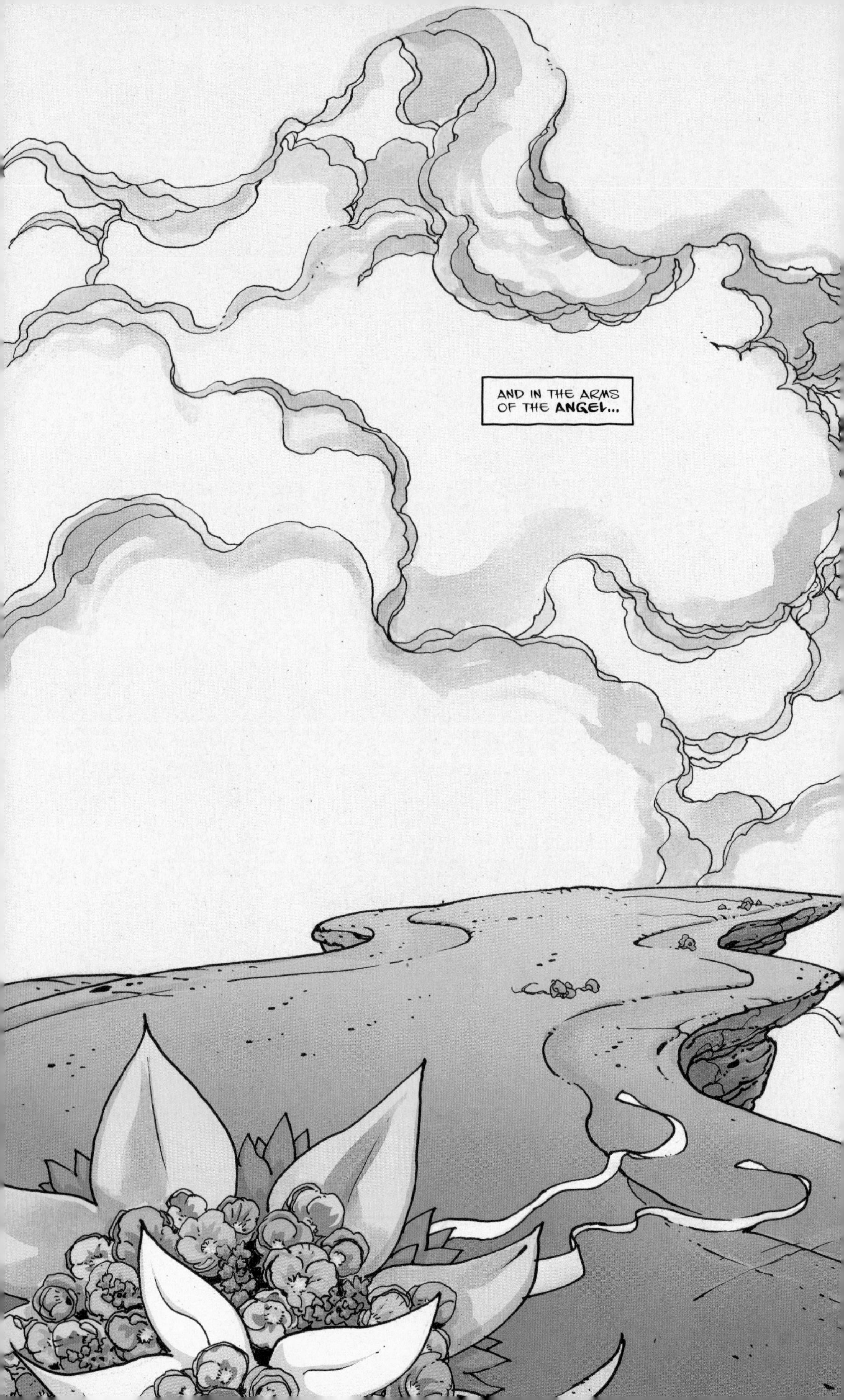
AND IN THE ARMS OF THE **ANGEL...**

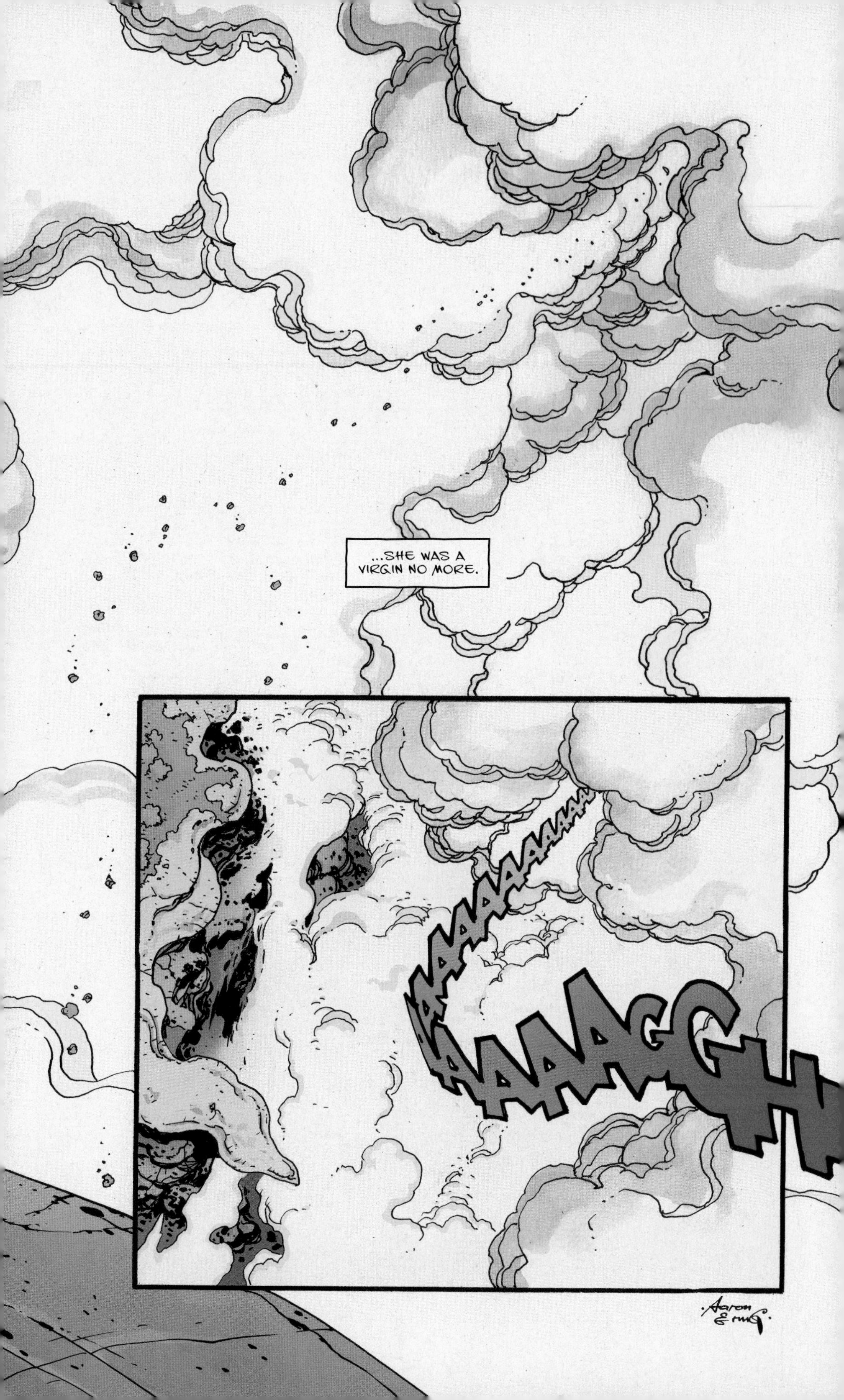
...SHE WAS A VIRGIN NO MORE.
AAAAAAAAAAAAAAAAAAAAAAAAGH

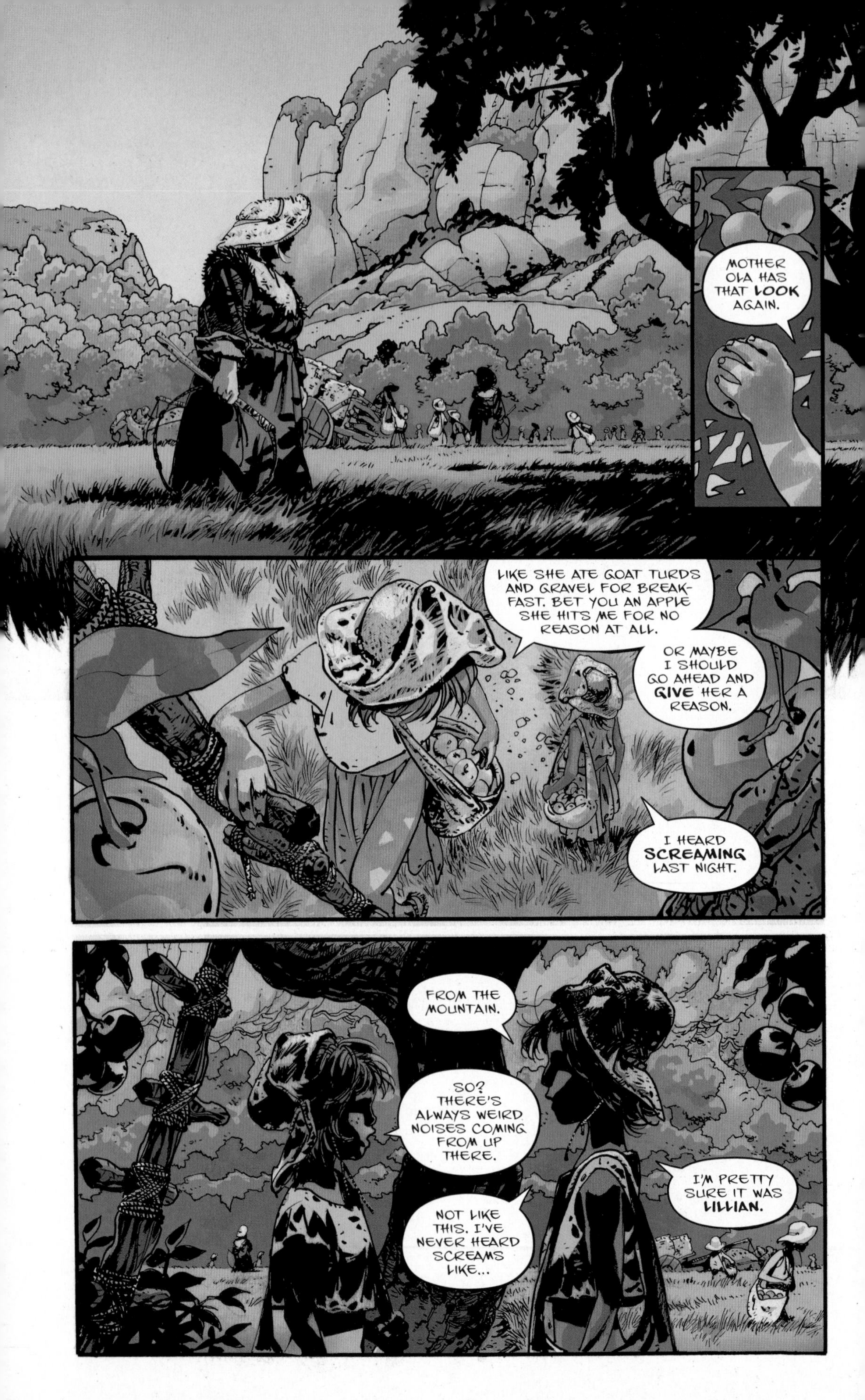
MOTHER OLA HAS THAT LOOK AGAIN.
LIKE SHE ATE GOAT TURDS AND GRAVEL FOR BREAK-FAST. BET YOU AN APPLE SHE HITS ME FOR NO REASON AT ALL.
OR MAYBE I SHOULD GO AHEAD AND GIVE HER A REASON.
I HEARD SCREAMING LAST NIGHT.
FROM THE MOUNTAIN.
SO? THERE'S ALWAYS WEIRD NOISES COMING FROM UP THERE.
NOT LIKE THIS. I'VE NEVER HEARD SCREAMS LIKE...
I'M PRETTY SURE IT WAS LILLIAN.

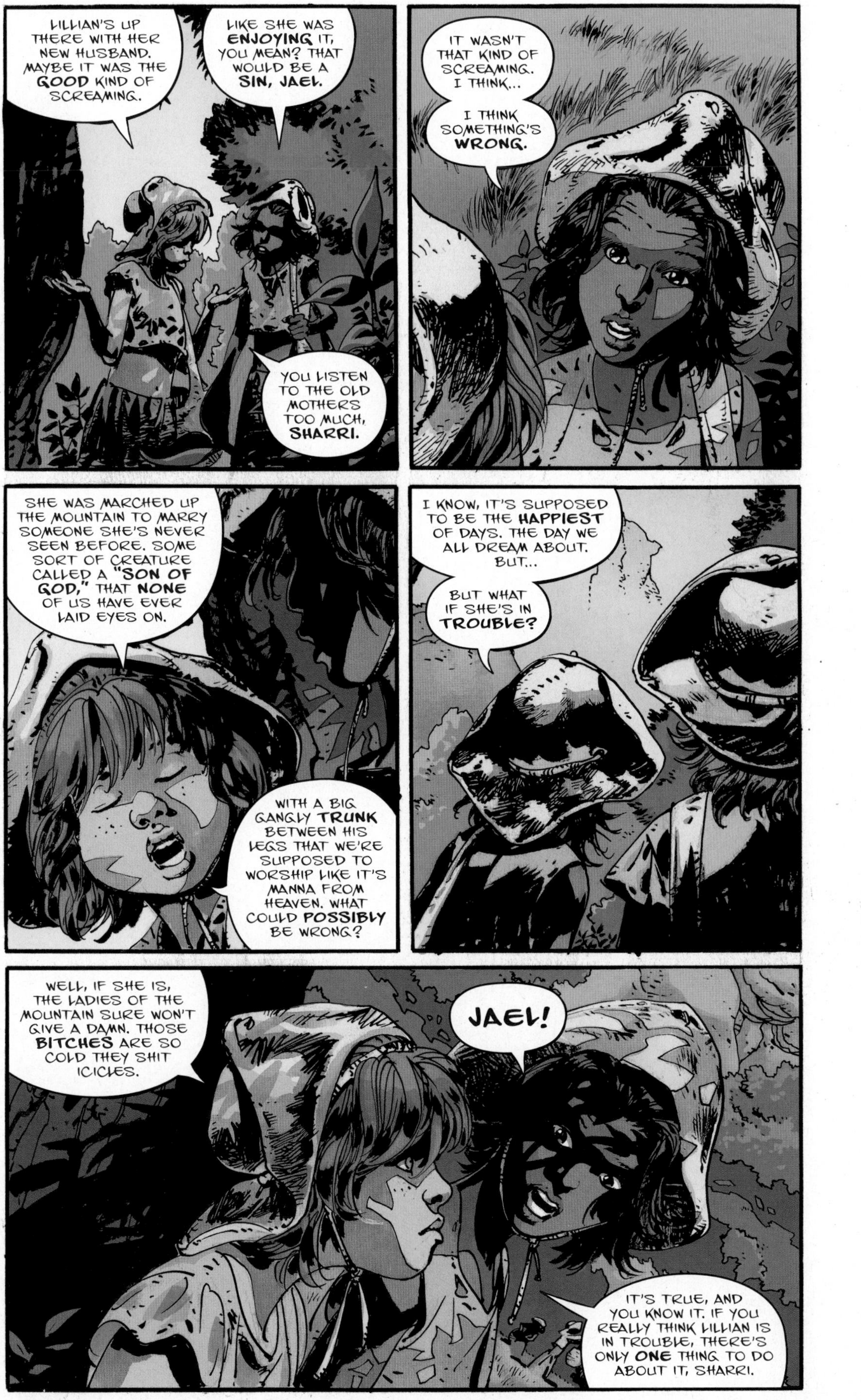
LILLIAN'S UP THERE WITH HER NEW HUSBAND. MAYBE IT WAS THE GOOD KIND OF SCREAMING.
LIKE SHE WAS ENJOYING IT, YOU MEAN? THAT WOULD BE A SIN, JAEL.
YOU LISTEN TO THE OLD MOTHERS TOO MUCH, SHARRI.
IT WASN'T THAT KIND OF SCREAMING. I THINK...
I THINK SOMETHING'S WRONG.
SHE WAS MARCHED UP THE MOUNTAIN TO MARRY SOMEONE SHE'S NEVER SEEN BEFORE. SOME SORT OF CREATURE CALLED A "SON OF GOD," THAT NONE OF US HAVE EVER LAID EYES ON.
WITH A BIG GANGLY TRUNK BETWEEN HIS LEGS THAT WE'RE SUPPOSED TO WORSHIP LIKE IT'S MANNA FROM HEAVEN. WHAT COULD POSSIBLY BE WRONG?
I KNOW, IT'S SUPPOSED TO BE THE HAPPIEST OF DAYS. THE DAY WE ALL DREAM ABOUT. BUT...
BUT WHAT IF SHE'S IN TROUBLE?
WELL, IF SHE IS, THE LADIES OF THE MOUNTAIN SURE WON'T GIVE A DAMN. THOSE BITCHES ARE SO COLD THEY SHIT ICICLES.
JAEL!
IT'S TRUE, AND YOU KNOW IT. IF YOU REALLY THINK LILLIAN IS IN TROUBLE, THERE'S ONLY ONE THING TO DO ABOUT IT, SHARRI.

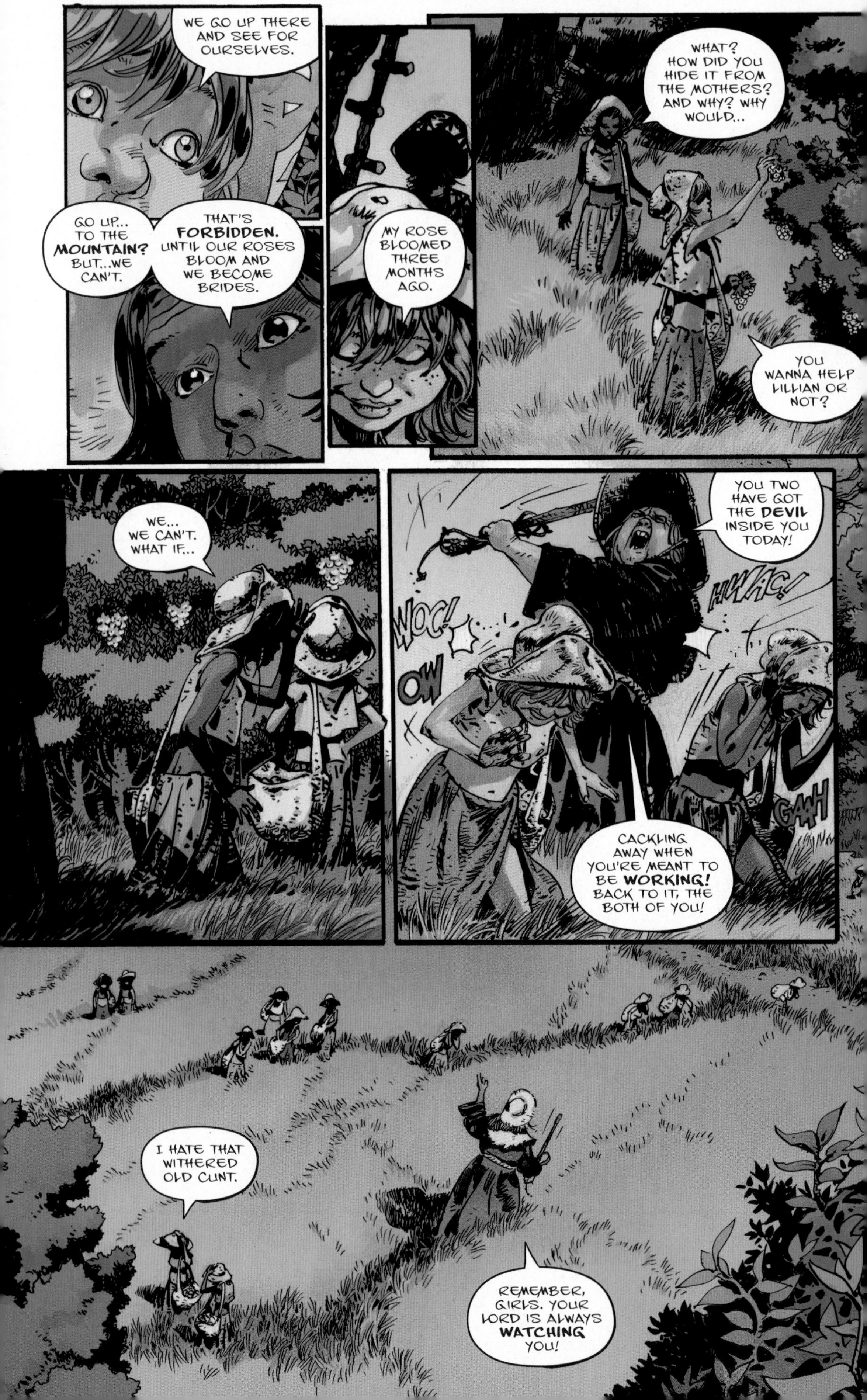
WE GO UP THERE AND SEE FOR OURSELVES.
GO UP... TO THE MOUNTAIN? BUT...WE CAN'T.
THAT'S FORBIDDEN. UNTIL OUR ROSES BLOOM AND WE BECOME BRIDES.
MY ROSE BLOOMED THREE MONTHS AGO.
WHAT? HOW DID YOU HIDE IT FROM THE MOTHERS? AND WHY? WHY WOULD...
YOU WANNA HELP LILLIAN OR NOT?
WE... WE CAN'T. WHAT IF...
YOU TWO HAVE GOT THE DEVIL INSIDE YOU TODAY!
HWAC!
WOC!
OW
GAAH
CACKLING AWAY WHEN YOU'RE MEANT TO BE WORKING! BACK TO IT, THE BOTH OF YOU!
I HATE THAT WITHERED OLD CUNT.
REMEMBER, GIRLS. YOUR LORD IS ALWAYS WATCHING YOU!

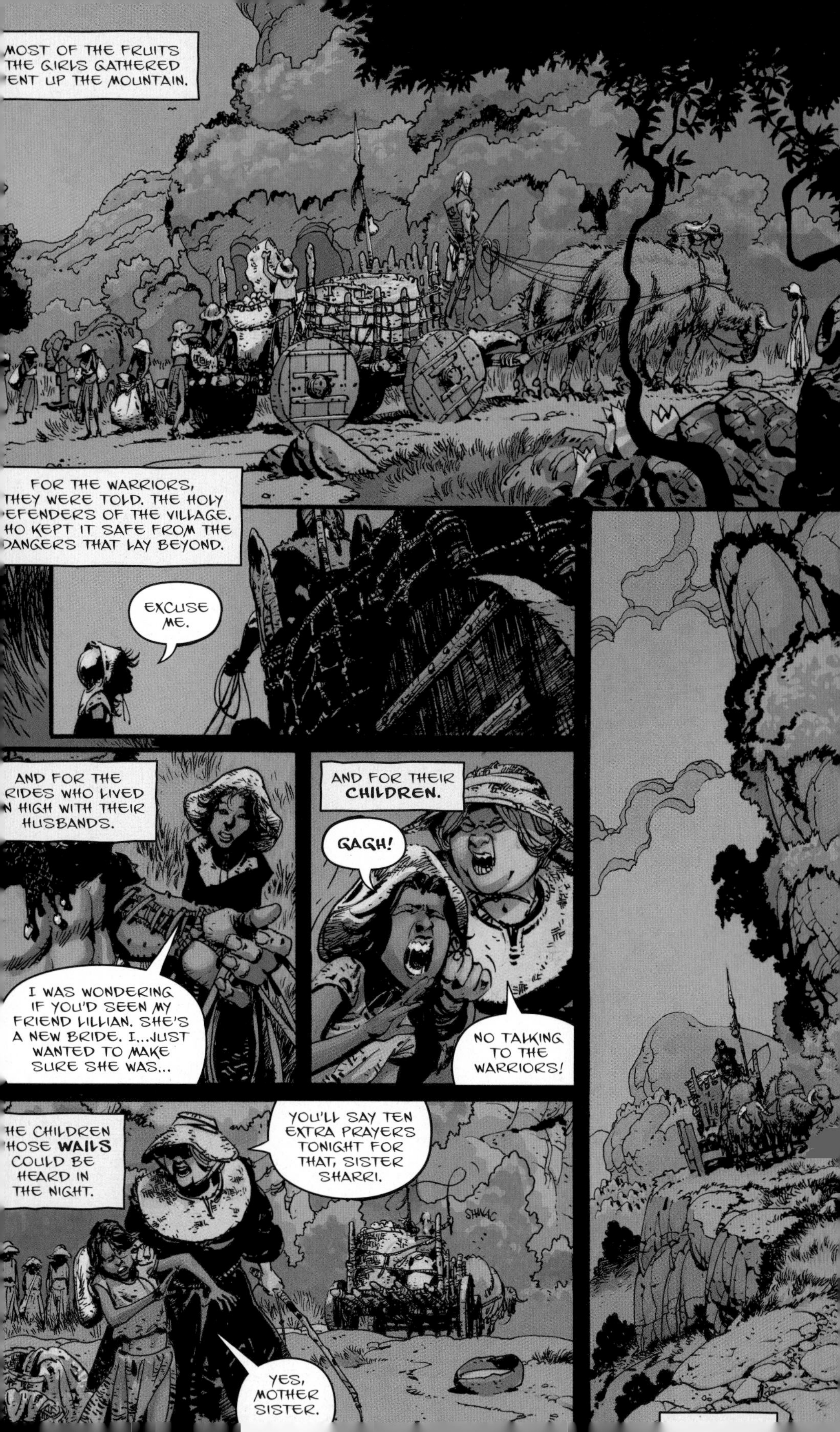
MOST OF THE FRUITS THE GIRLS GATHERED ENT UP THE MOUNTAIN.
FOR THE WARRIORS, THEY WERE TOLD. THE HOLY EFENDERS OF THE VILLAGE. HO KEPT IT SAFE FROM THE DANGERS THAT LAY BEYOND.
EXCUSE ME.
AND FOR THE RIDES WHO LIVED N HIGH WITH THEIR HUSBANDS.
I WAS WONDERING IF YOU'D SEEN MY FRIEND LILLIAN. SHE'S A NEW BRIDE. I...JUST WANTED TO MAKE SURE SHE WAS...
AND FOR THEIR CHILDREN.
GAGH!
NO TALKING TO THE WARRIORS!
HE CHILDREN HOSE WAILS COULD BE HEARD IN THE NIGHT.
YOU'LL SAY TEN EXTRA PRAYERS TONIGHT FOR THAT, SISTER SHARRI.
YES, MOTHER SISTER.

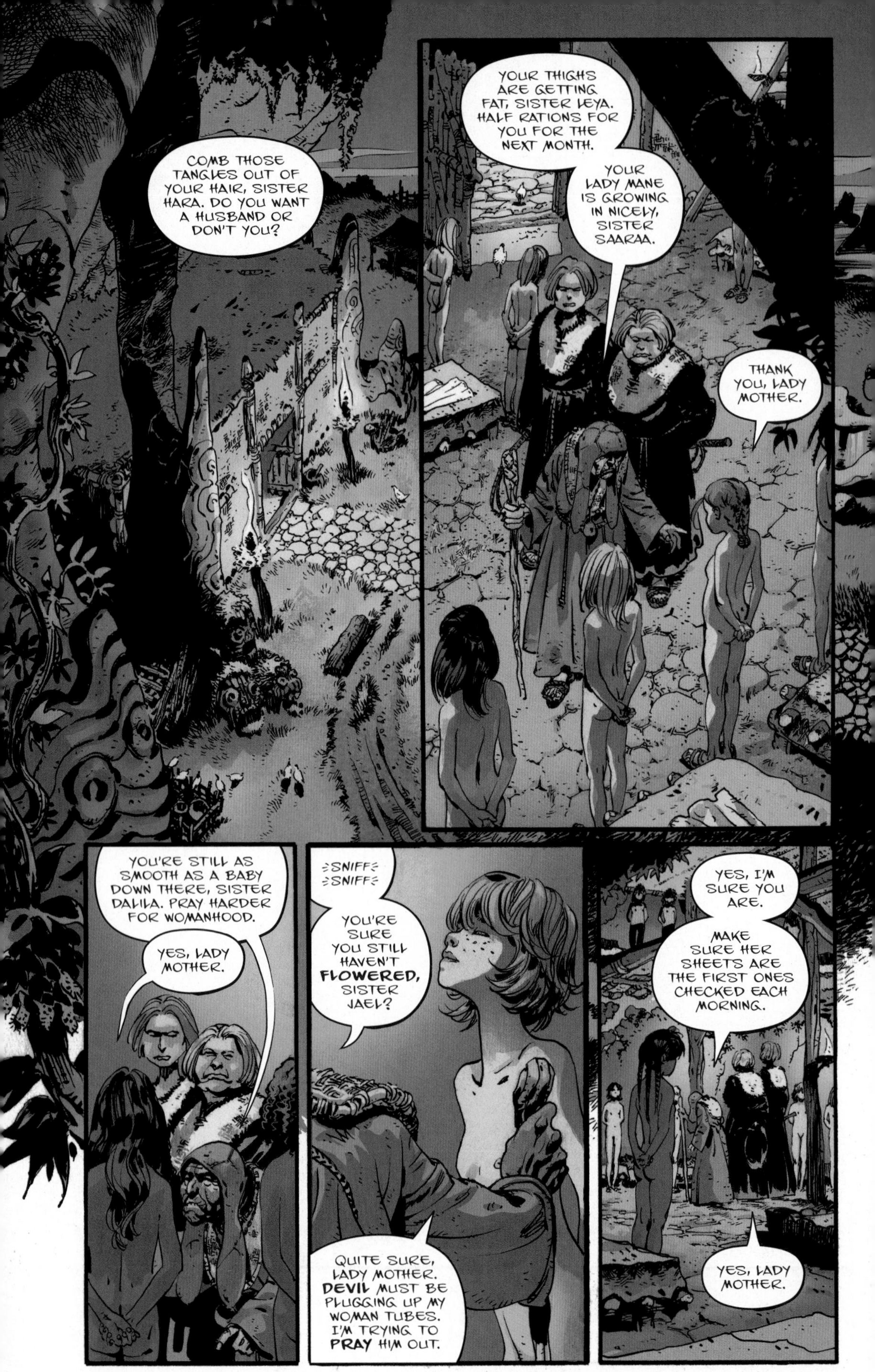
COMB THOSE TANGLES OUT OF YOUR HAIR, SISTER HARA. DO YOU WANT A HUSBAND OR DON'T YOU?
YOUR THIGHS ARE GETTING FAT, SISTER LEYA. HALF RATIONS FOR YOU FOR THE NEXT MONTH.
YOUR LADY MANE IS GROWING IN NICELY, SISTER SAARAA.
THANK YOU, LADY MOTHER.
YOU'RE STILL AS SMOOTH AS A BABY DOWN THERE, SISTER DALILA. PRAY HARDER FOR WOMANHOOD.
YES, LADY MOTHER.
SNIFF
SNIFF
YOU'RE SURE YOU STILL HAVEN'T **FLOWERED,** SISTER JAEL?
QUITE SURE, LADY MOTHER. **DEVIL** MUST BE PLUGGING UP MY WOMAN TUBES. I'M TRYING TO **PRAY** HIM OUT.
YES, I'M SURE YOU ARE.
MAKE SURE HER SHEETS ARE THE FIRST ONES CHECKED EACH MORNING.
YES, LADY MOTHER.

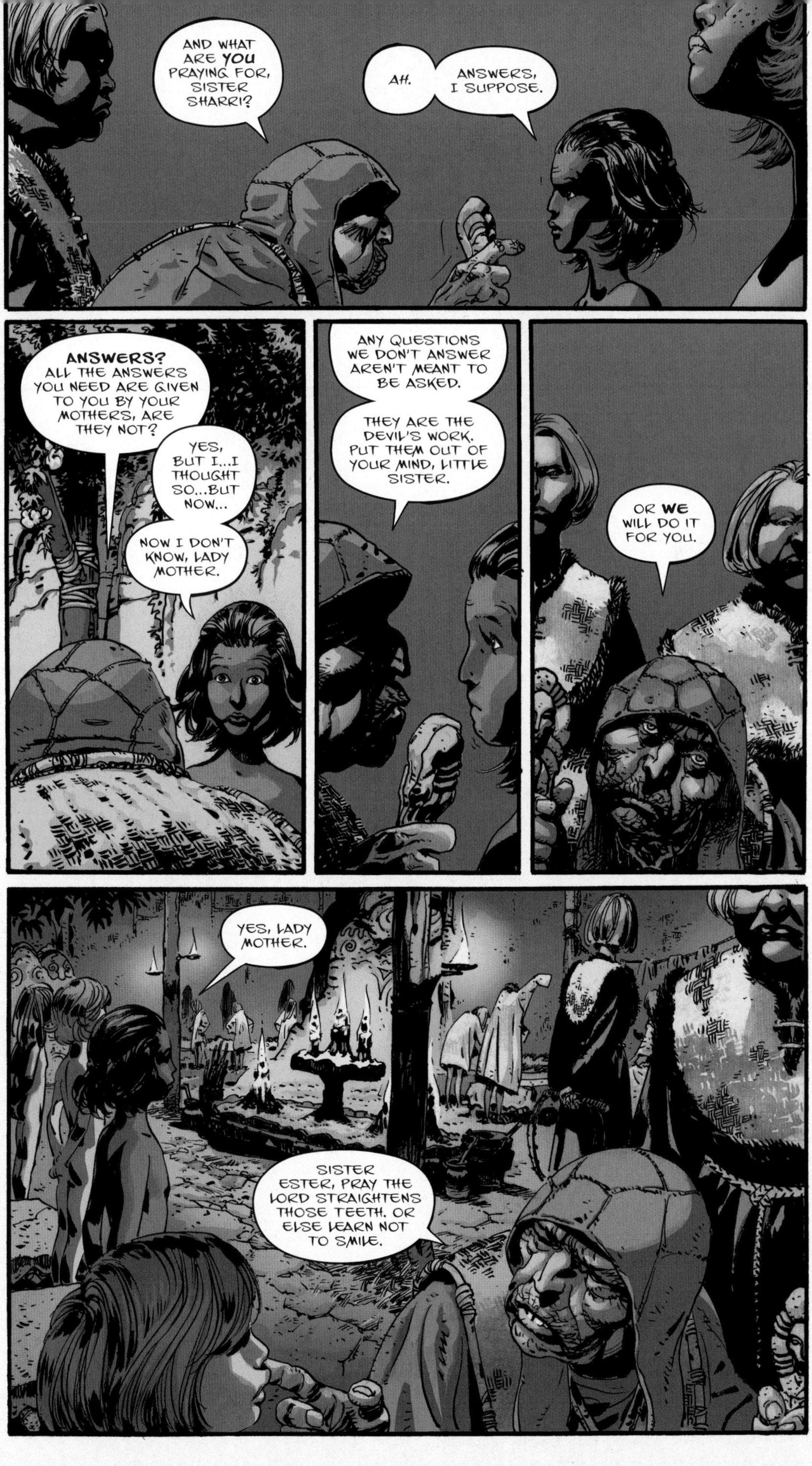
AND WHAT ARE YOU PRAYING FOR, SISTER SHARRI?
AH.
ANSWERS, I SUPPOSE.
ANSWERS? ALL THE ANSWERS YOU NEED ARE GIVEN TO YOU BY YOUR MOTHERS, ARE THEY NOT?
YES, BUT I...I THOUGHT SO...BUT NOW...
NOW I DON'T KNOW, LADY MOTHER.
ANY QUESTIONS WE DON'T ANSWER AREN'T MEANT TO BE ASKED.
THEY ARE THE DEVIL'S WORK. PUT THEM OUT OF YOUR MIND, LITTLE SISTER.
OR WE WILL DO IT FOR YOU.
YES, LADY MOTHER.
SISTER ESTER, PRAY THE LORD STRAIGHTENS THOSE TEETH. OR ELSE LEARN NOT TO SMILE.

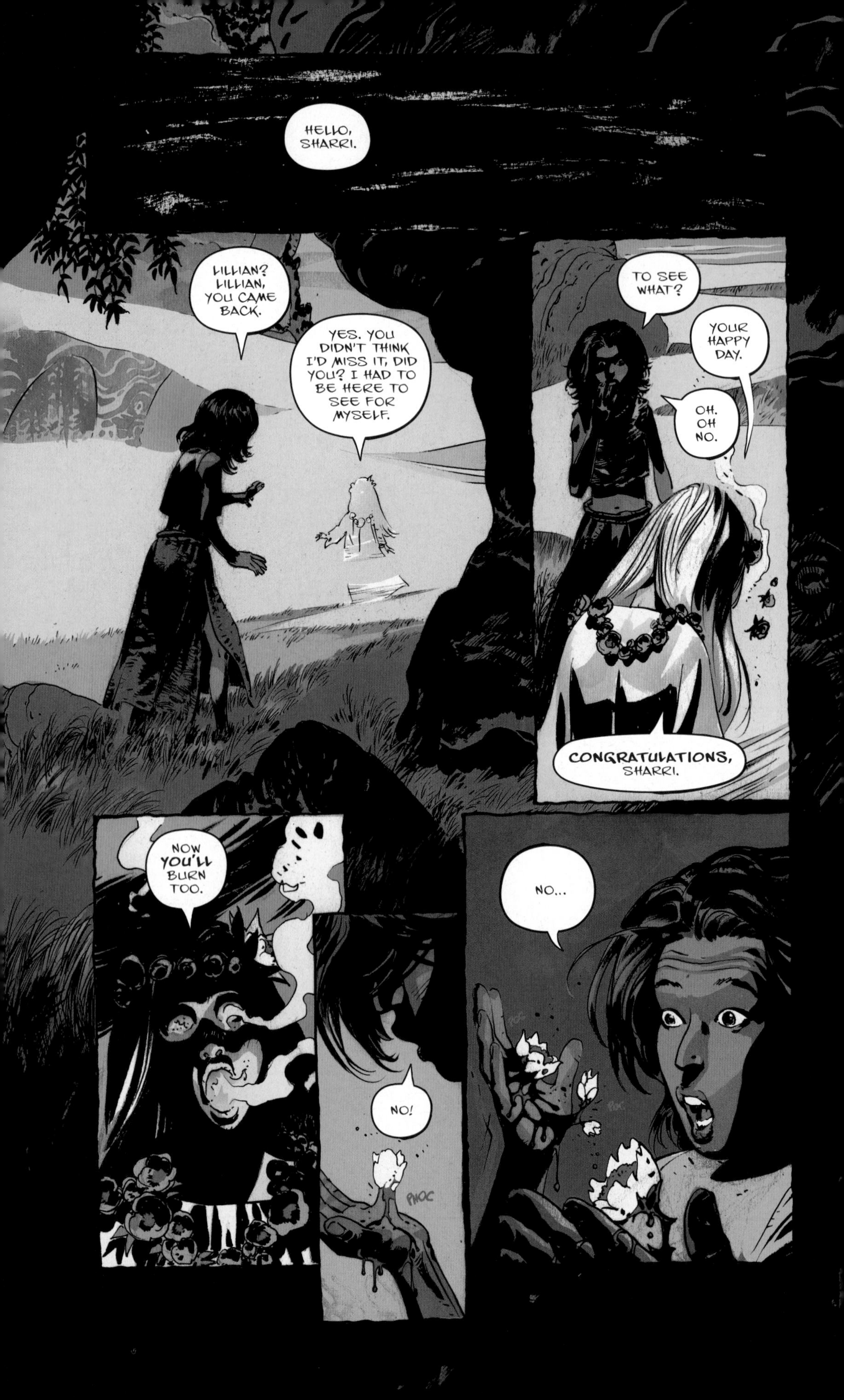
HELLO, SHARRI.
LILLIAN? LILLIAN, YOU CAME BACK.
YES. YOU DIDN'T THINK I'D MISS IT, DID YOU? I HAD TO BE HERE TO SEE FOR MYSELF.
TO SEE WHAT?
YOUR HAPPY DAY.
OH. OH NO.
CONGRATULATIONS, SHARRI.
NOW YOU'LL BURN TOO.
NO!
PHOC
NO...

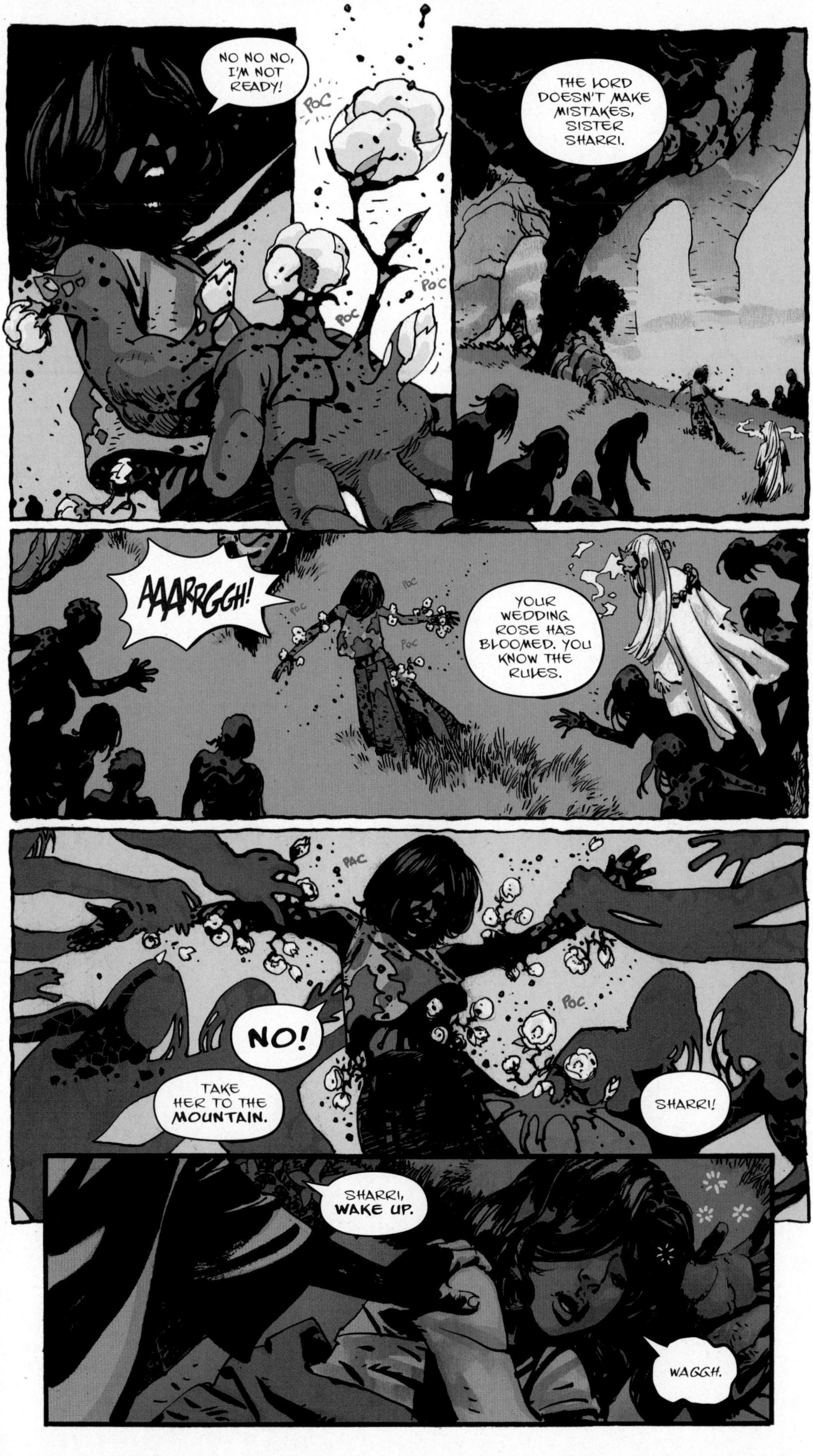

NO NO NO, I'M NOT READY!
POC
POC
POC
THE LORD DOESN'T MAKE MISTAKES, SISTER SHARRI.
AAARRGGH!
POC
POC
YOUR WEDDING ROSE HAS BLOOMED. YOU KNOW THE RULES.
PAC
POC
NO!
TAKE HER TO THE MOUNTAIN.
SHARRI!
SHARRI, WAKE UP.
WAGGH.

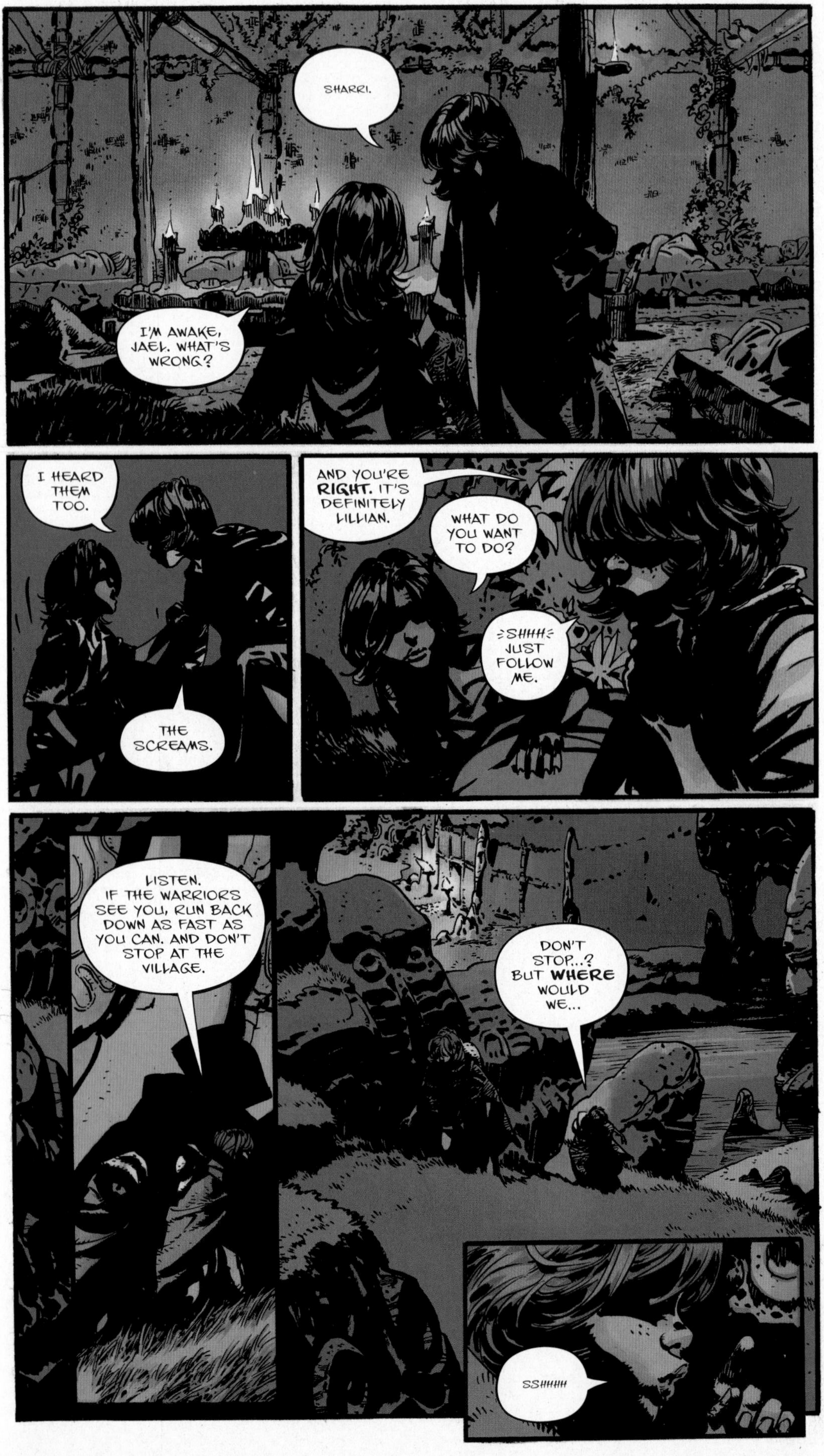
SHARRI.
I'M AWAKE, JAEL. WHAT'S WRONG?
I HEARD THEM TOO.
THE SCREAMS.
AND YOU'RE RIGHT. IT'S DEFINITELY LILLIAN.
WHAT DO YOU WANT TO DO?
SHHH JUST FOLLOW ME.
LISTEN. IF THE WARRIORS SEE YOU, RUN BACK DOWN AS FAST AS YOU CAN. AND DON'T STOP AT THE VILLAGE.
DON'T STOP...? BUT WHERE WOULD WE...
SSHHHH

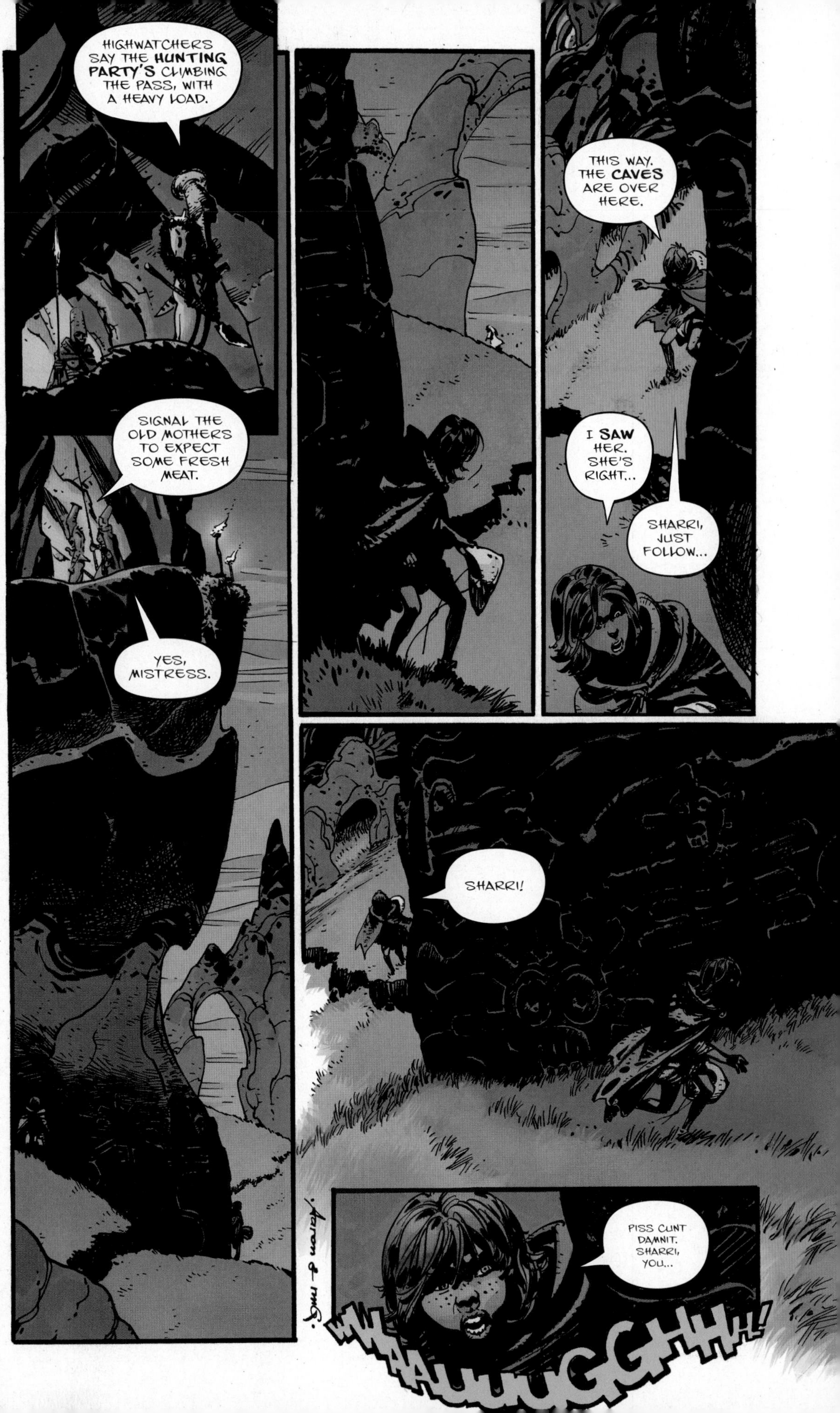
HIGHWATCHERS SAY THE HUNTING PARTY'S CLIMBING THE PASS, WITH A HEAVY LOAD.
SIGNAL THE OLD MOTHERS TO EXPECT SOME FRESH MEAT.
YES, MISTRESS.
THIS WAY. THE CAVES ARE OVER HERE.
I SAW HER. SHE'S RIGHT...
SHARRI, JUST FOLLOW...
SHARRI!
PISS CUNT DAMNIT. SHARRI, YOU...
WHAAUUUGGHHH!

WHAT THE **SHIT** IS THAT...

A-WAAAUUGGHHHH!

WE'D BETTER **HURRY!** SOUNDS LIKE THEY NEED HELP HOLDING HER DOWN!

LILLIAN!

LILLIAN, IT'S SHARRI. ARE YOU OKAY? I...I THOUGHT I HEARD YOU **SCREAMING.**

SHARRI...

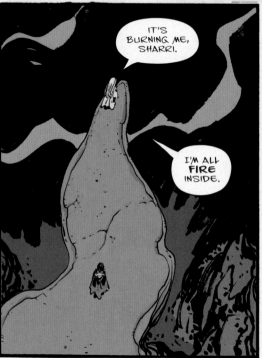

IT'S **BURNING** ME, SHARRI.

I'M ALL **FIRE** INSIDE.

AAAAARRGGHH!

HOLD HER DOWN!

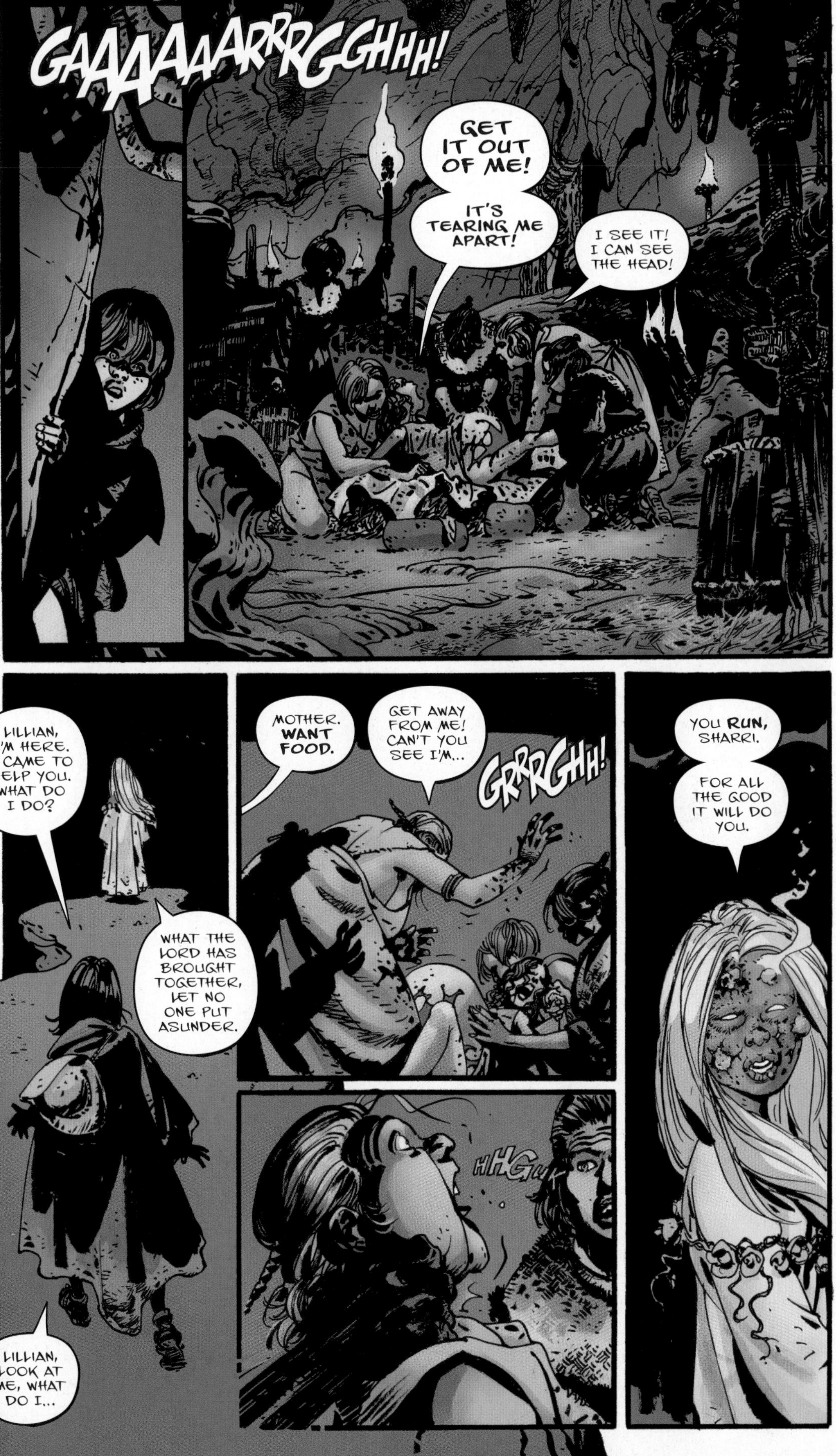
GAAAAAARRRGGHHH!
GET IT OUT OF ME!
IT'S TEARING ME APART!
I SEE IT! I CAN SEE THE HEAD!
LILLIAN, I'M HERE. I CAME TO HELP YOU. WHAT DO I DO?
WHAT THE LORD HAS BROUGHT TOGETHER, LET NO ONE PUT ASUNDER.
LILLIAN, LOOK AT ME, WHAT DO I...
MOTHER. WANT FOOD.
GET AWAY FROM ME! CAN'T YOU SEE I'M...
GRRRGHH!
HHGU
YOU RUN, SHARRI.
FOR ALL THE GOOD IT WILL DO YOU.

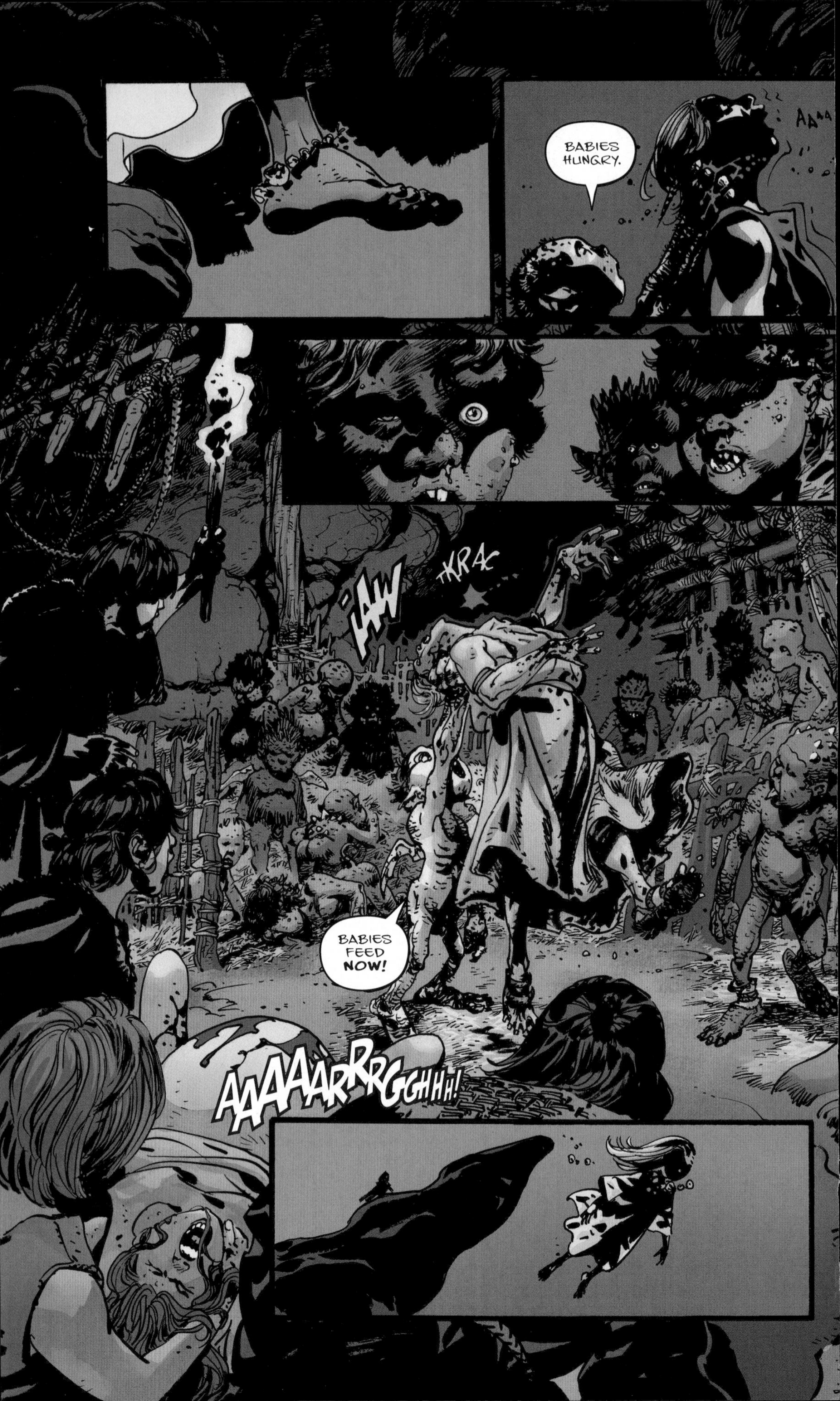
BABIES HUNGRY.
AAA
¡AW
TKRAC
BABIES FEED NOW!
AAAAARRRGGHHH!

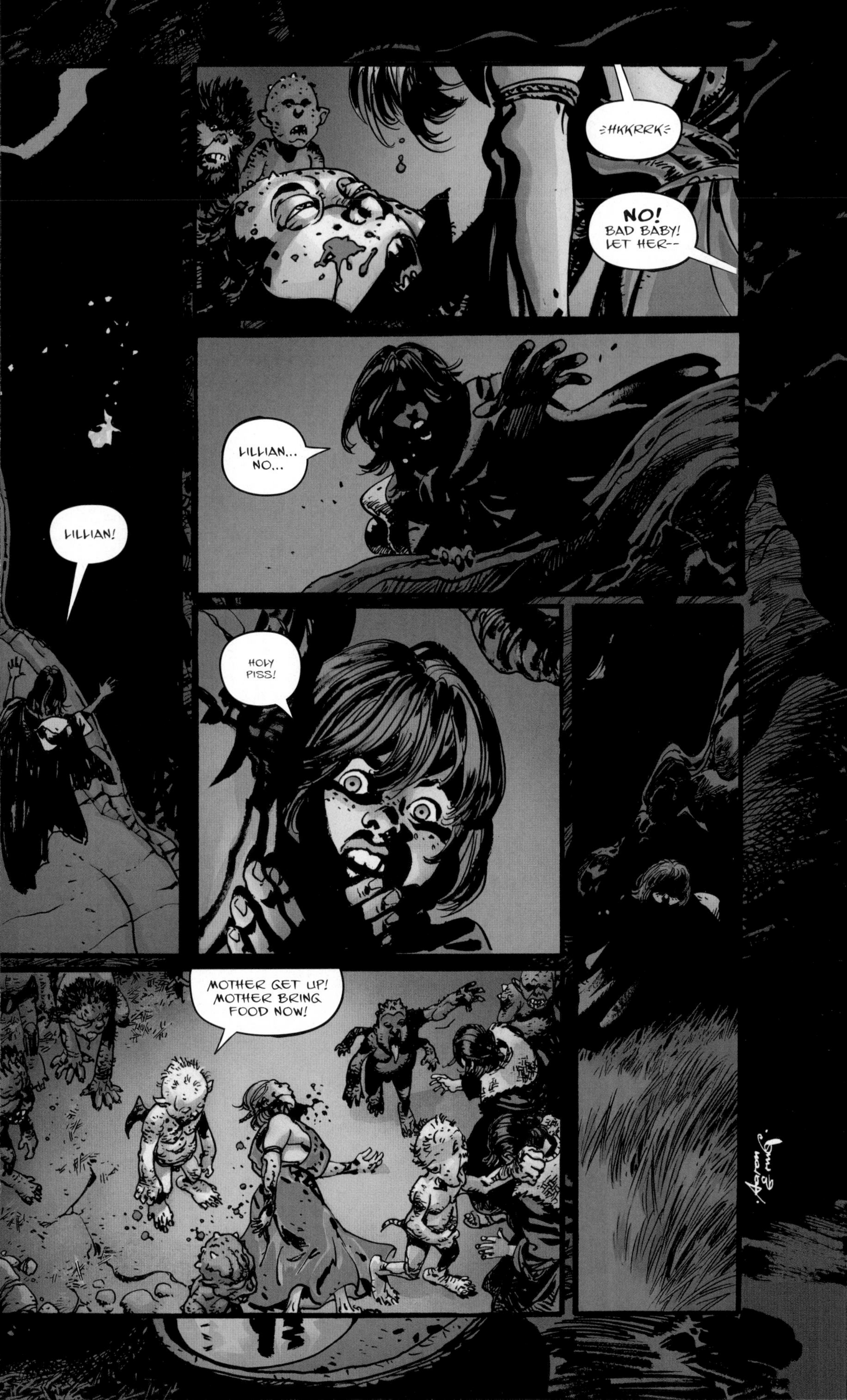
=HKKRRK=
NO! BAD BABY! LET HER--
LILLIAN... NO...
LILLIAN!
HOLY PISS!
MOTHER GET UP! MOTHER BRING FOOD NOW!

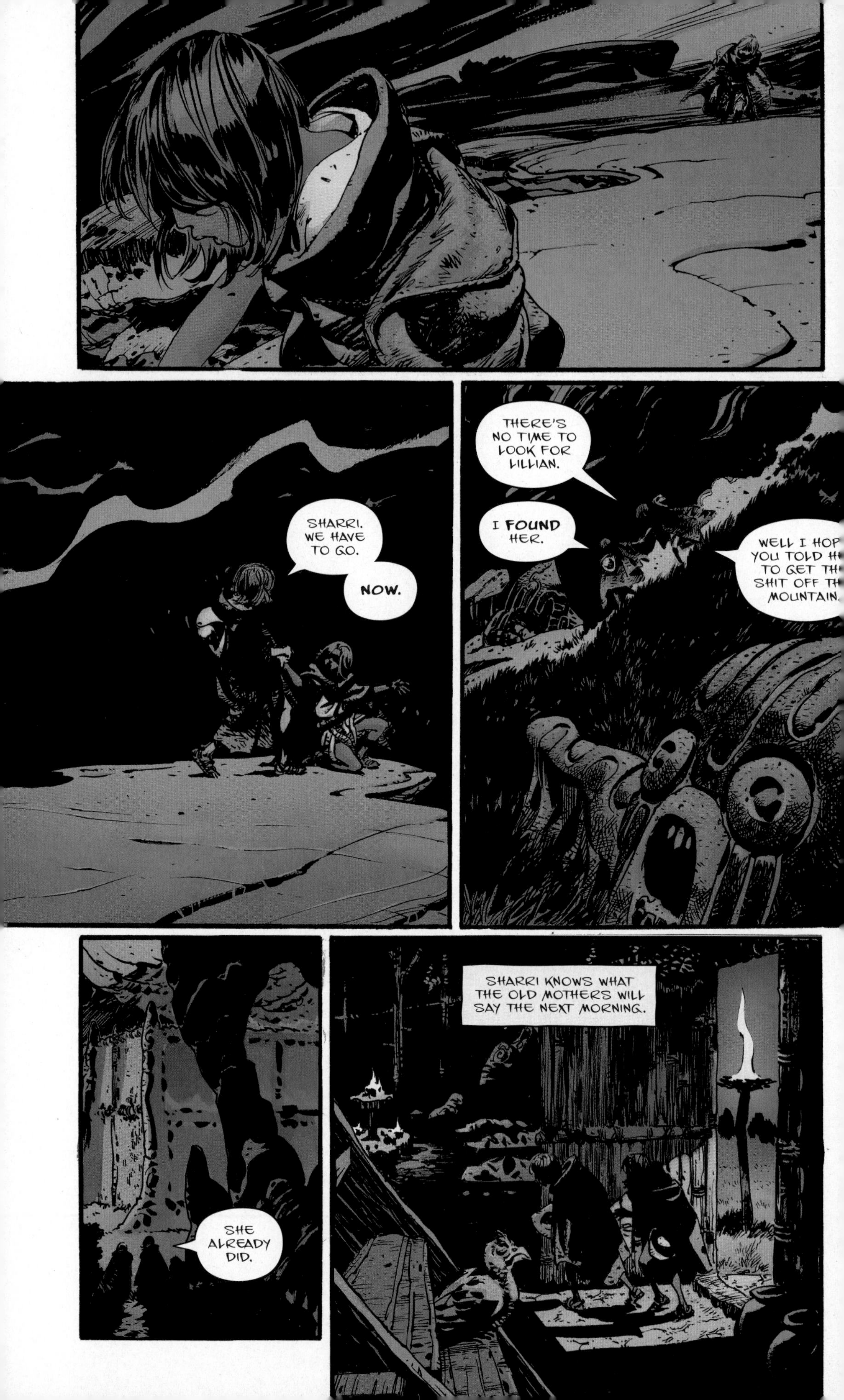
SHARRI. WE HAVE TO GO.
NOW.
THERE'S NO TIME TO LOOK FOR LILLIAN.
I FOUND HER.
WELL I HOP YOU TOLD H TO GET TH SHIT OFF TH MOUNTAIN.
SHE ALREADY DID.
SHARRI KNOWS WHAT THE OLD MOTHERS WILL SAY THE NEXT MORNING.

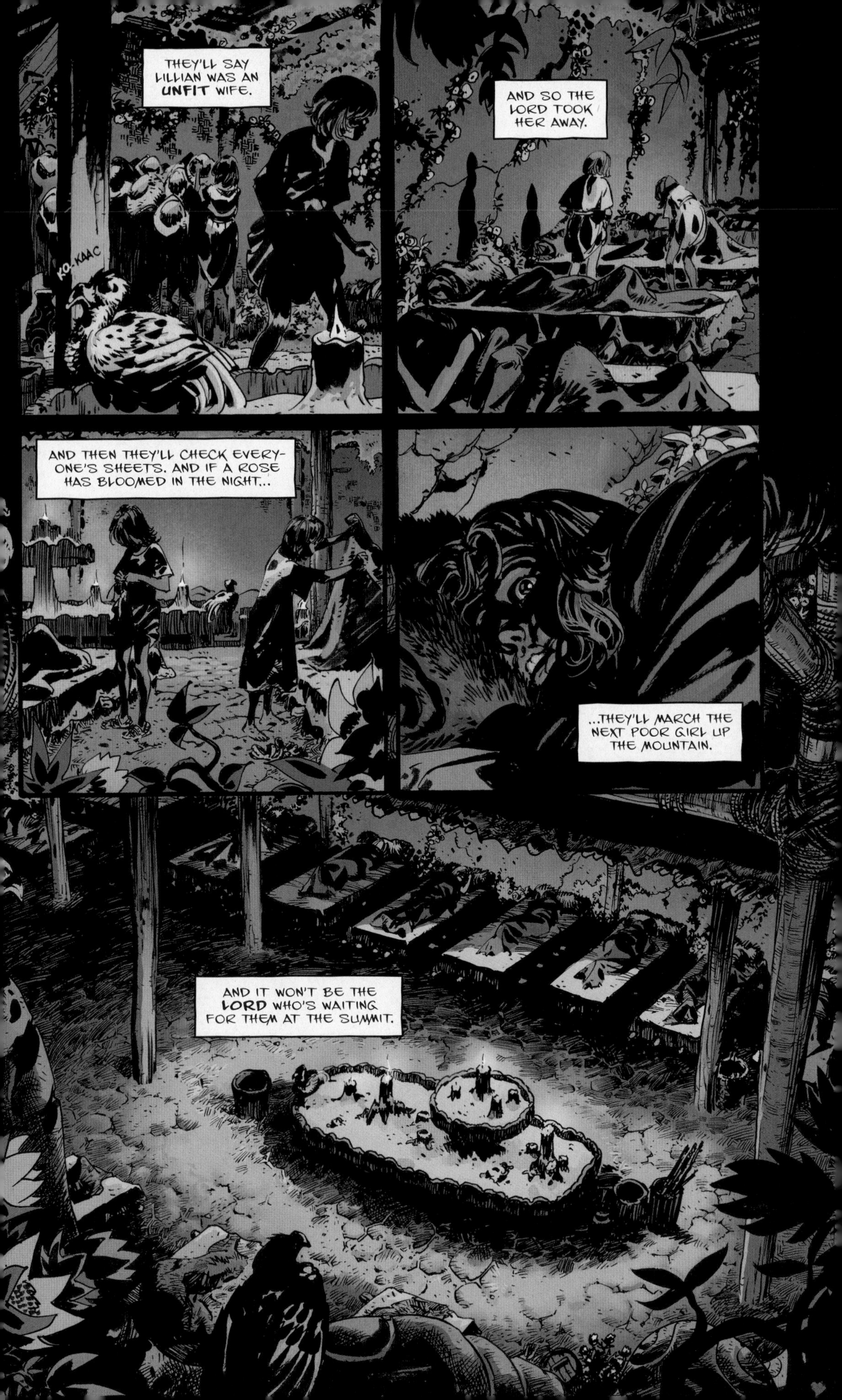
THEY'LL SAY LILLIAN WAS AN UNFIT WIFE.
KO-KAAC
AND SO THE LORD TOOK HER AWAY.
AND THEN THEY'LL CHECK EVERY-ONE'S SHEETS. AND IF A ROSE HAS BLOOMED IN THE NIGHT...
...THEY'LL MARCH THE NEXT POOR GIRL UP THE MOUNTAIN.
AND IT WON'T BE THE LORD WHO'S WAITING FOR THEM AT THE SUMMIT.

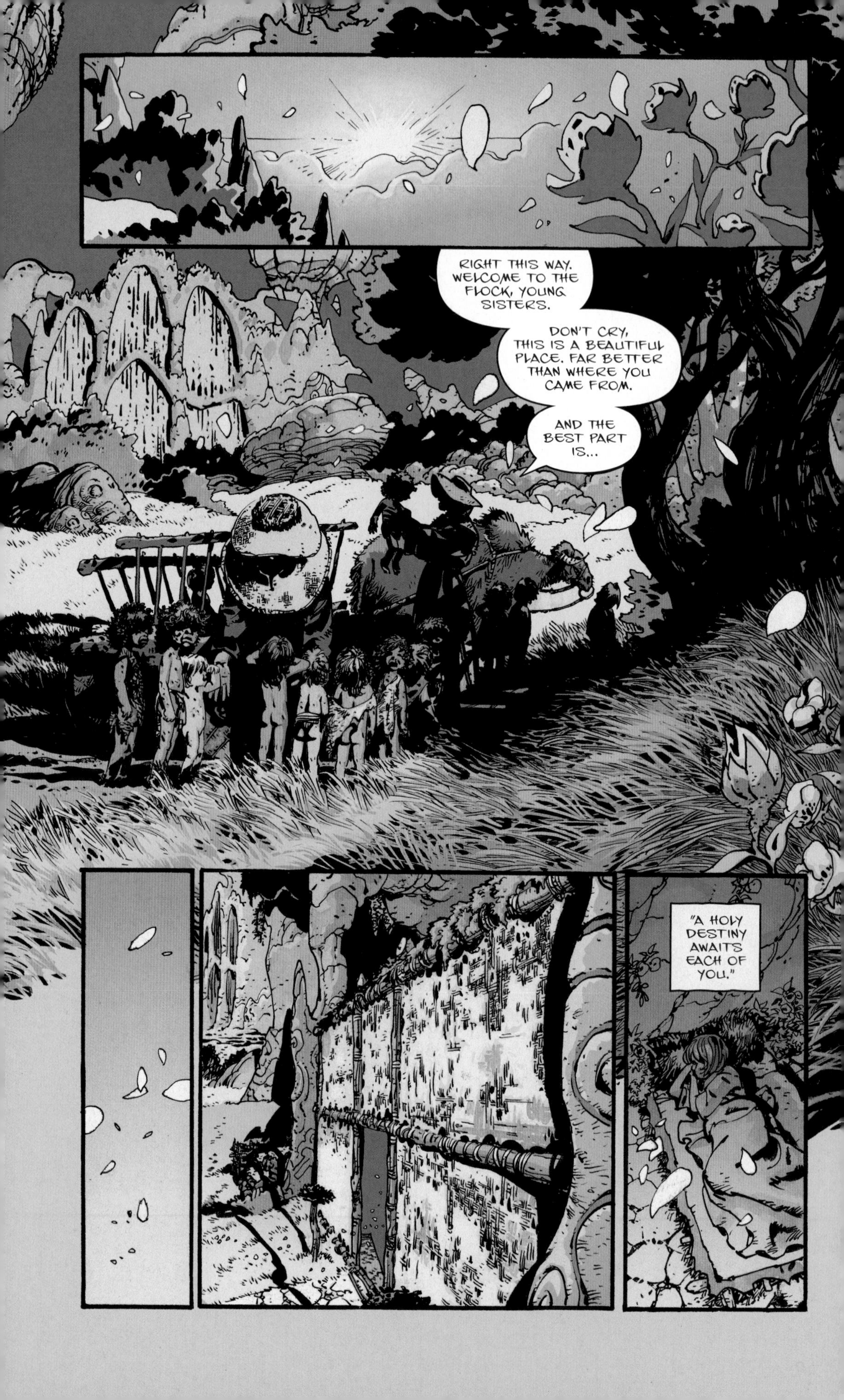

RIGHT THIS WAY. WELCOME TO THE FLOCK, YOUNG SISTERS.
DON'T CRY, THIS IS A BEAUTIFUL PLACE. FAR BETTER THAN WHERE YOU CAME FROM.
AND THE BEST PART IS...
"A HOLY DESTINY AWAITS EACH OF YOU."

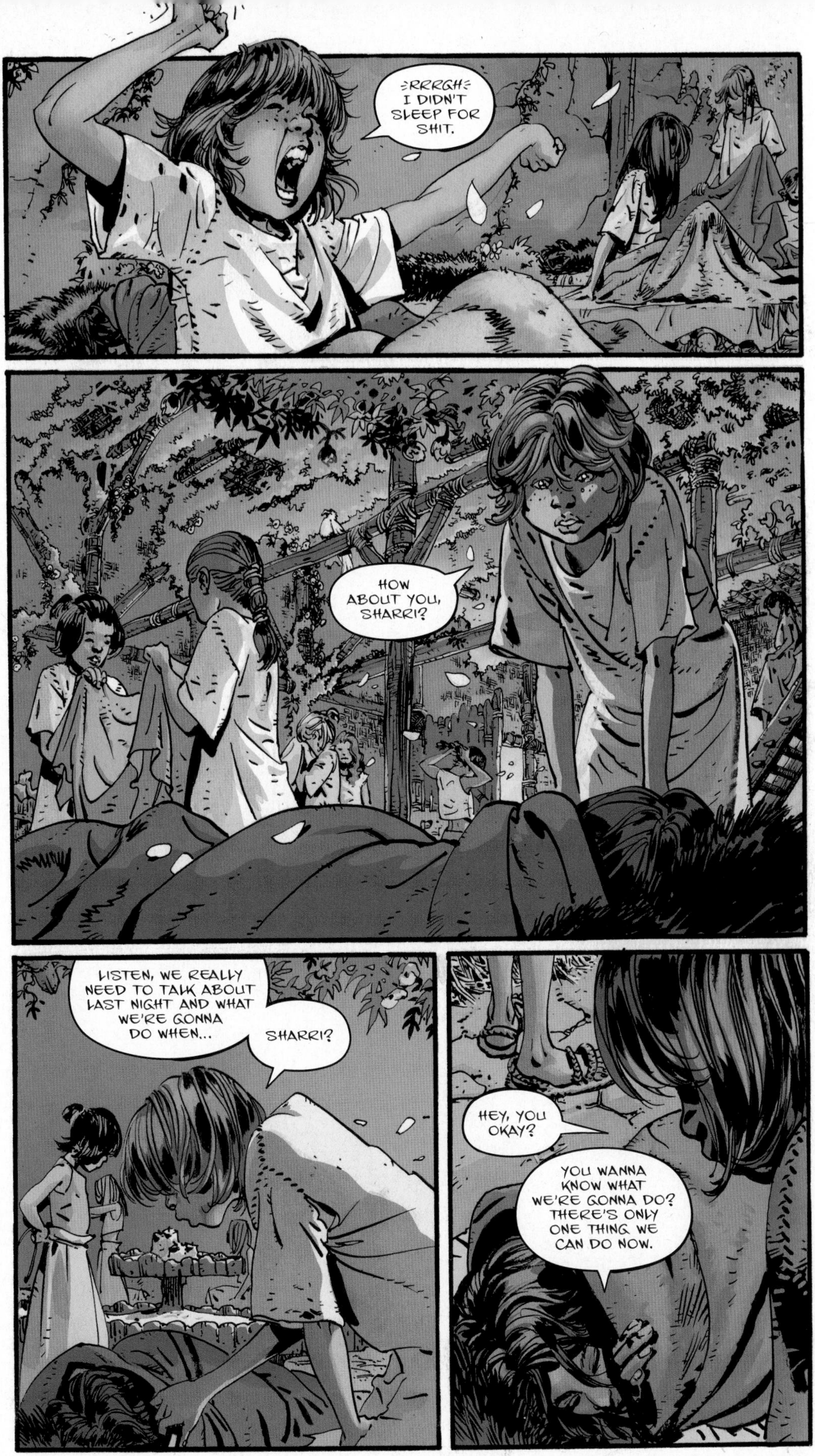
RRRGH I DIDN'T SLEEP FOR SHIT.
HOW ABOUT YOU, SHARRI?
LISTEN, WE REALLY NEED TO TALK ABOUT LAST NIGHT AND WHAT WE'RE GONNA DO WHEN...
SHARRI?
HEY, YOU OKAY?
YOU WANNA KNOW WHAT WE'RE GONNA DO? THERE'S ONLY ONE THING WE CAN DO NOW.

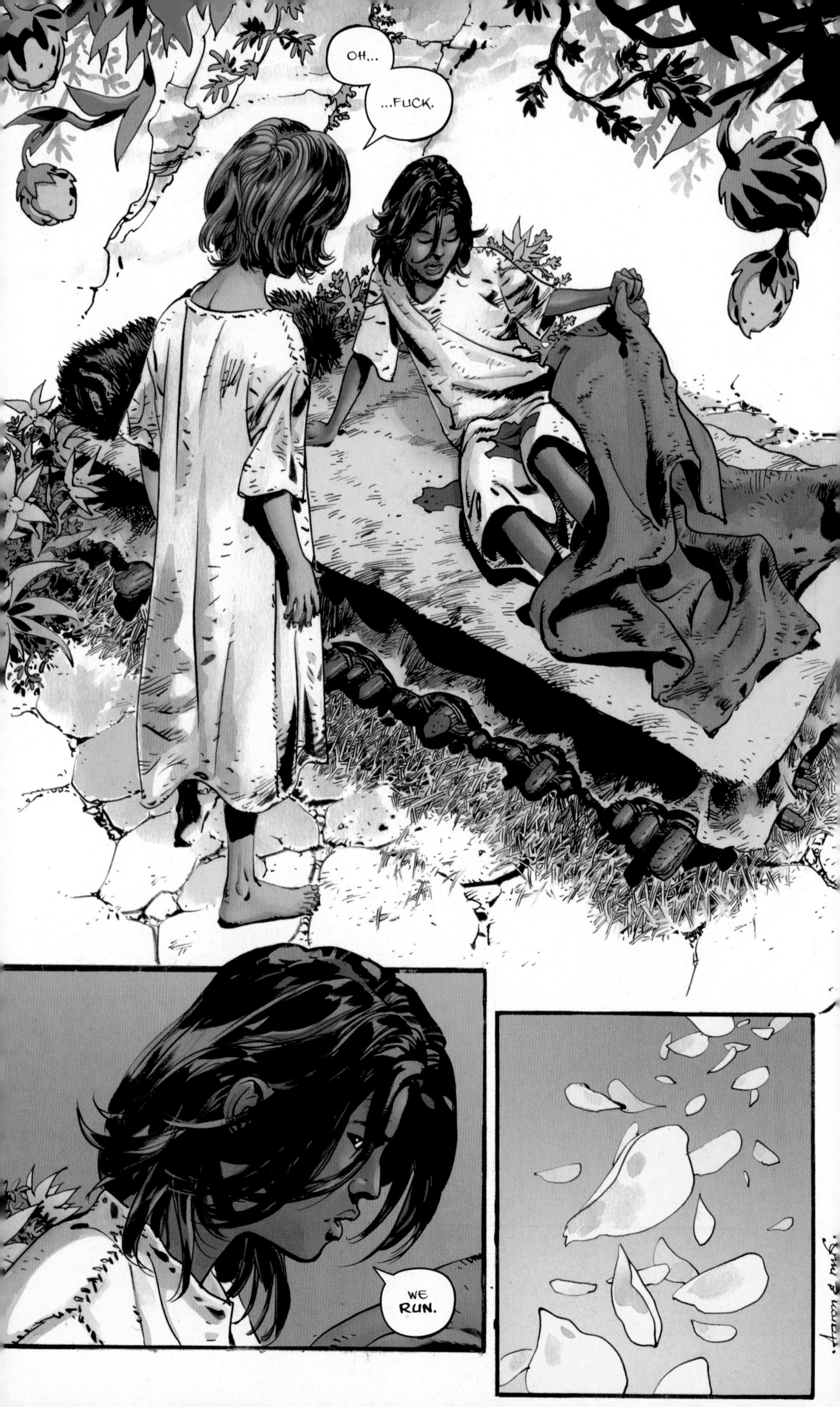
OH...
...FUCK.
WE RUN.

# Chapter Two
## "Running with the Devil"

**A**ND ADAM SAID, THIS IS
NOW BONE OF MY BONES,
AND FLESH OF MY FLESH:
SHE SHALL BE CALLED WOMAN.

--**G**ENESIS 2:23

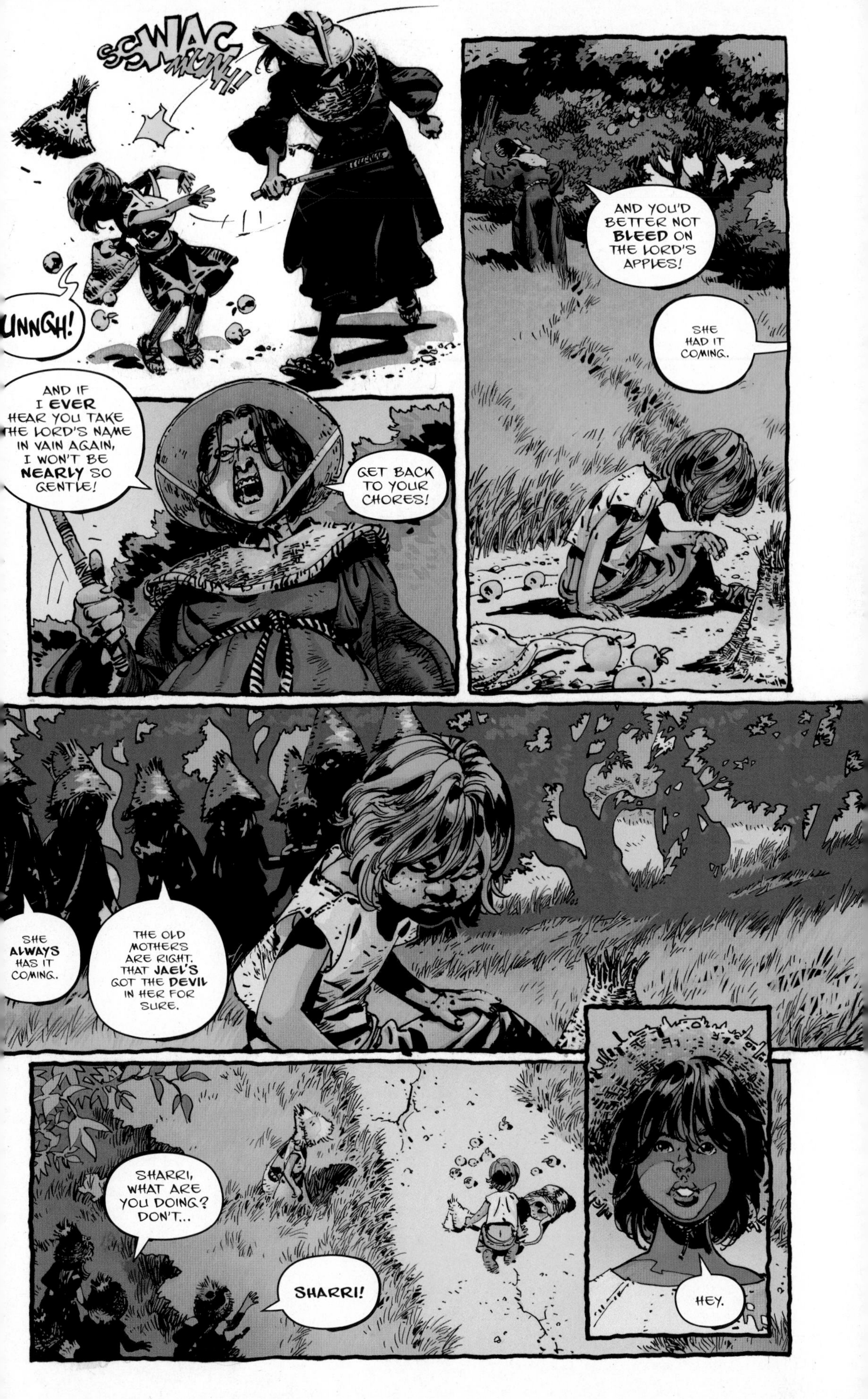
SCWAC
SMUNH!
UNNGH!
AND YOU'D BETTER NOT BLEED ON THE LORD'S APPLES!
SHE HAD IT COMING.
AND IF I EVER HEAR YOU TAKE THE LORD'S NAME IN VAIN AGAIN, I WON'T BE NEARLY SO GENTLE!
GET BACK TO YOUR CHORES!
SHE ALWAYS HAS IT COMING.
THE OLD MOTHERS ARE RIGHT. THAT JAEL'S GOT THE DEVIL IN HER FOR SURE.
SHARRI, WHAT ARE YOU DOING? DON'T...
SHARRI!
HEY.

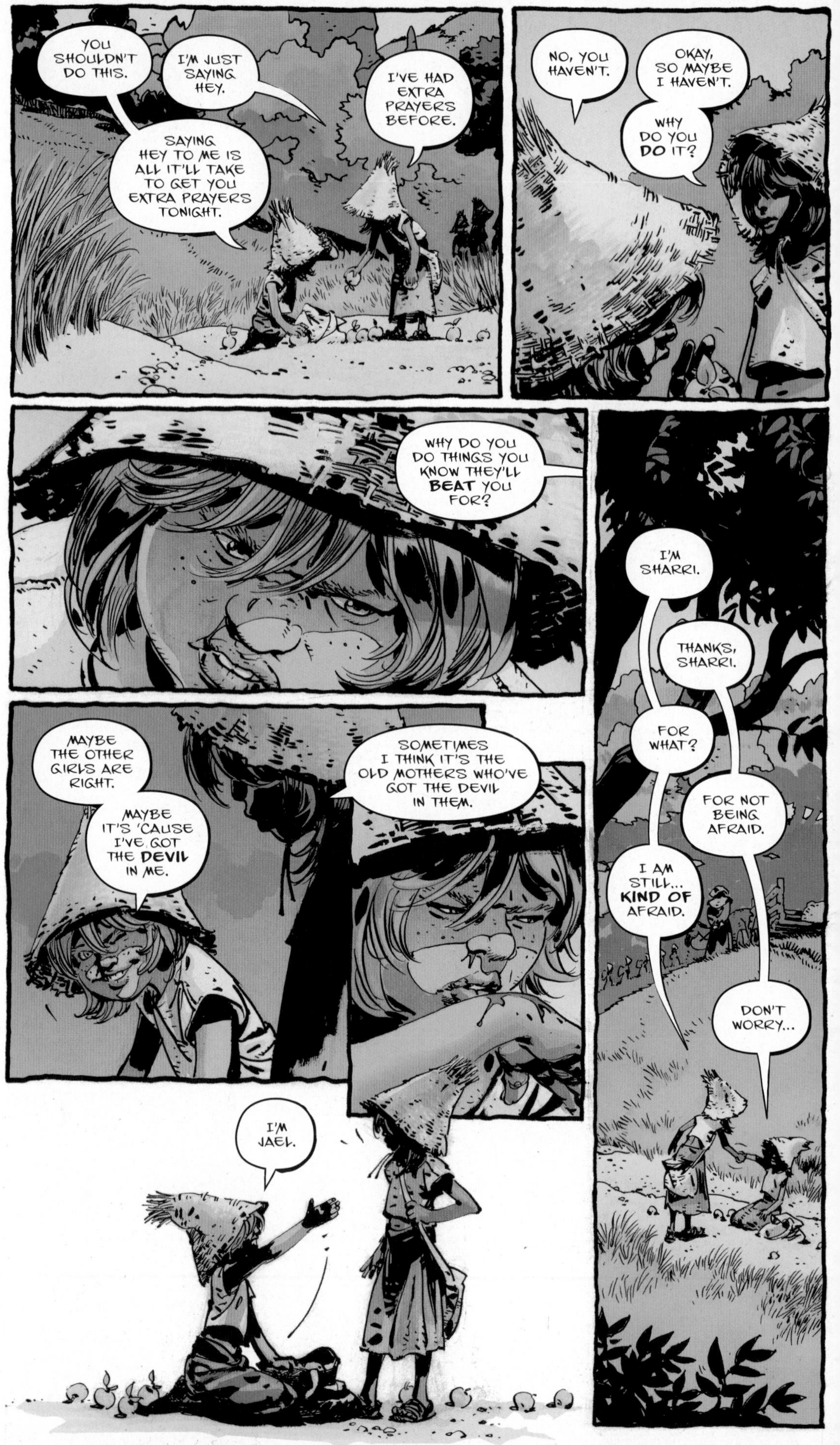
YOU SHOULDN'T DO THIS.
I'M JUST SAYING HEY.
SAYING HEY TO ME IS ALL IT'LL TAKE TO GET YOU EXTRA PRAYERS TONIGHT.
I'VE HAD EXTRA PRAYERS BEFORE.
NO, YOU HAVEN'T.
OKAY, SO MAYBE I HAVEN'T.
WHY DO YOU DO IT?
WHY DO YOU DO THINGS YOU KNOW THEY'LL BEAT YOU FOR?
MAYBE THE OTHER GIRLS ARE RIGHT.
MAYBE IT'S 'CAUSE I'VE GOT THE DEVIL IN ME.
SOMETIMES I THINK IT'S THE OLD MOTHERS WHO'VE GOT THE DEVIL IN THEM.
I'M JAEL.
I'M SHARRI.
THANKS, SHARRI.
FOR WHAT?
FOR NOT BEING AFRAID.
I AM STILL... KIND OF AFRAID.
DON'T WORRY...

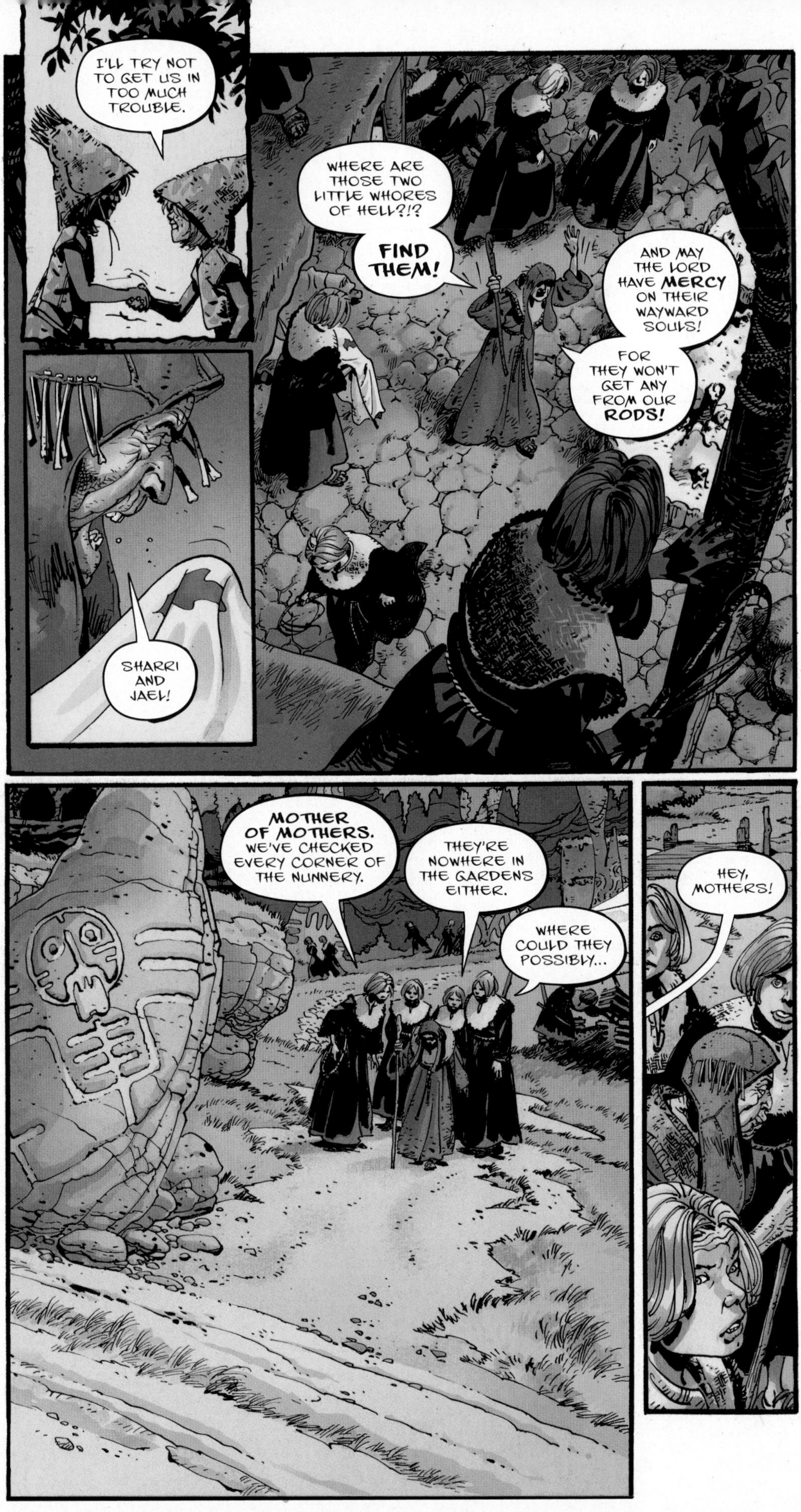
I'LL TRY NOT TO GET US IN TOO MUCH TROUBLE.
WHERE ARE THOSE TWO LITTLE WHORES OF HELL?!?
FIND THEM!
AND MAY THE LORD HAVE MERCY ON THEIR WAYWARD SOULS!
FOR THEY WON'T GET ANY FROM OUR RODS!
SHARRI AND JAEL!
MOTHER OF MOTHERS. WE'VE CHECKED EVERY CORNER OF THE NUNNERY.
THEY'RE NOWHERE IN THE GARDENS EITHER.
WHERE COULD THEY POSSIBLY...
HEY, MOTHERS!

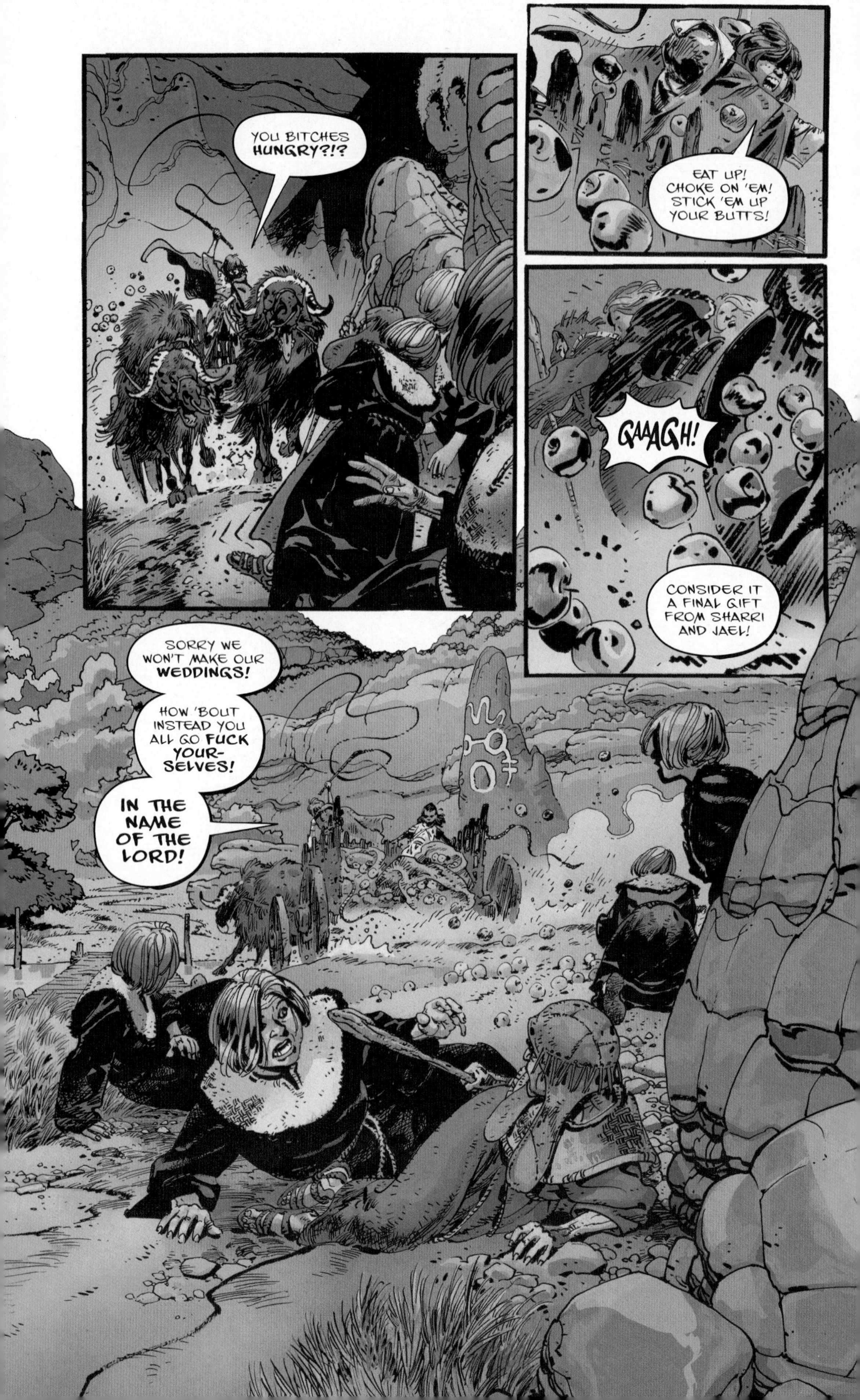

YOU BITCHES HUNGRY?!?
EAT UP! CHOKE ON 'EM! STICK 'EM UP YOUR BUTTS!
GAAAGH!
CONSIDER IT A FINAL GIFT FROM SHARRI AND JAEL!
SORRY WE WON'T MAKE OUR WEDDINGS!
HOW 'BOUT INSTEAD YOU ALL GO FUCK YOURSELVES!
IN THE NAME OF THE LORD!

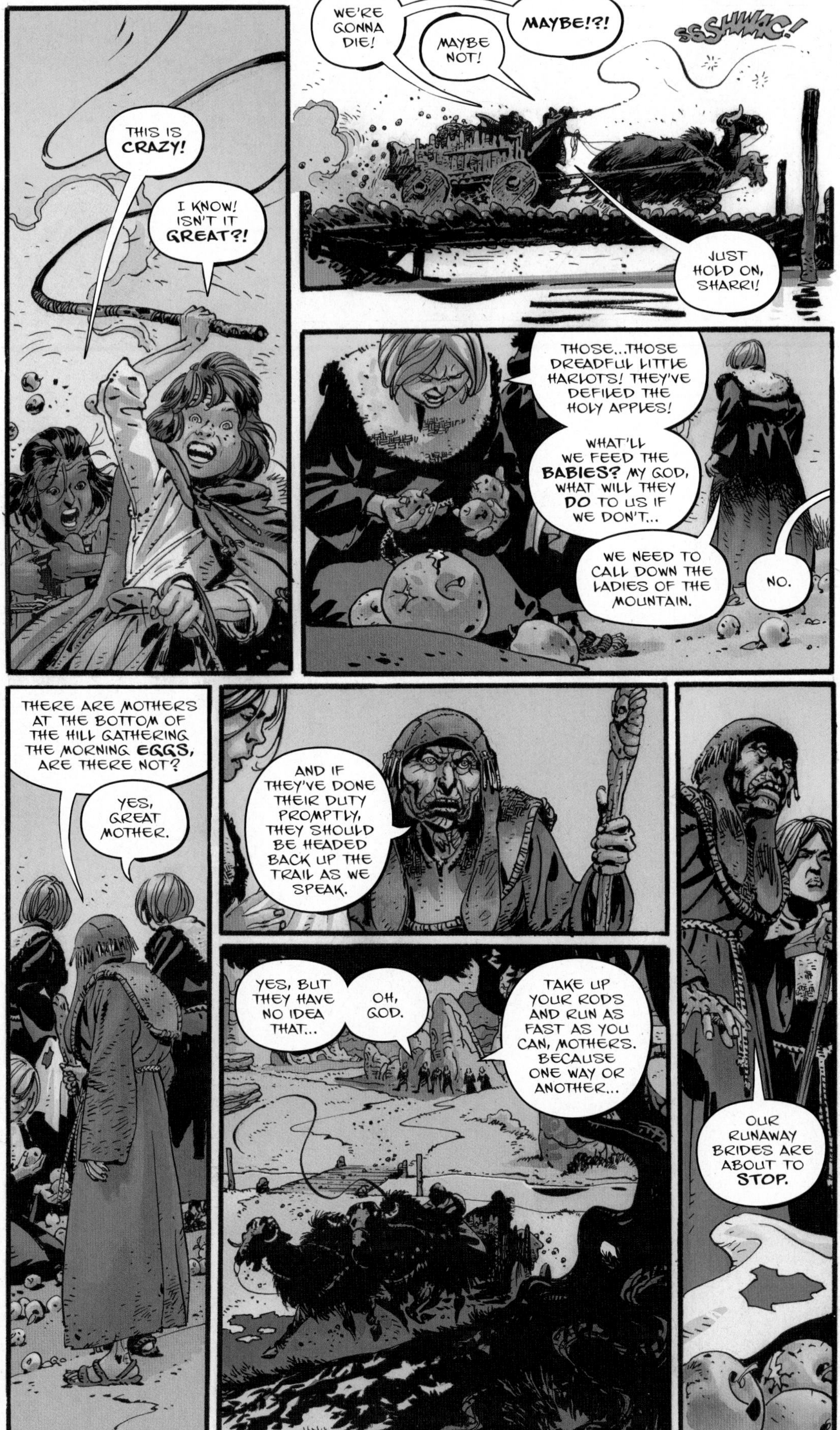

THIS IS CRAZY!
I KNOW! ISN'T IT GREAT?!
WE'RE GONNA DIE!
MAYBE NOT!
MAYBE!?!
SSSHWAC!
JUST HOLD ON, SHARRI!
THOSE...THOSE DREADFUL LITTLE HARLOTS! THEY'VE DEFILED THE HOLY APPLES!
WHAT'LL WE FEED THE BABIES? MY GOD, WHAT WILL THEY DO TO US IF WE DON'T...
WE NEED TO CALL DOWN THE LADIES OF THE MOUNTAIN.
NO.
THERE ARE MOTHERS AT THE BOTTOM OF THE HILL GATHERING THE MORNING EGGS, ARE THERE NOT?
YES, GREAT MOTHER.
AND IF THEY'VE DONE THEIR DUTY PROMPTLY, THEY SHOULD BE HEADED BACK UP THE TRAIL AS WE SPEAK.
YES, BUT THEY HAVE NO IDEA THAT...
OH, GOD.
TAKE UP YOUR RODS AND RUN AS FAST AS YOU CAN, MOTHERS. BECAUSE ONE WAY OR ANOTHER...
OUR RUNAWAY BRIDES ARE ABOUT TO STOP.

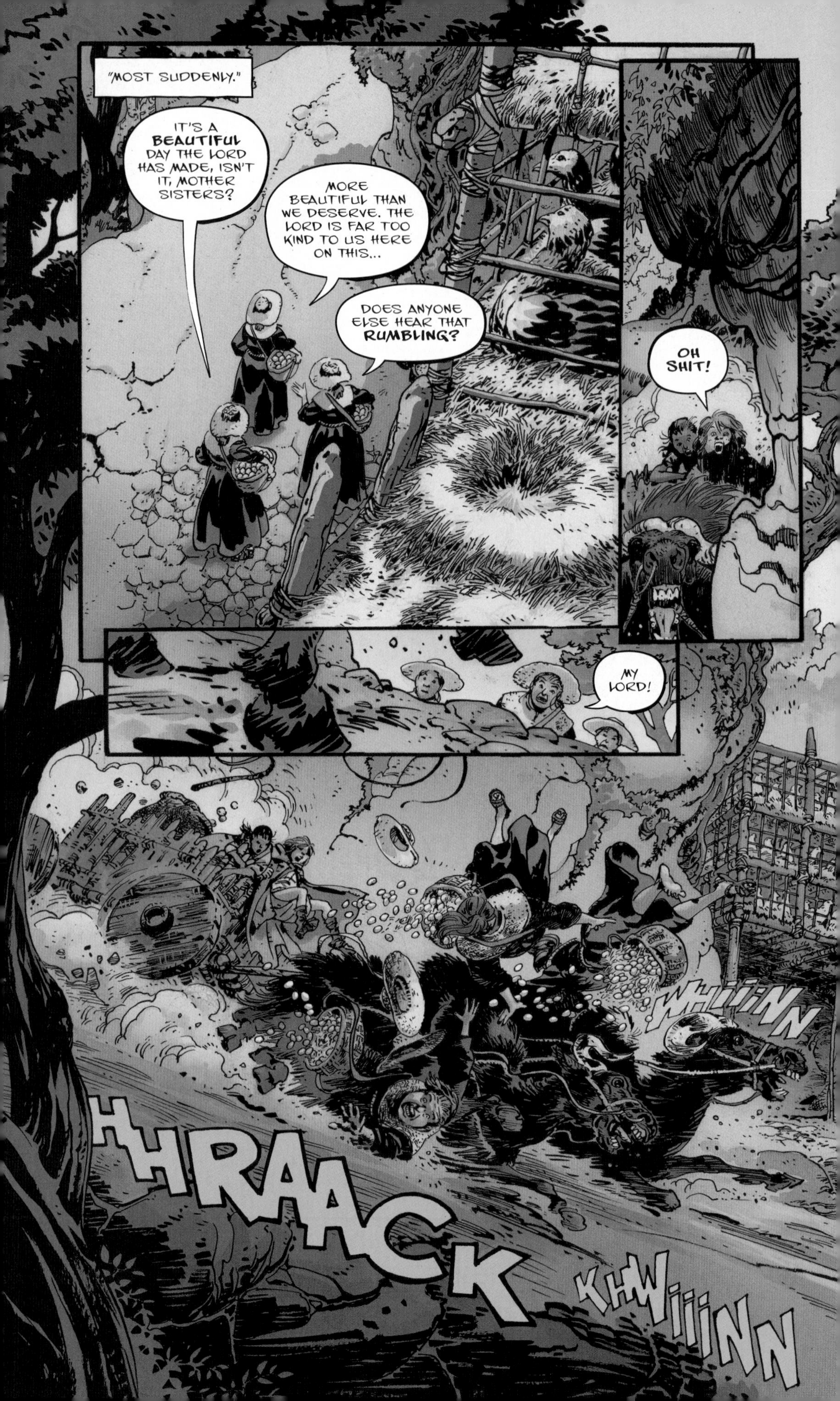

"MOST SUDDENLY."
IT'S A BEAUTIFUL DAY THE LORD HAS MADE, ISN'T IT, MOTHER SISTERS?
MORE BEAUTIFUL THAN WE DESERVE. THE LORD IS FAR TOO KIND TO US HERE ON THIS...
DOES ANYONE ELSE HEAR THAT RUMBLING?
OH SHIT!
MY LORD!
WHIIINN
HHRAACK
KHWIIINN

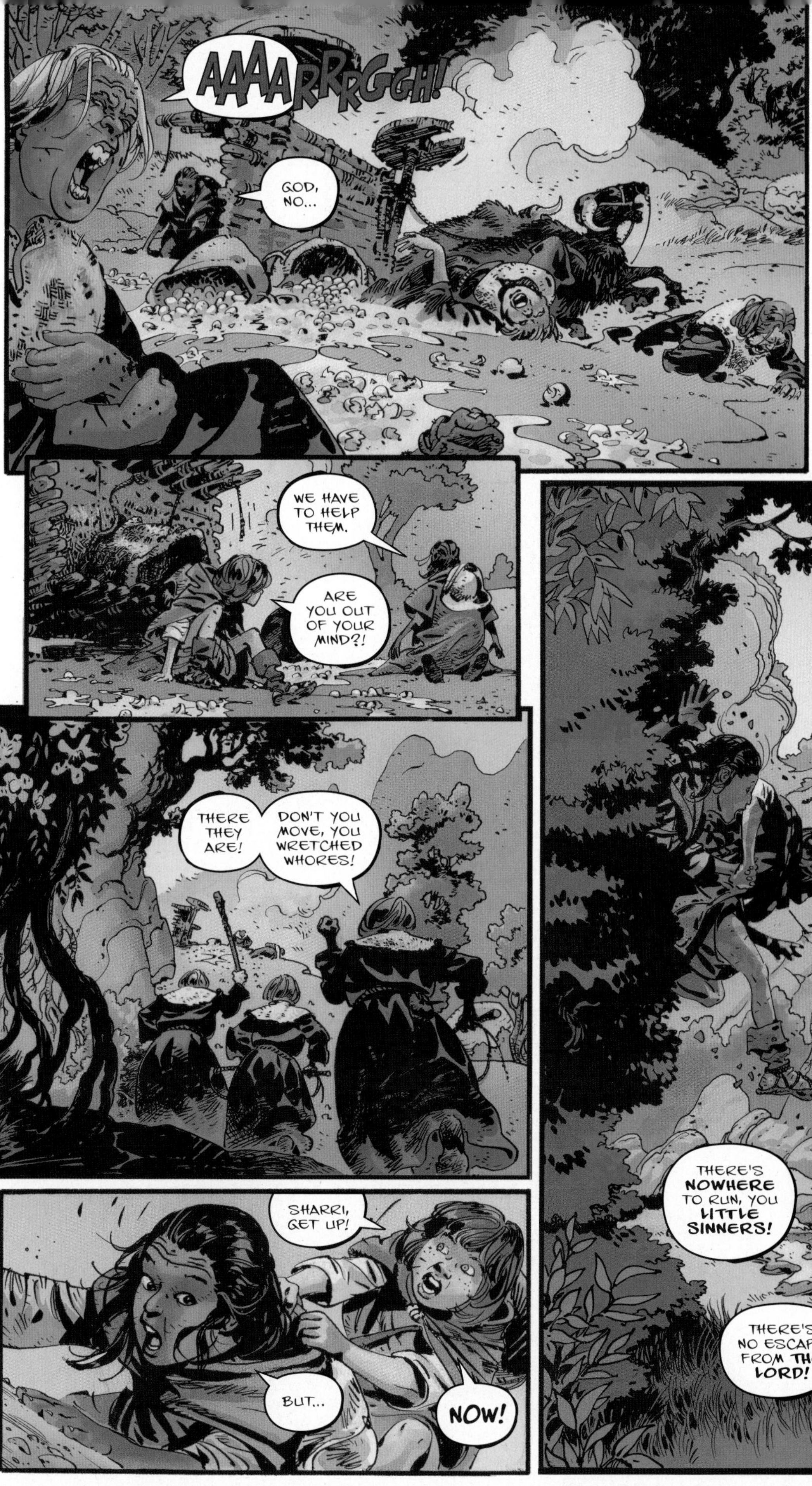
AAAARRRGGH!
GOD, NO...
WE HAVE TO HELP THEM.
ARE YOU OUT OF YOUR MIND?!
THERE THEY ARE!
DON'T YOU MOVE, YOU WRETCHED WHORES!
SHARRI, GET UP!
BUT...
NOW!
THERE'S NOWHERE TO RUN, YOU LITTLE SINNERS!
THERE'S NO ESCAPE FROM THE LORD!

YOU INCOMPETENTS!

SINCE YOU'VE BROUGHT BACK NO **RUNAWAY BRIDES** FOR US TO WHIP, I EXPECT YOU LOT TO SPEND THE REST OF YOUR EVENING FLOGGING YOURSELVES.

MOST **VIGOROUSLY.**

OUR APOLOGIES, GREAT MOTHER. WE SEARCHED ALL THROUGH THE GARDENS, BUT...

BUT WE'RE JUST NOT **HUNTERS.**

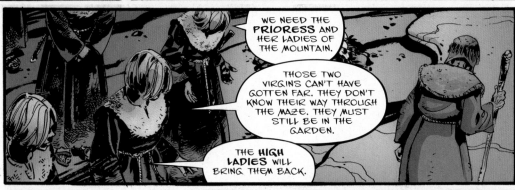

WE NEED THE **PRIORESS** AND HER LADIES OF THE MOUNTAIN.

THOSE TWO VIRGINS CAN'T HAVE GOTTEN FAR. THEY DON'T KNOW THEIR WAY THROUGH THE MAZE. THEY MUST STILL BE IN THE GARDEN.

THE **HIGH LADIES** WILL BRING THEM BACK.

VERY WELL. SEND THE SIGNAL.

GOD, THOSE HALF-NAKED SOWS WILL NEVER LET ME HEAR THE END OF THIS.

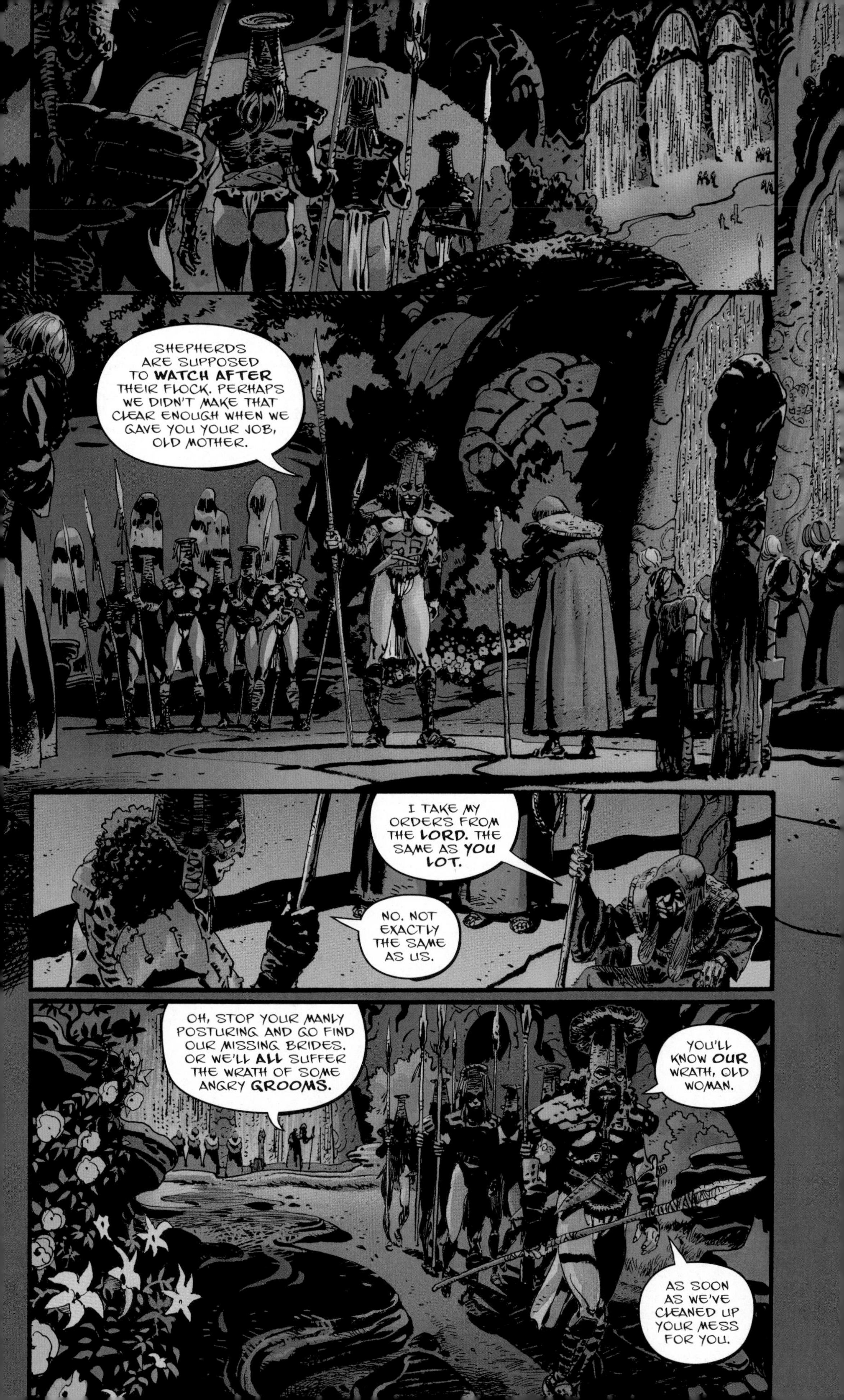
SHEPHERDS ARE SUPPOSED TO WATCH AFTER THEIR FLOCK. PERHAPS WE DIDN'T MAKE THAT CLEAR ENOUGH WHEN WE GAVE YOU YOUR JOB, OLD MOTHER.
I TAKE MY ORDERS FROM THE LORD. THE SAME AS YOU LOT.
NO. NOT EXACTLY THE SAME AS US.
OH, STOP YOUR MANLY POSTURING AND GO FIND OUR MISSING BRIDES. OR WE'LL ALL SUFFER THE WRATH OF SOME ANGRY GROOMS.
YOU'LL KNOW OUR WRATH, OLD WOMAN.
AS SOON AS WE'VE CLEANED UP YOUR MESS FOR YOU.

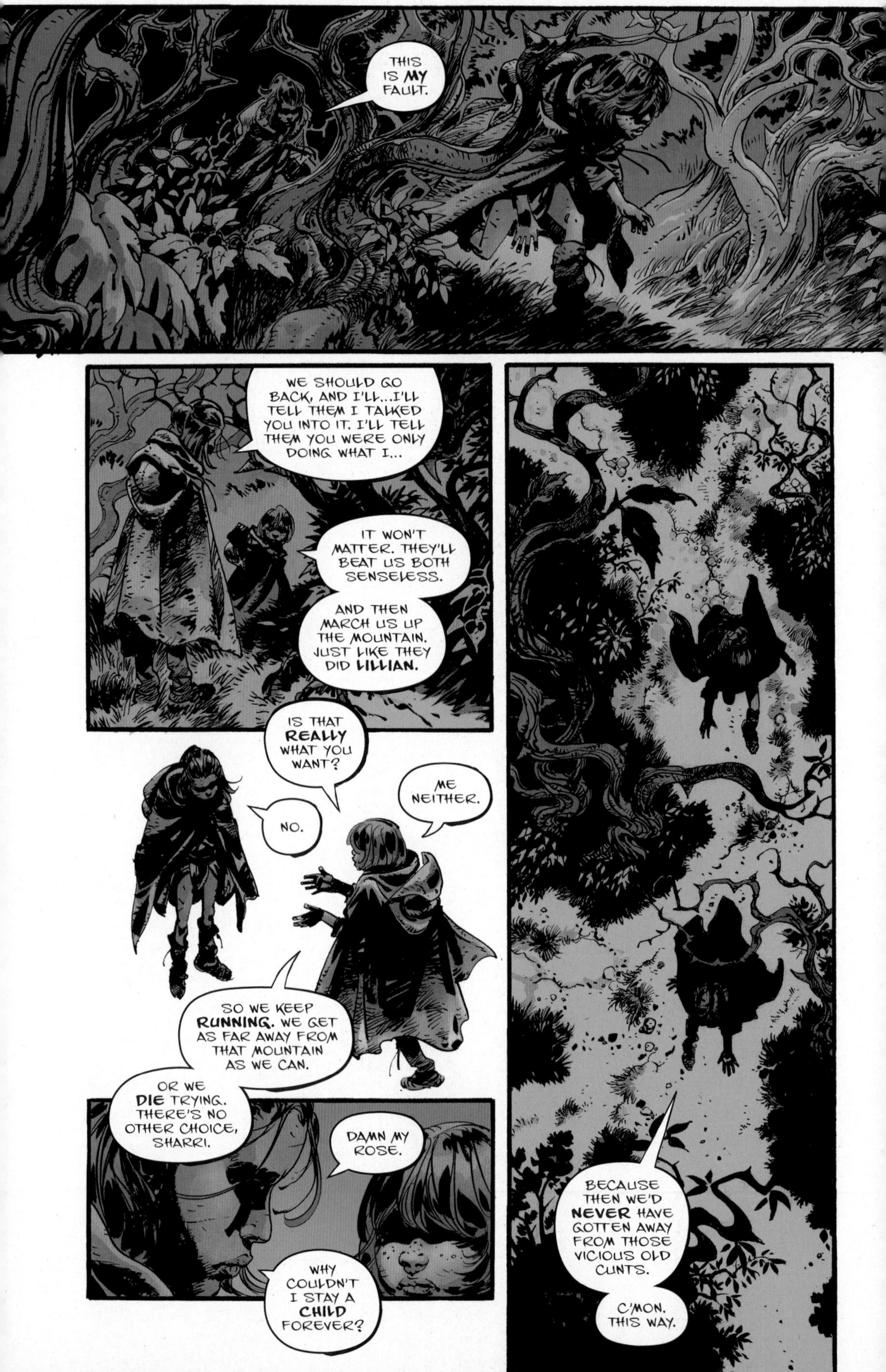
THIS IS MY FAULT.
WE SHOULD GO BACK, AND I'LL...I'LL TELL THEM I TALKED YOU INTO IT. I'LL TELL THEM YOU WERE ONLY DOING WHAT I...
IT WON'T MATTER. THEY'LL BEAT US BOTH SENSELESS.
AND THEN MARCH US UP THE MOUNTAIN. JUST LIKE THEY DID LILLIAN.
IS THAT REALLY WHAT YOU WANT?
NO.
ME NEITHER.
SO WE KEEP RUNNING. WE GET AS FAR AWAY FROM THAT MOUNTAIN AS WE CAN.
OR WE DIE TRYING. THERE'S NO OTHER CHOICE, SHARRI.
DAMN MY ROSE.
WHY COULDN'T I STAY A CHILD FOREVER?
BECAUSE THEN WE'D NEVER HAVE GOTTEN AWAY FROM THOSE VICIOUS OLD CUNTS.
C'MON. THIS WAY.

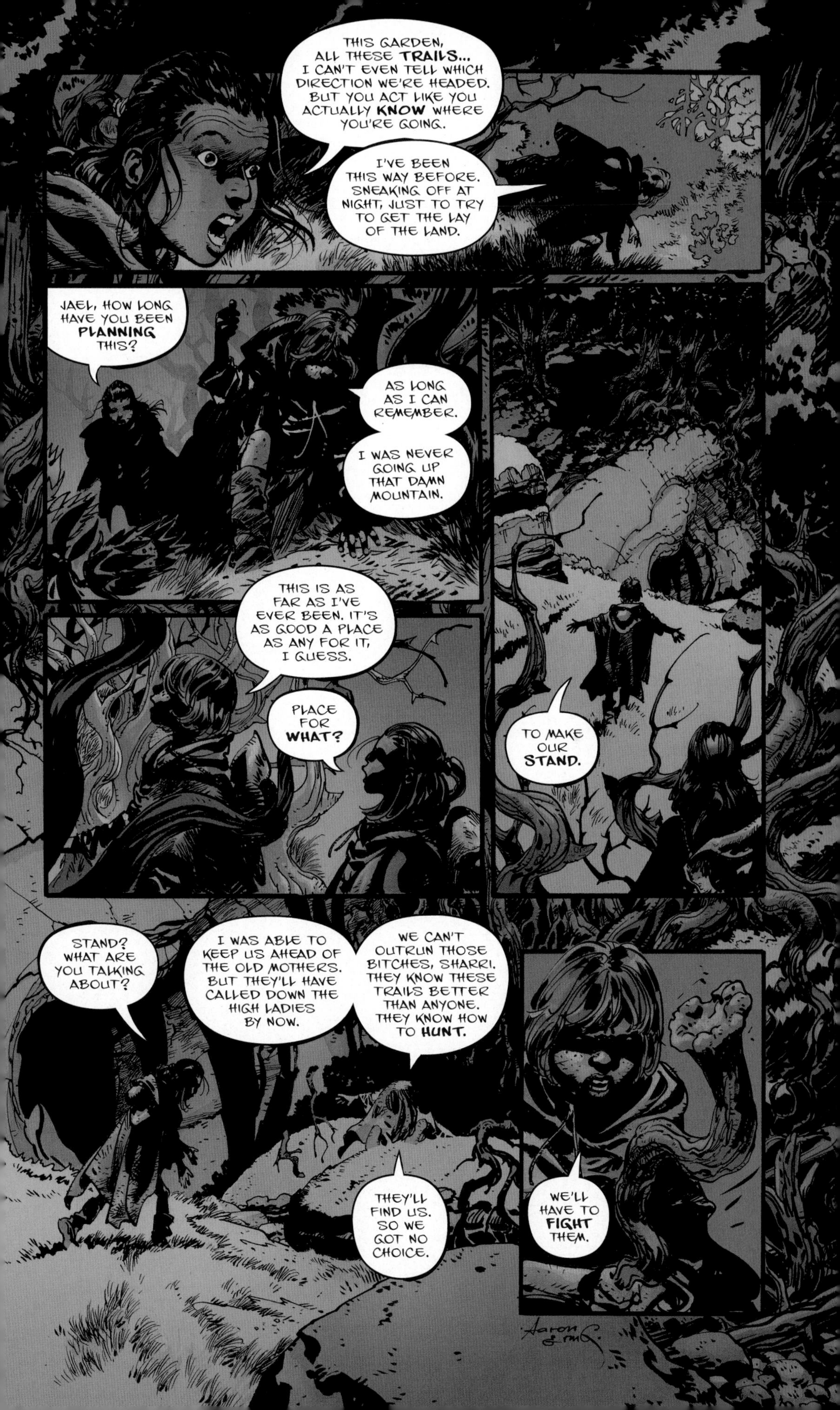

THIS GARDEN, ALL THESE **TRAILS...** I CAN'T EVEN TELL WHICH DIRECTION WE'RE HEADED. BUT YOU ACT LIKE YOU ACTUALLY **KNOW** WHERE YOU'RE GOING.
I'VE BEEN THIS WAY BEFORE. SNEAKING OFF AT NIGHT, JUST TO TRY TO GET THE LAY OF THE LAND.
JAEL, HOW LONG HAVE YOU BEEN **PLANNING** THIS?
AS LONG AS I CAN REMEMBER.
I WAS NEVER GOING UP THAT DAMN MOUNTAIN.
THIS IS AS FAR AS I'VE EVER BEEN. IT'S AS GOOD A PLACE AS ANY FOR IT, I GUESS.
PLACE FOR **WHAT?**
TO MAKE OUR **STAND.**
STAND? WHAT ARE YOU TALKING ABOUT?
I WAS ABLE TO KEEP US AHEAD OF THE OLD MOTHERS. BUT THEY'LL HAVE CALLED DOWN THE HIGH LADIES BY NOW.
WE CAN'T OUTRUN THOSE BITCHES, SHARRI. THEY KNOW THESE TRAILS BETTER THAN ANYONE. THEY KNOW HOW TO **HUNT.**
THEY'LL FIND US. SO WE GOT NO CHOICE.
WE'LL HAVE TO **FIGHT** THEM.

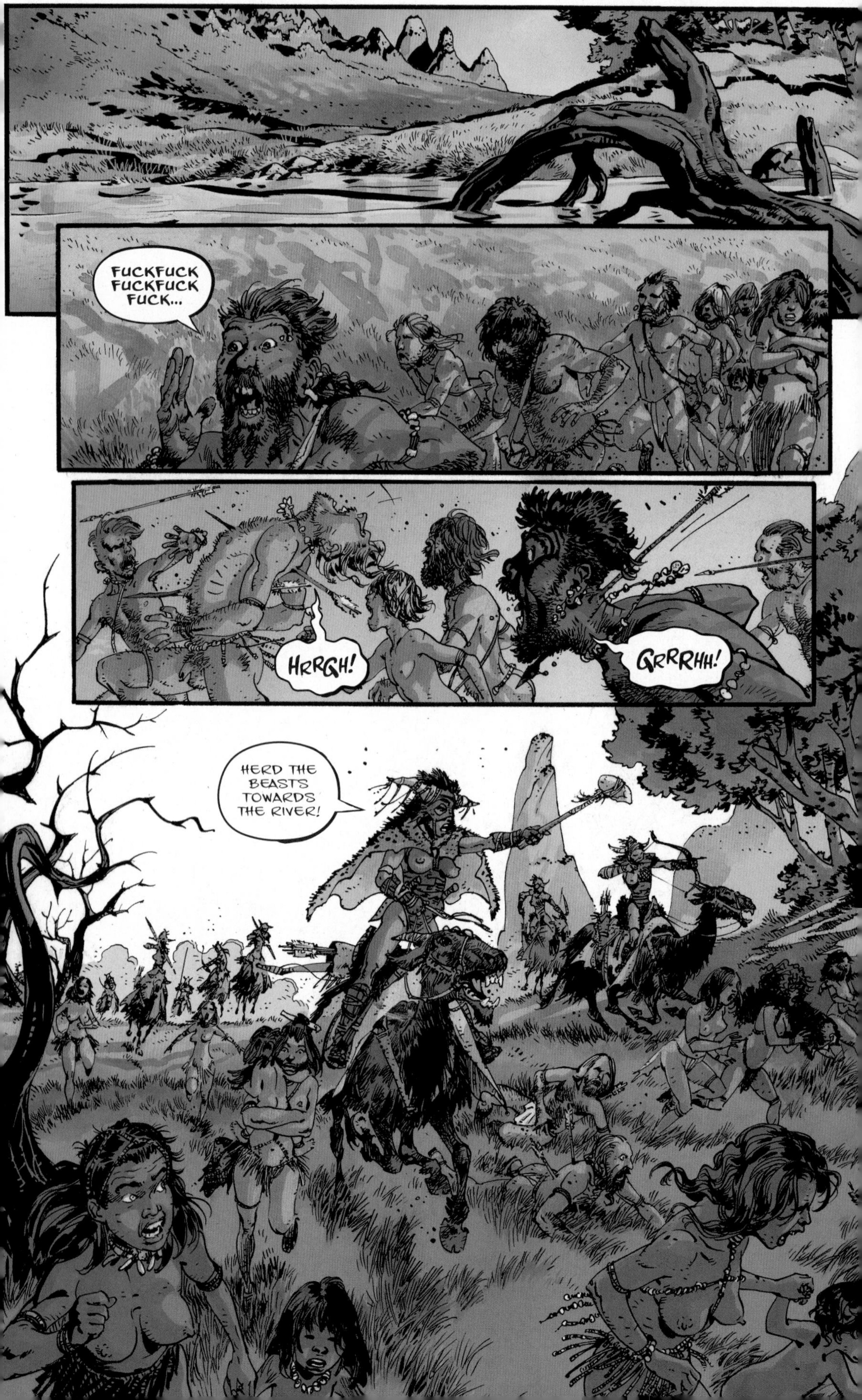
FUCKFUCK FUCKFUCK FUCK...
HRRGH!
GRRRHH!
HERD THE BEASTS TOWARDS THE RIVER!

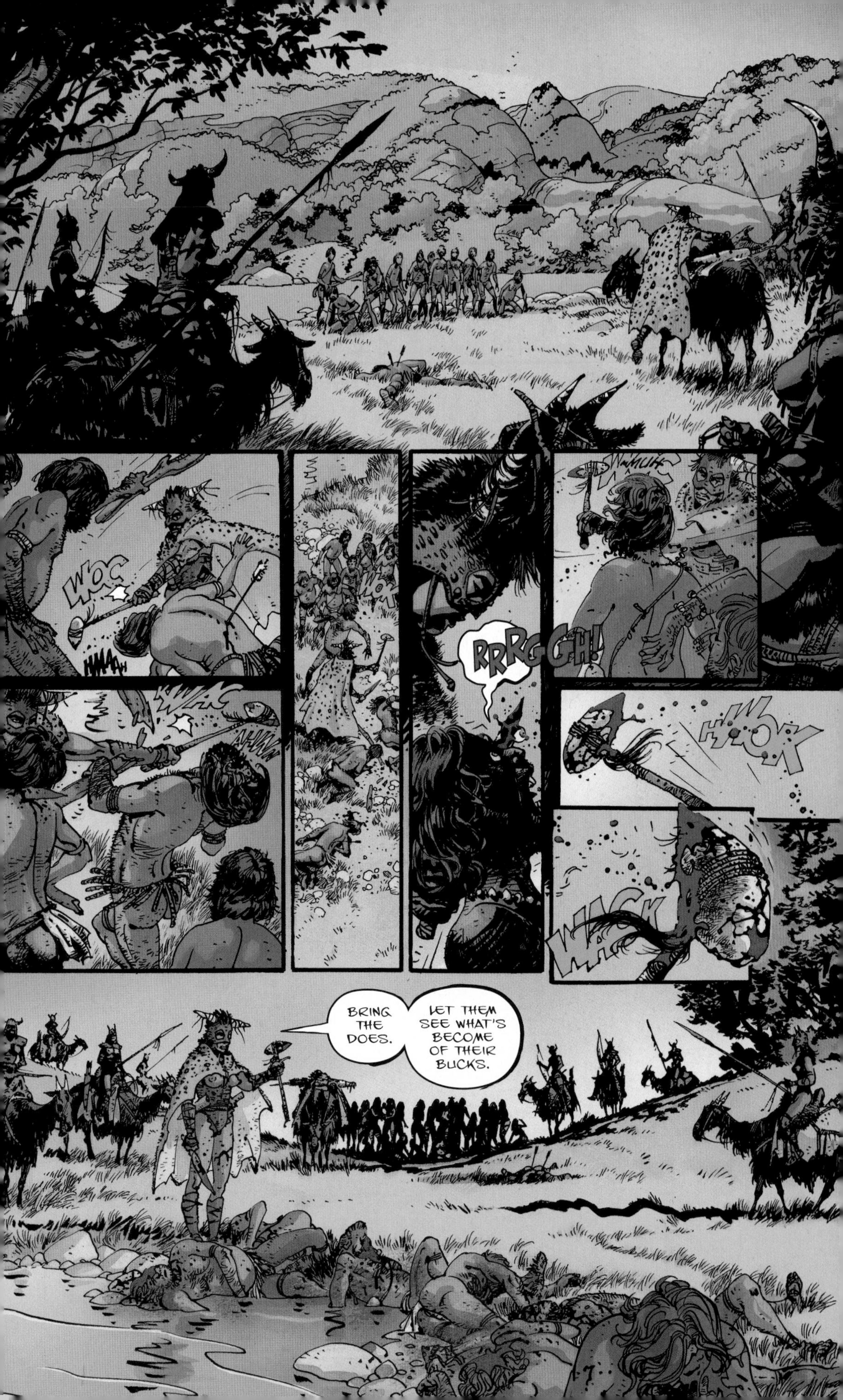
WOC
HWAAH
WOK
RRRGGH!
WHAC
HWOK
WACK
BRING THE DOES.
LET THEM SEE WHAT'S BECOME OF THEIR BUCKS.

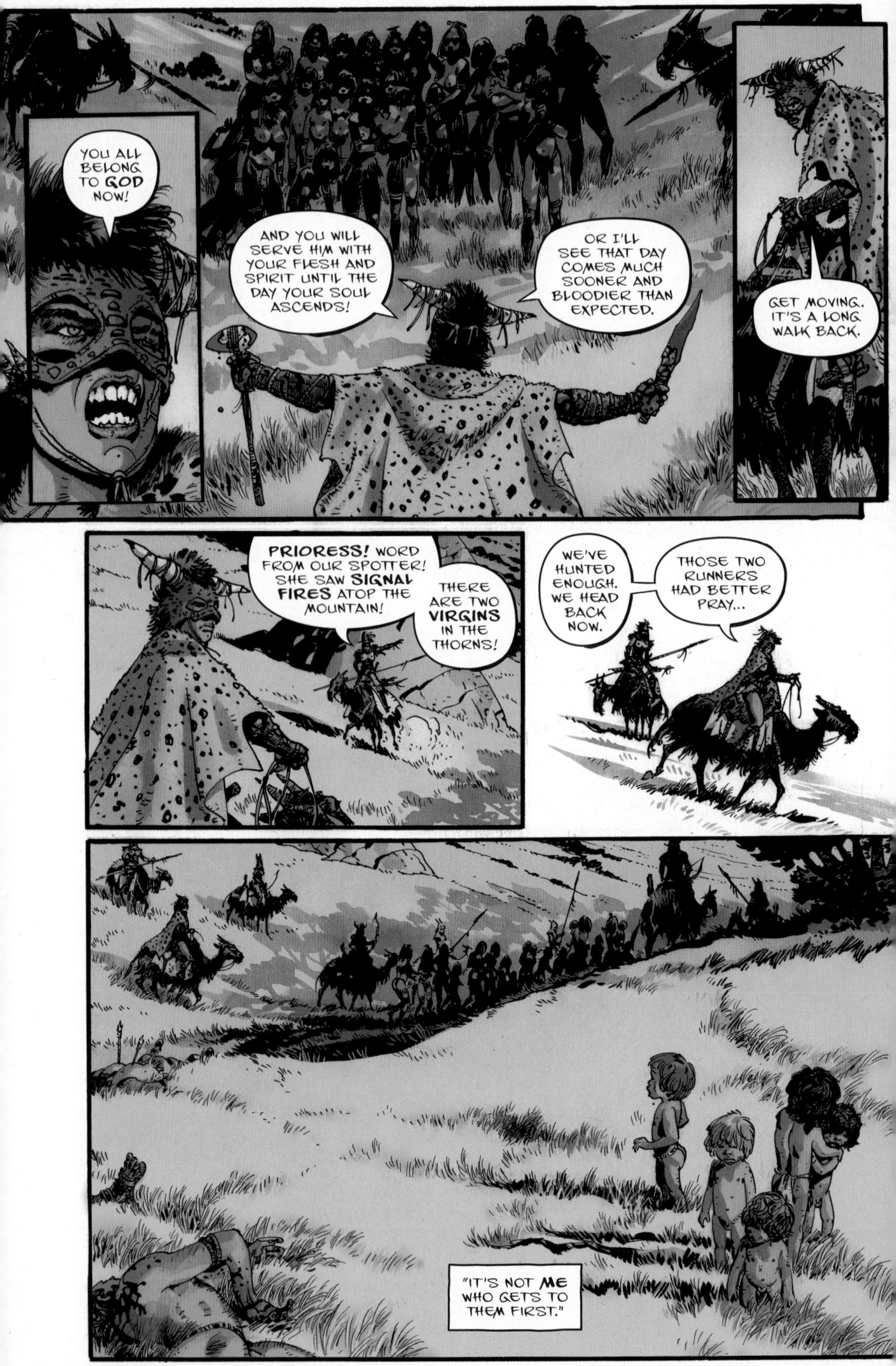
YOU ALL BELONG TO GOD NOW!
AND YOU WILL SERVE HIM WITH YOUR FLESH AND SPIRIT UNTIL THE DAY YOUR SOUL ASCENDS!
OR I'LL SEE THAT DAY COMES MUCH SOONER AND BLOODIER THAN EXPECTED.
GET MOVING. IT'S A LONG WALK BACK.
PRIORESS! WORD FROM OUR SPOTTER! SHE SAW SIGNAL FIRES ATOP THE MOUNTAIN!
THERE ARE TWO VIRGINS IN THE THORNS!
WE'VE HUNTED ENOUGH. WE HEAD BACK NOW.
THOSE TWO RUNNERS HAD BETTER PRAY...
"IT'S NOT ME WHO GETS TO THEM FIRST."

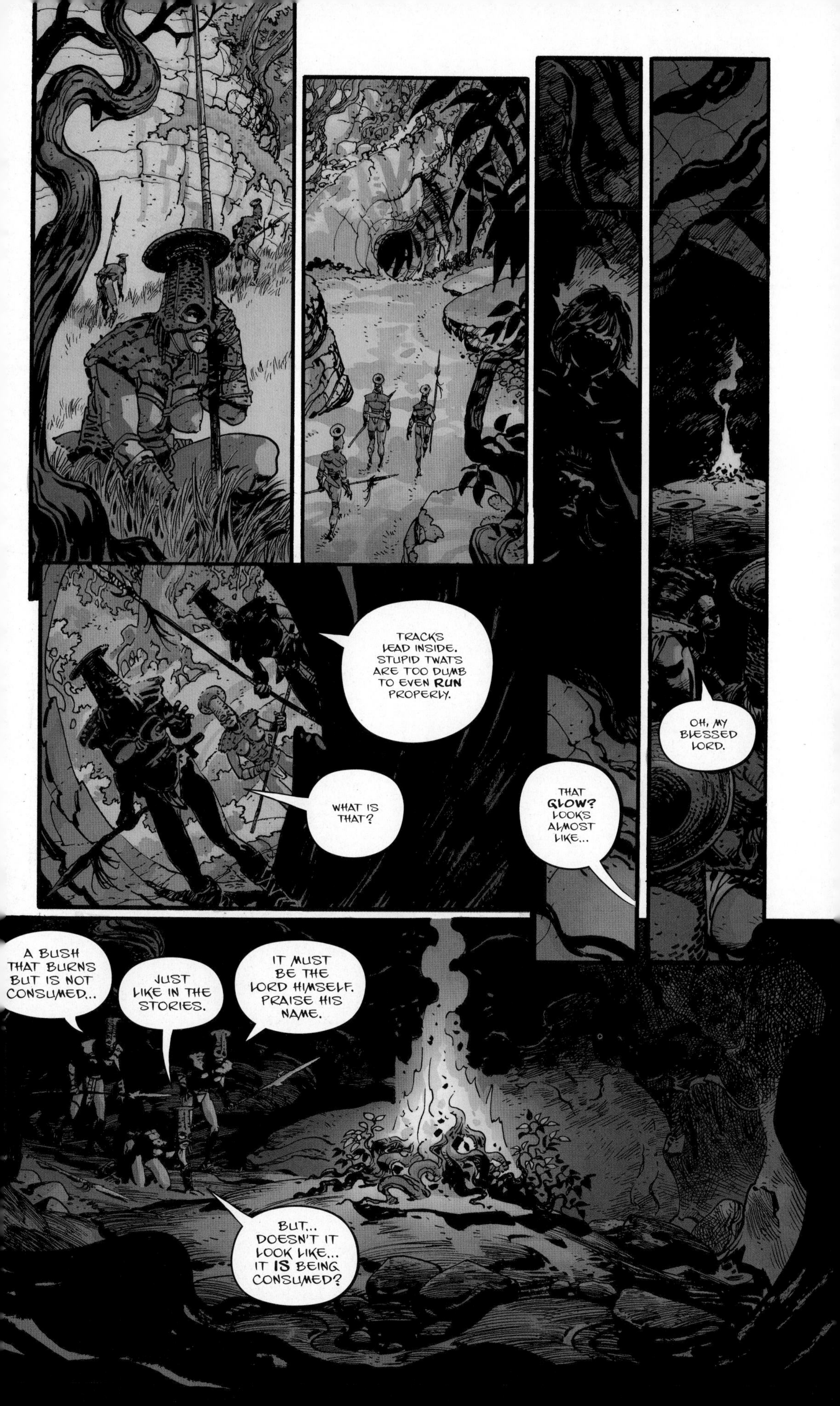
TRACKS LEAD INSIDE. STUPID TWATS ARE TOO DUMB TO EVEN **RUN** PROPERLY.
WHAT IS THAT?
THAT **GLOW?** LOOKS ALMOST LIKE...
OH, MY BLESSED LORD.
A BUSH THAT BURNS BUT IS NOT CONSUMED...
JUST LIKE IN THE STORIES.
IT MUST BE THE LORD HIMSELF. PRAISE HIS NAME.
BUT... DOESN'T IT LOOK LIKE... IT **IS** BEING CONSUMED?

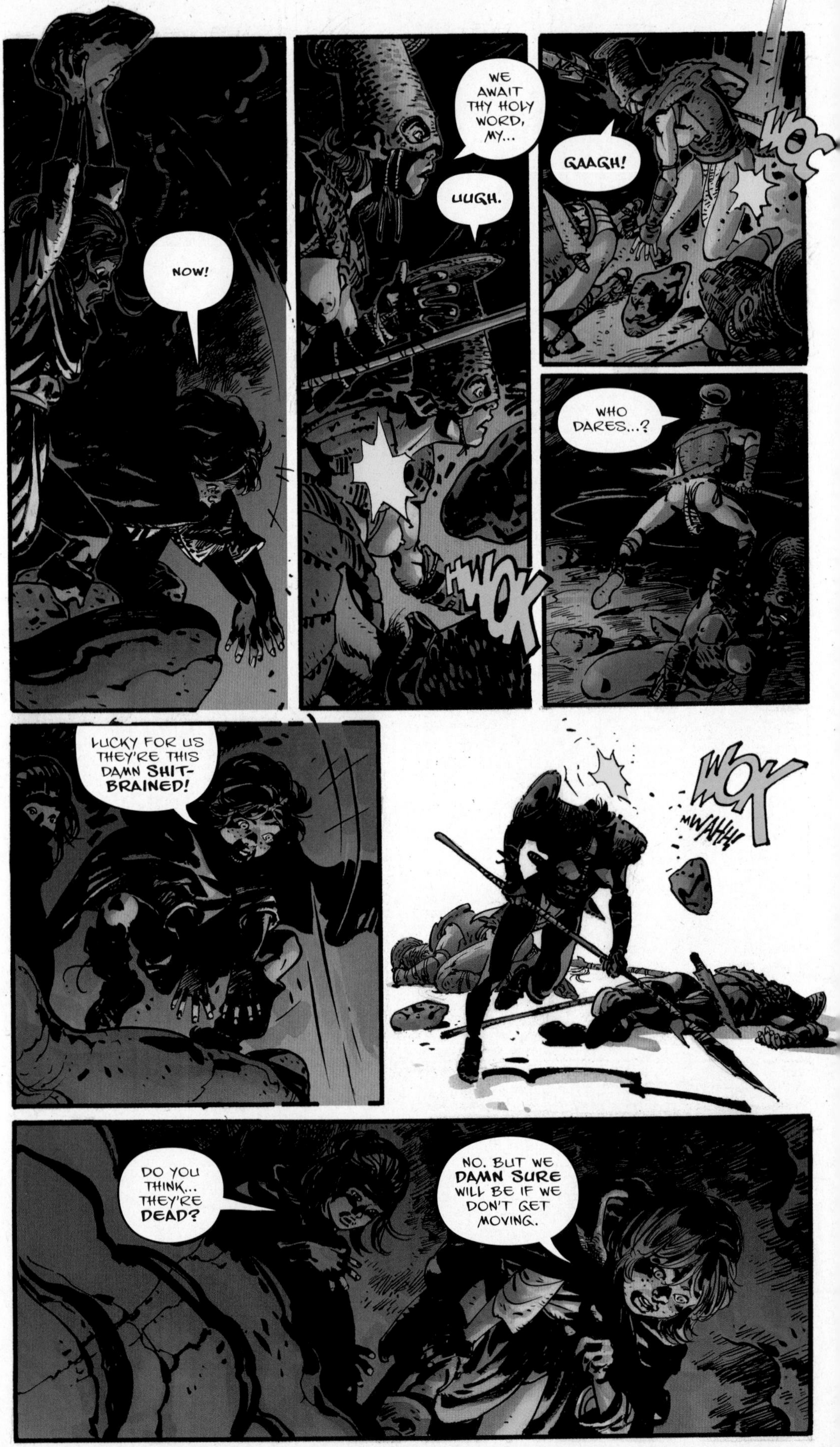
NOW!
WE AWAIT THY HOLY WORD, MY...
UUGH.
HWOK
GAAGH!
WOC
WHO DARES...?
LUCKY FOR US THEY'RE THIS DAMN SHIT-BRAINED!
WOK
MWAHH!
DO YOU THINK... THEY'RE DEAD?
NO. BUT WE DAMN SURE WILL BE IF WE DON'T GET MOVING.

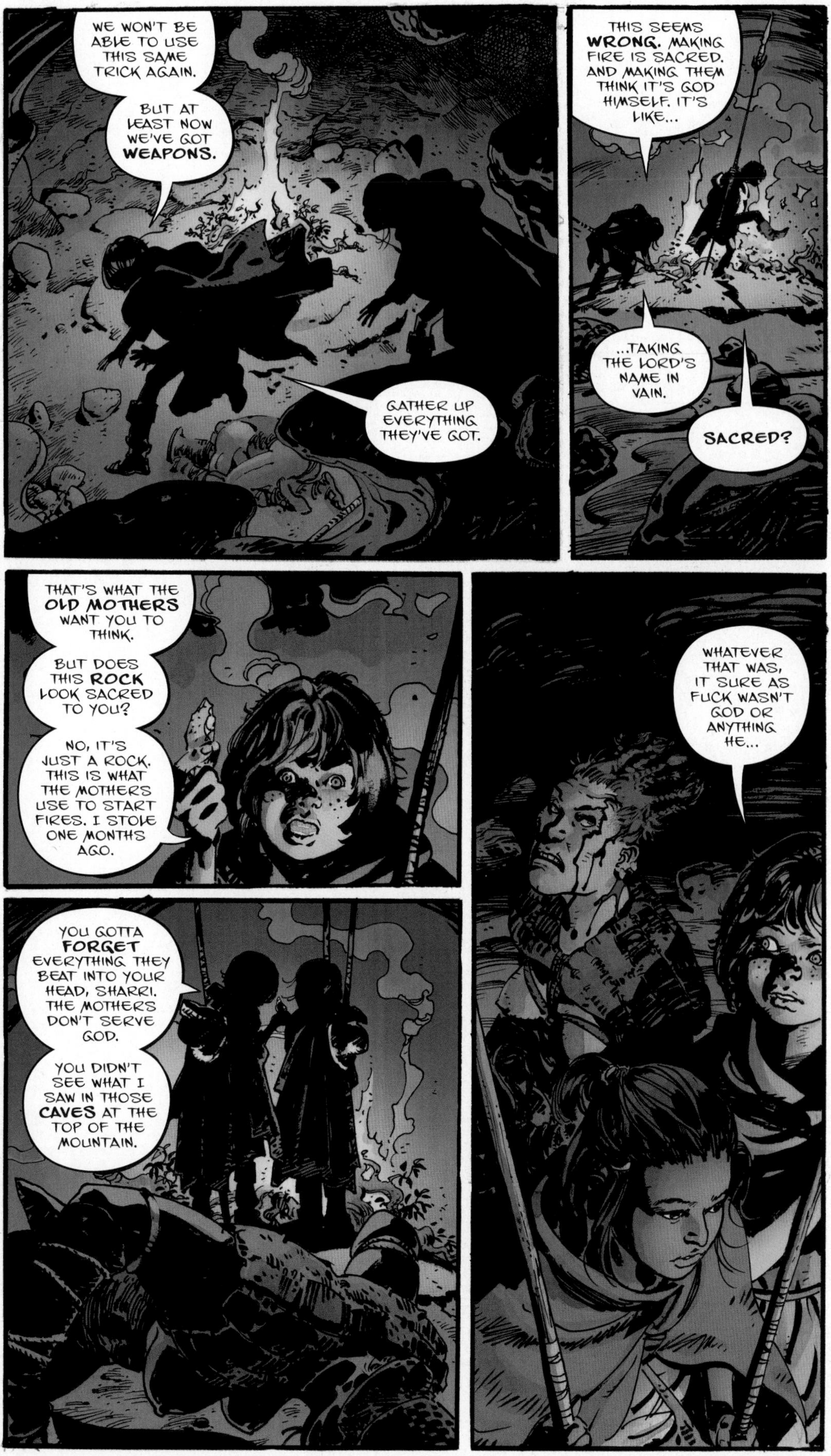
WE WON'T BE ABLE TO USE THIS SAME TRICK AGAIN.
BUT AT LEAST NOW WE'VE GOT **WEAPONS.**
GATHER UP EVERYTHING THEY'VE GOT.
THIS SEEMS **WRONG.** MAKING FIRE IS SACRED. AND MAKING THEM THINK IT'S GOD HIMSELF. IT'S LIKE...
...TAKING THE LORD'S NAME IN VAIN.
**SACRED?**
THAT'S WHAT THE **OLD MOTHERS** WANT YOU TO THINK.
BUT DOES THIS **ROCK** LOOK SACRED TO YOU?
NO, IT'S JUST A ROCK. THIS IS WHAT THE MOTHERS USE TO START FIRES. I STOLE ONE MONTHS AGO.
YOU GOTTA **FORGET** EVERYTHING THEY BEAT INTO YOUR HEAD, SHARRI. THE MOTHERS DON'T SERVE GOD.
YOU DIDN'T SEE WHAT I SAW IN THOSE **CAVES** AT THE TOP OF THE MOUNTAIN.
WHATEVER THAT WAS, IT SURE AS FUCK WASN'T GOD OR ANYTHING HE...

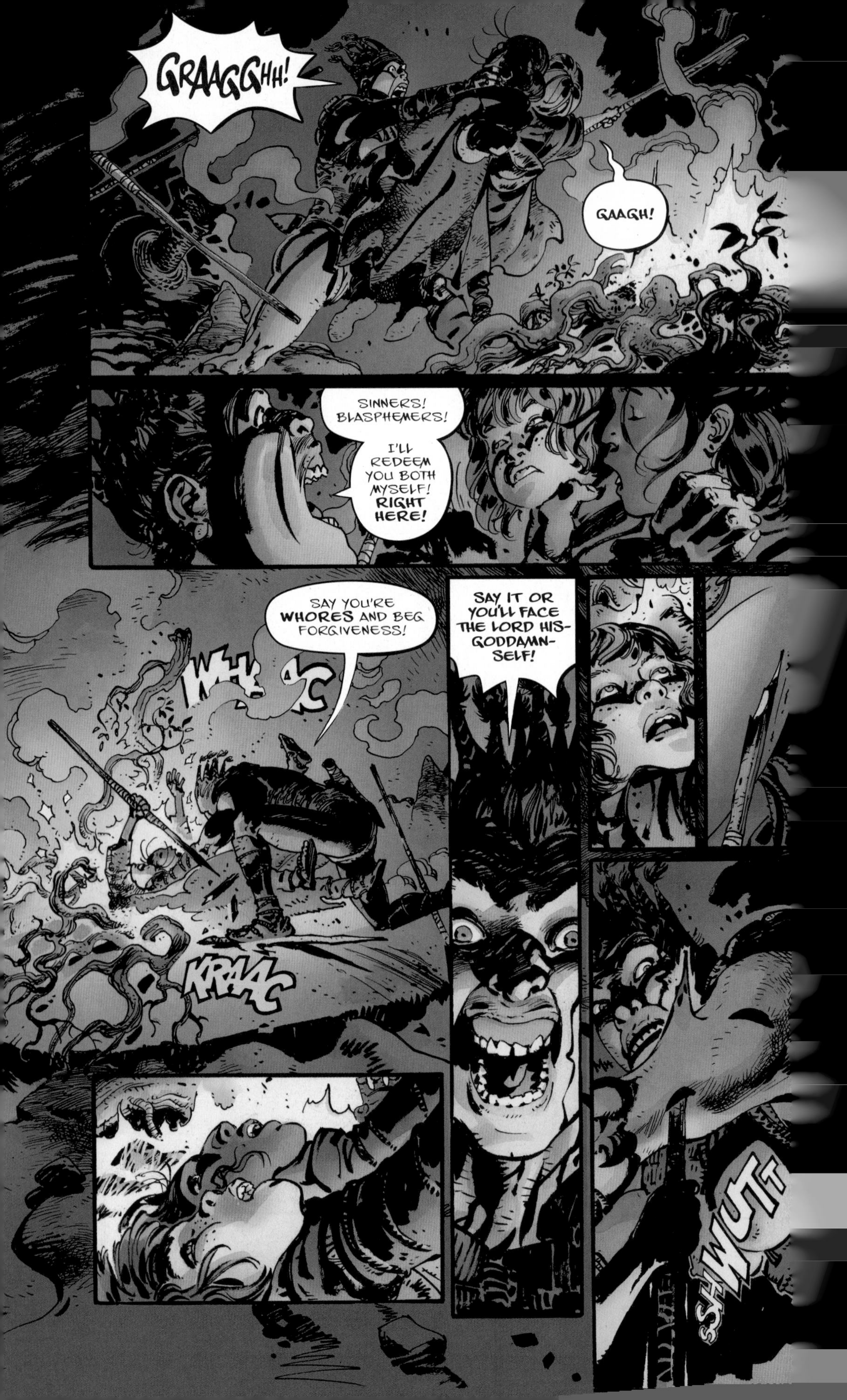
GRAAGGHH!
GAAGH!
SINNERS! BLASPHEMERS!
I'LL REDEEM YOU BOTH MYSELF! RIGHT HERE!
SAY YOU'RE WHORES AND BEG FORGIVENESS!
KRAAC
SAY IT OR YOU'LL FACE THE LORD HIS-GODDAMN-SELF!
SSHWUT

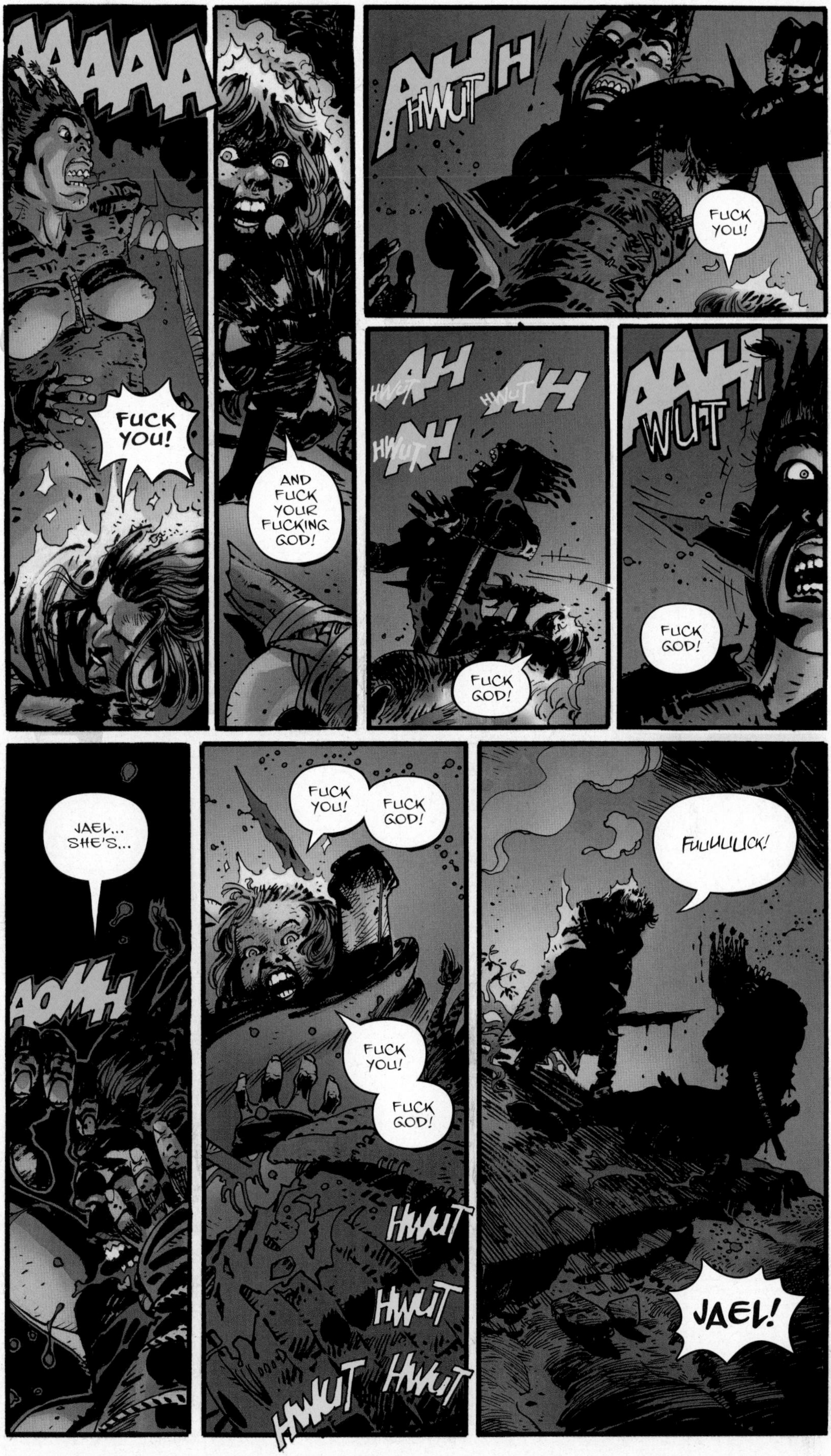
AAAAA
FUCK YOU!
AND FUCK YOUR FUCKING GOD!
AHH
HWUT
FUCK YOU!
AH
HWUT
AH
HWUT
AH
HWUT
FUCK GOD!
AAH
WUT
FUCK GOD!
JAEL... SHE'S...
AOMH
FUCK YOU!
FUCK GOD!
FUCK YOU!
FUCK GOD!
HWUT
HWUT
HWUT
HWUT
FUUUUUCK!
JAEL!

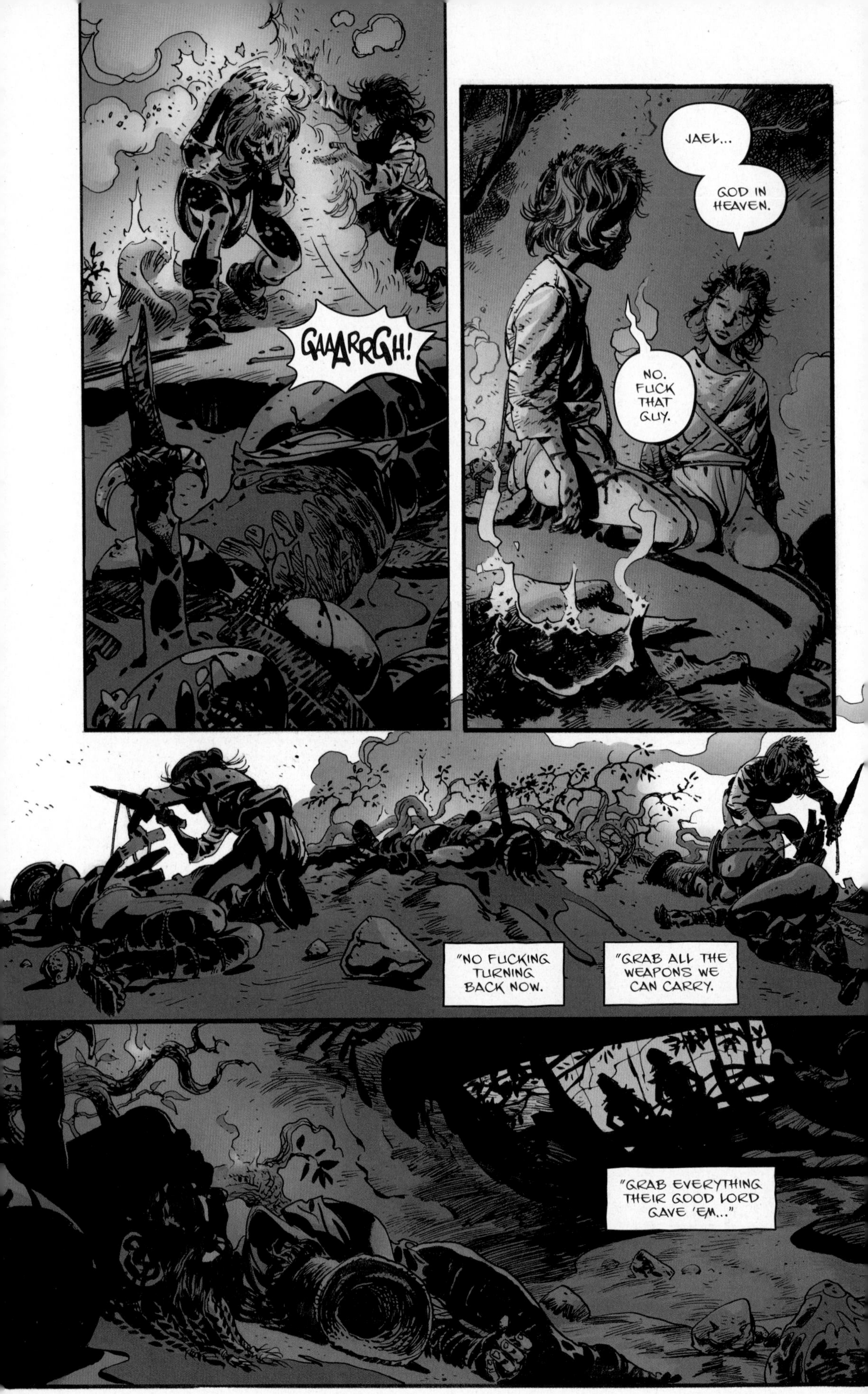
GAAARRGH!
JAEL...
GOD IN HEAVEN.
NO. FUCK THAT GUY.
"NO FUCKING TURNING BACK NOW.
"GRAB ALL THE WEAPONS WE CAN CARRY.
"GRAB EVERYTHING THEIR GOOD LORD GAVE 'EM..."

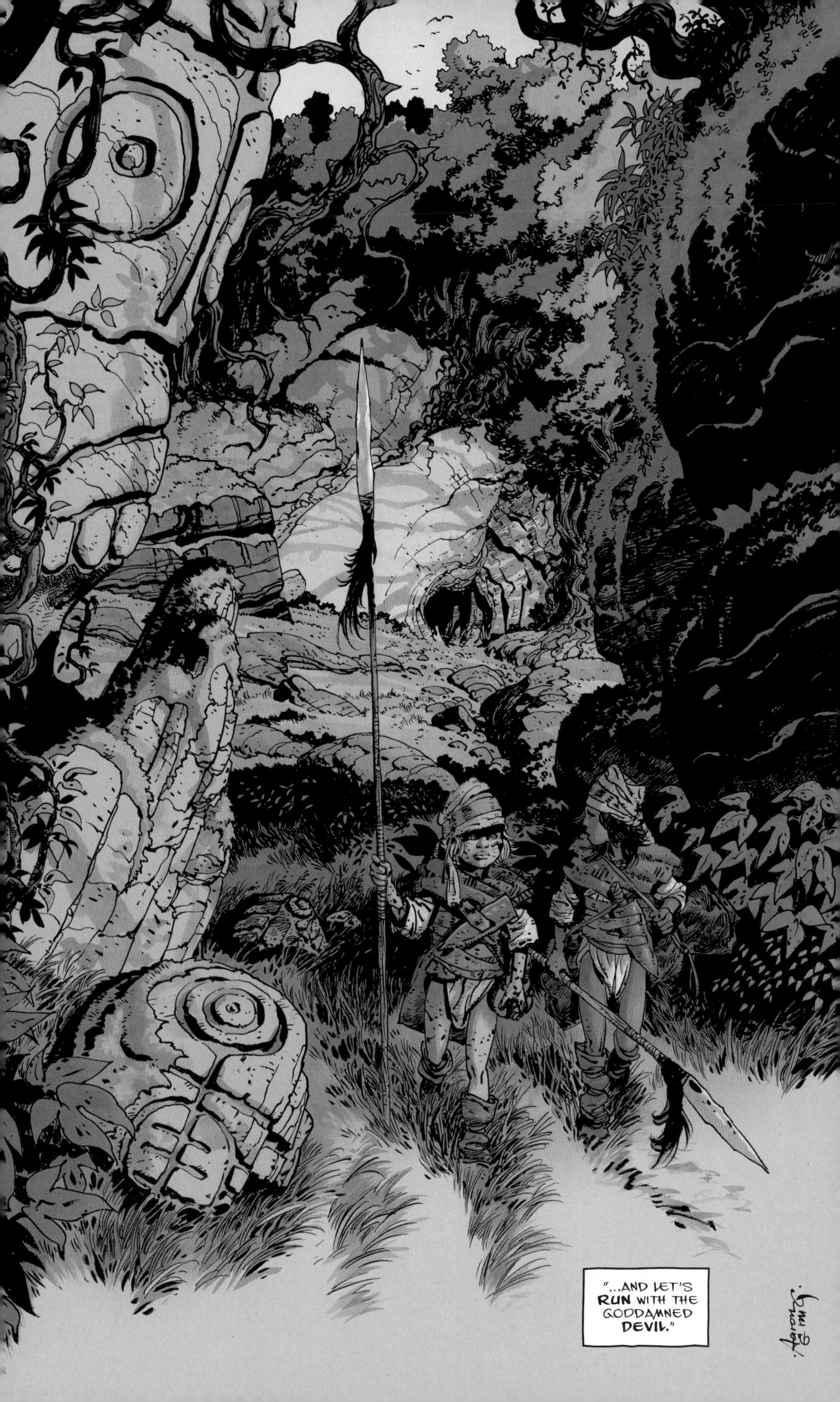
"...AND LET'S **RUN** WITH THE GODDAMNED **DEVIL.**"

# Chapter Three

## "Into the Thorns"

**B**UT THEY THAT WAIT UPON THE LORD SHALL RENEW THEIR STRENGTH; THEY SHALL MOUNT UP WITH WINGS AS EAGLES; THEY SHALL RUN, AND NOT BE WEARY; AND THEY SHALL WALK, AND NOT FAINT.

--ISAIAH 40:313

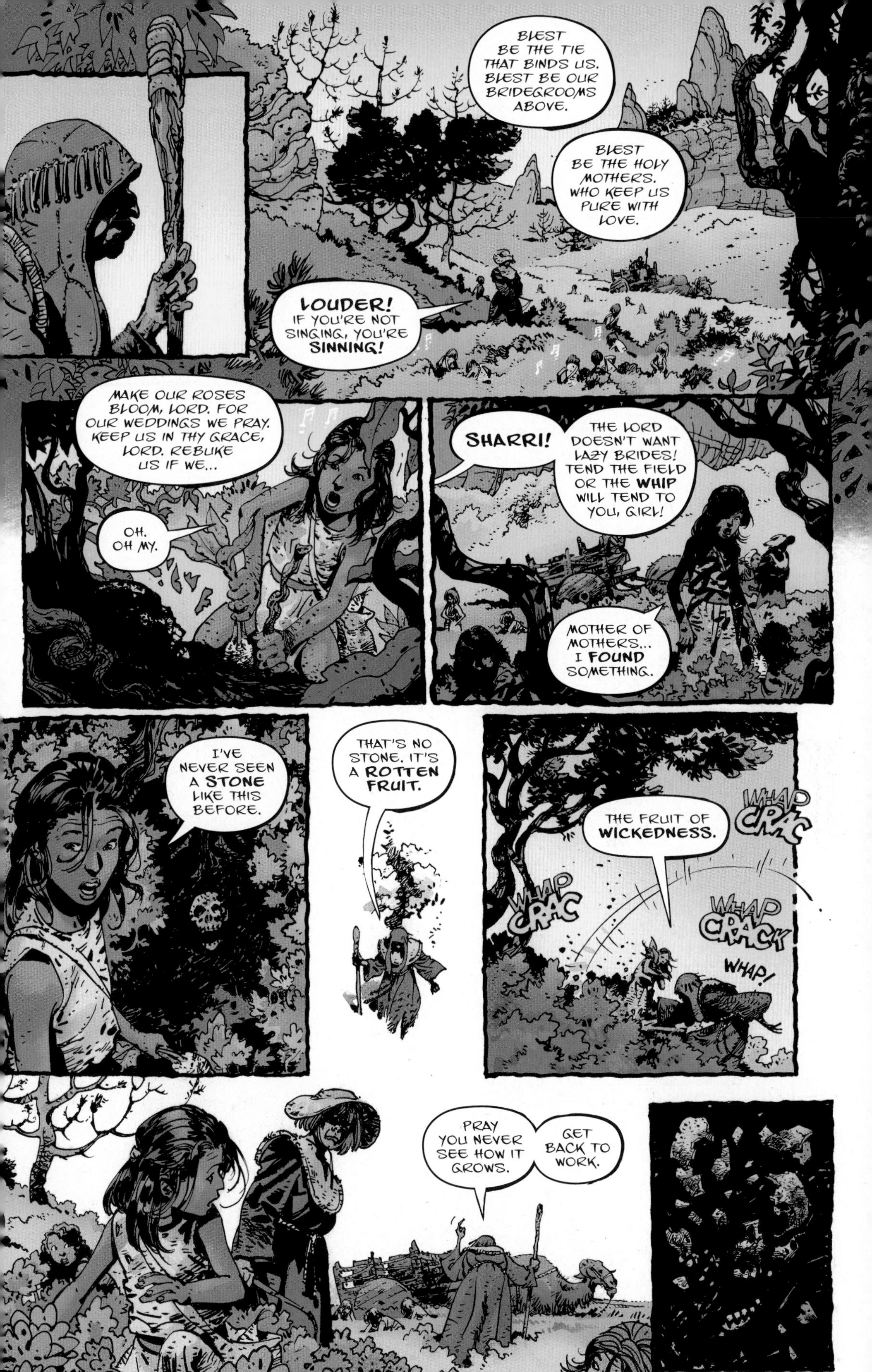

BLEST BE THE TIE THAT BINDS US. BLEST BE OUR BRIDEGROOMS ABOVE.
BLEST BE THE HOLY MOTHERS. WHO KEEP US PURE WITH LOVE.
LOUDER! IF YOU'RE NOT SINGING, YOU'RE SINNING!
MAKE OUR ROSES BLOOM, LORD. FOR OUR WEDDINGS WE PRAY. KEEP US IN THY GRACE, LORD. REBUKE US IF WE...
OH. OH MY.
SHARRI!
THE LORD DOESN'T WANT LAZY BRIDES! TEND THE FIELD OR THE WHIP WILL TEND TO YOU, GIRL!
MOTHER OF MOTHERS... I FOUND SOMETHING.
I'VE NEVER SEEN A STONE LIKE THIS BEFORE.
THAT'S NO STONE. IT'S A ROTTEN FRUIT.
THE FRUIT OF WICKEDNESS.
WHAP
CRAC
WHAP
CRAC
WHAP
CRACK
WHAP!
PRAY YOU NEVER SEE HOW IT GROWS.
GET BACK TO WORK.

KEEP MOVING!

EACH OF YOU MUST SAY A PRAYER OVER YOUR RUNAWAY SISTER!

PRAY FOR HER LOST, **WHORE** SOUL!

OH, MY LORD.

EZRAH SAT NEXT TO ME IN THE CHOIR. I CAN'T BELIEVE SHE WOULD RUN AWAY. WHAT IN THE WORLD COULD MAKE HER ALL **SWOLLEN** LIKE THAT?

MOTHERS SAY **SNAKES** IN THE THORNS. BUT **I'VE** NEVER SEEN SNAKES DOWN THERE.

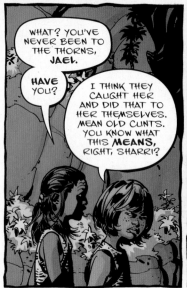

WHAT? YOU'VE NEVER BEEN TO THE THORNS, **JAEL.**

**HAVE** YOU?

I THINK THEY CAUGHT HER AND DID THAT TO HER THEMSELVES. MEAN OLD CUNTS. YOU KNOW WHAT THIS **MEANS,** RIGHT, SHARRI?

YES. NEVER LEAVE THE GARDEN. AND **NEVER EVER** GO INTO THE **THORNS.**

IT ME_ WHEN RUN... NEVE STO

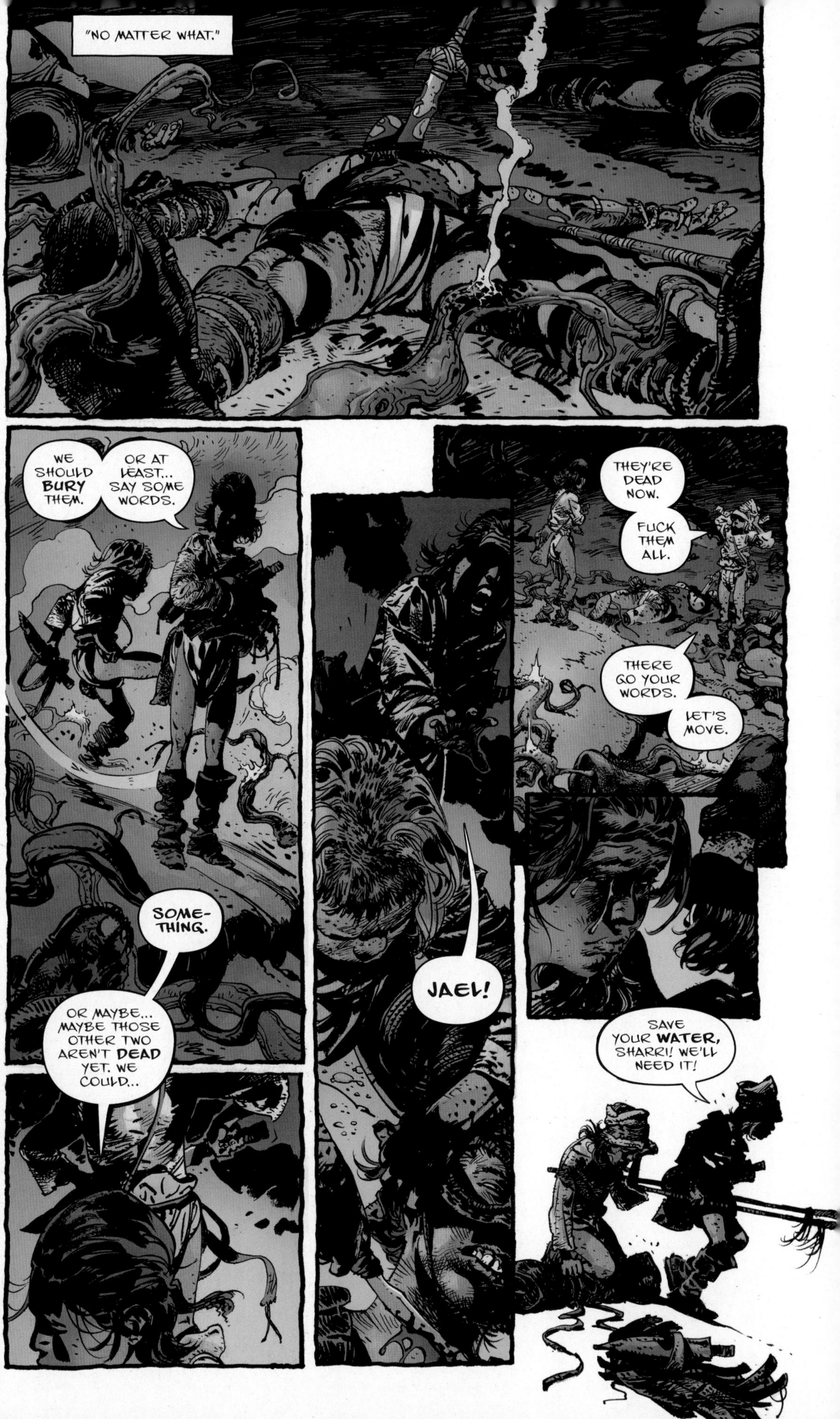
"NO MATTER WHAT."
WE SHOULD BURY THEM.
OR AT LEAST... SAY SOME WORDS.
SOME-THING.
OR MAYBE... MAYBE THOSE OTHER TWO AREN'T DEAD YET. WE COULD...
JAEL!
THEY'RE DEAD NOW.
FUCK THEM ALL.
THERE GO YOUR WORDS.
LET'S MOVE.
SAVE YOUR WATER, SHARRI! WE'LL NEED IT!

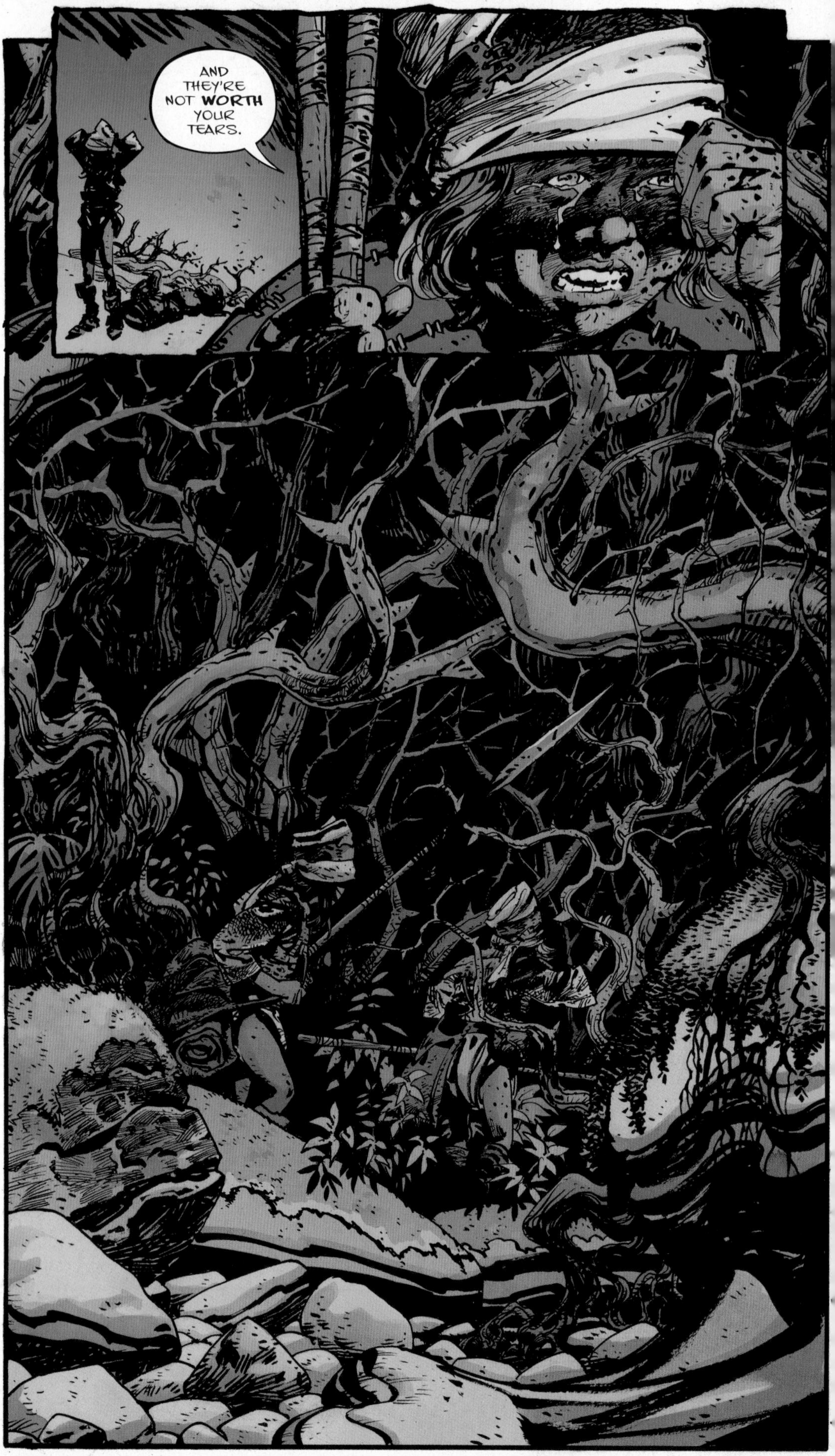
AND THEY'RE NOT **WORTH** YOUR TEARS.

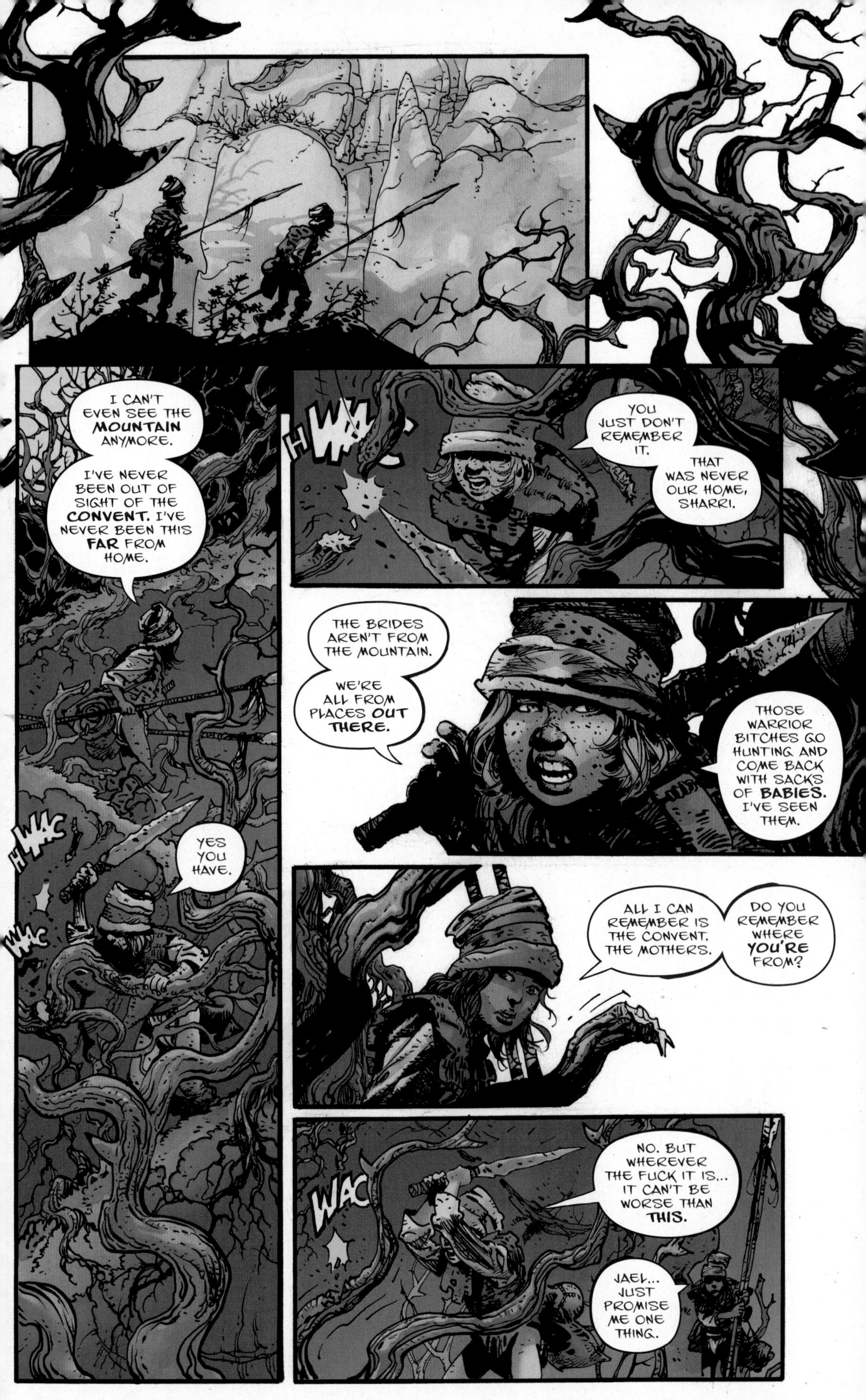
I CAN'T EVEN SEE THE MOUNTAIN ANYMORE.
I'VE NEVER BEEN OUT OF SIGHT OF THE CONVENT. I'VE NEVER BEEN THIS FAR FROM HOME.
HWAC
YOU JUST DON'T REMEMBER IT.
THAT WAS NEVER OUR HOME, SHARRI.
THE BRIDES AREN'T FROM THE MOUNTAIN.
WE'RE ALL FROM PLACES OUT THERE.
THOSE WARRIOR BITCHES GO HUNTING AND COME BACK WITH SACKS OF BABIES. I'VE SEEN THEM.
HWAC
YES YOU HAVE.
WAC
DO YOU REMEMBER WHERE YOU'RE FROM?
ALL I CAN REMEMBER IS THE CONVENT. THE MOTHERS.
WAC
NO. BUT WHEREVER THE FUCK IT IS... IT CAN'T BE WORSE THAN THIS.
JAEL... JUST PROMISE ME ONE THING.

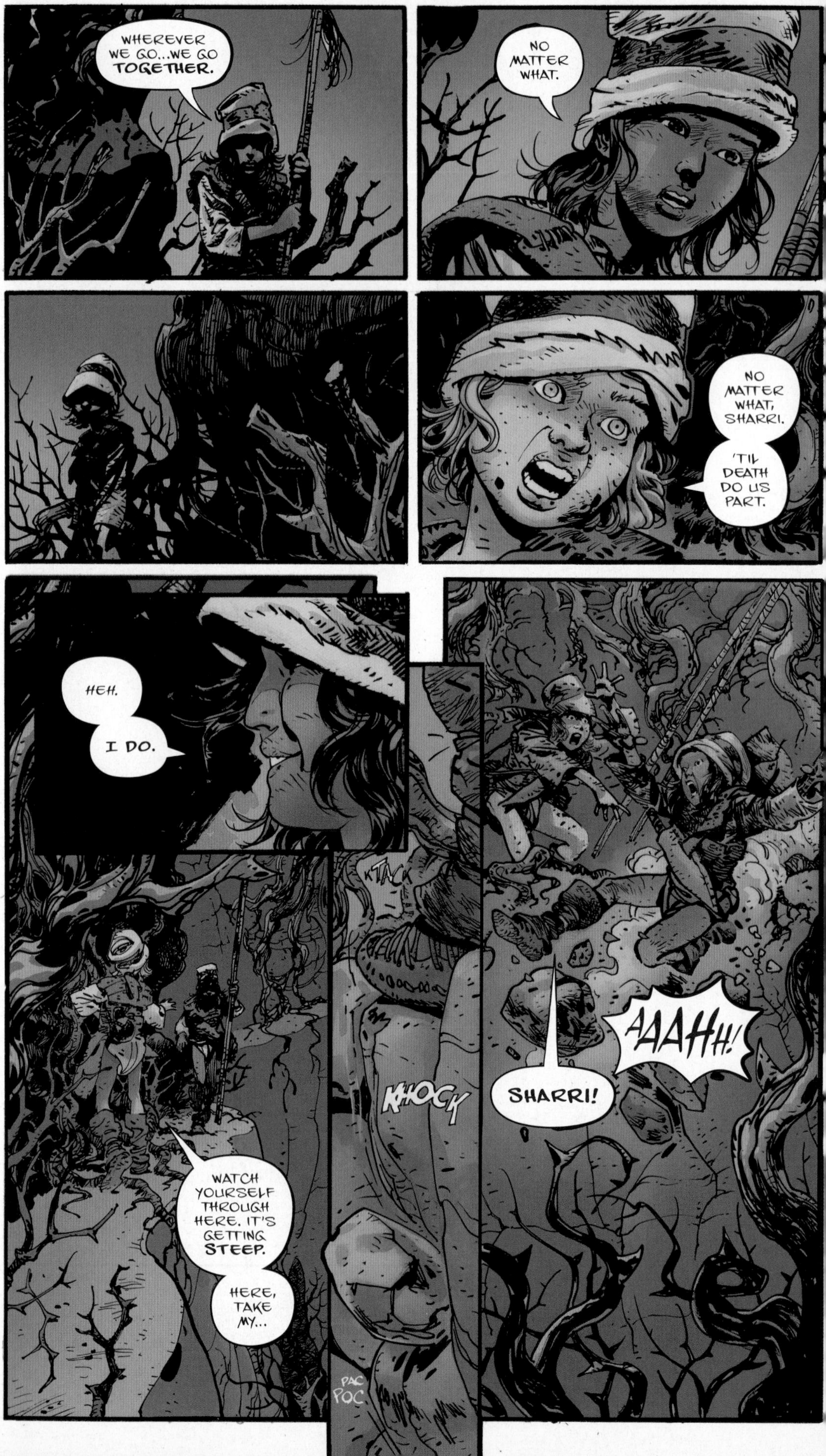

WHEREVER WE GO...WE GO TOGETHER.
NO MATTER WHAT.
NO MATTER WHAT, SHARRI.
'TIL DEATH DO US PART.
HEH.
I DO.
WATCH YOURSELF THROUGH HERE. IT'S GETTING STEEP.
HERE, TAKE MY...
KTACK
KHOCK
PAC POC
SHARRI!
AAAHH!

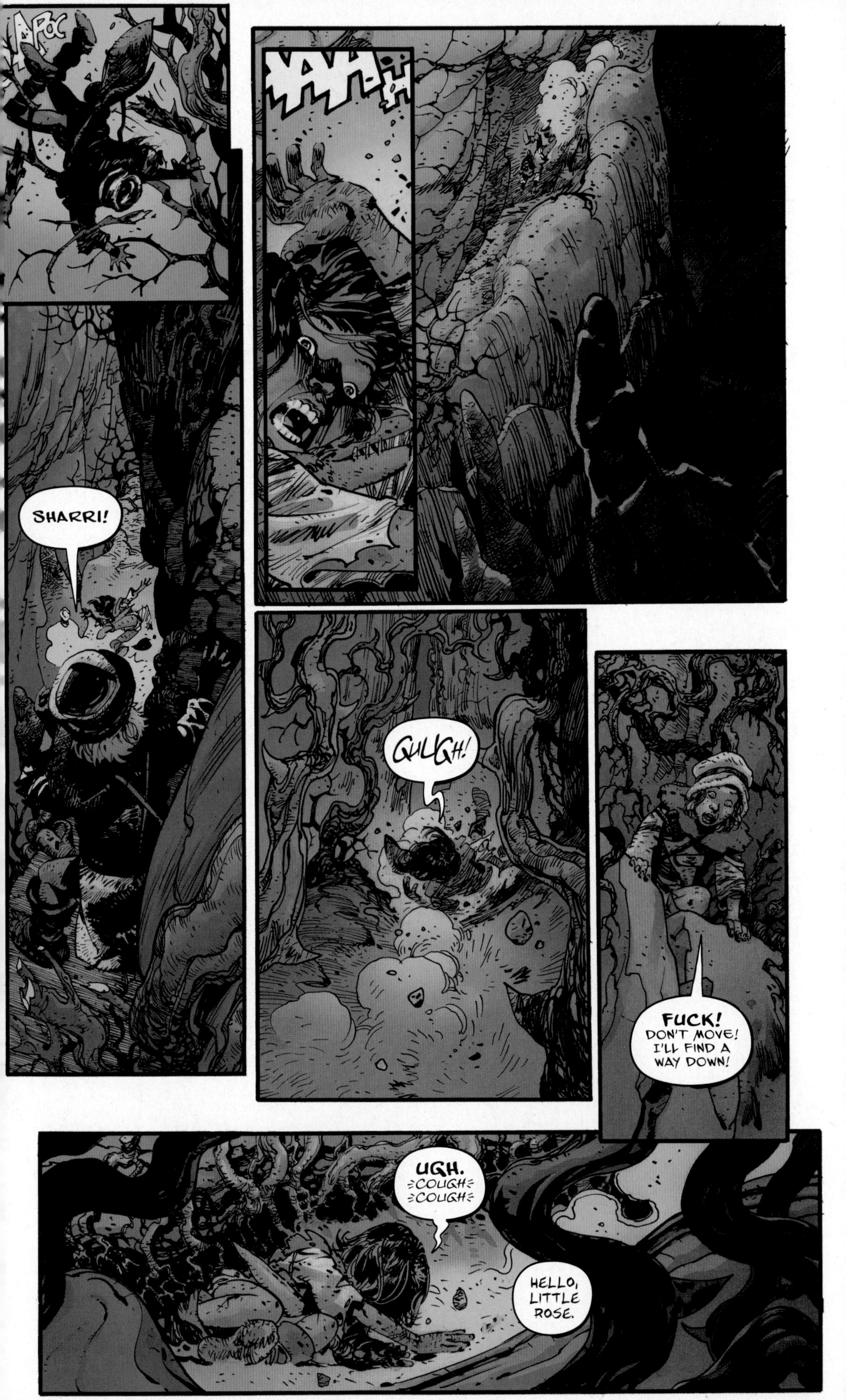

APOC
YAAAH
SHARRI!
GULGH!
FUCK! DON'T MOVE! I'LL FIND A WAY DOWN!
UGH. COUGH COUGH
HELLO, LITTLE ROSE.

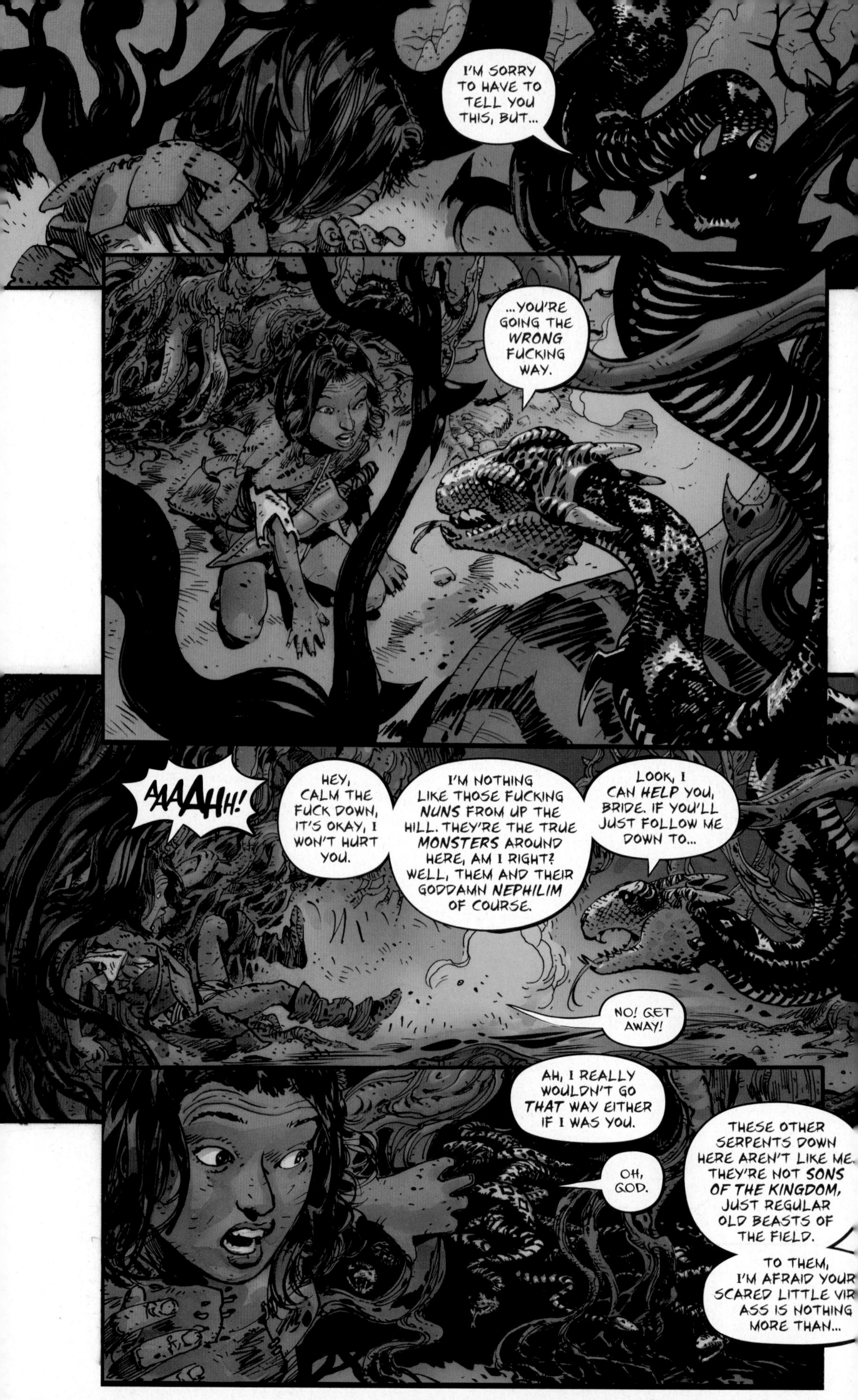
I'M SORRY TO HAVE TO TELL YOU THIS, BUT...
...YOU'RE GOING THE WRONG FUCKING WAY.
AAAAHH!
HEY, CALM THE FUCK DOWN, IT'S OKAY, I WON'T HURT YOU.
I'M NOTHING LIKE THOSE FUCKING NUNS FROM UP THE HILL. THEY'RE THE TRUE MONSTERS AROUND HERE, AM I RIGHT? WELL, THEM AND THEIR GODDAMN NEPHILIM OF COURSE.
LOOK, I CAN HELP YOU, BRIDE. IF YOU'LL JUST FOLLOW ME DOWN TO...
NO! GET AWAY!
AH, I REALLY WOULDN'T GO THAT WAY EITHER IF I WAS YOU.
OH, GOD.
THESE OTHER SERPENTS DOWN HERE AREN'T LIKE ME. THEY'RE NOT SONS OF THE KINGDOM, JUST REGULAR OLD BEASTS OF THE FIELD.
TO THEM, I'M AFRAID YOUR SCARED LITTLE VIR ASS IS NOTHING MORE THAN...

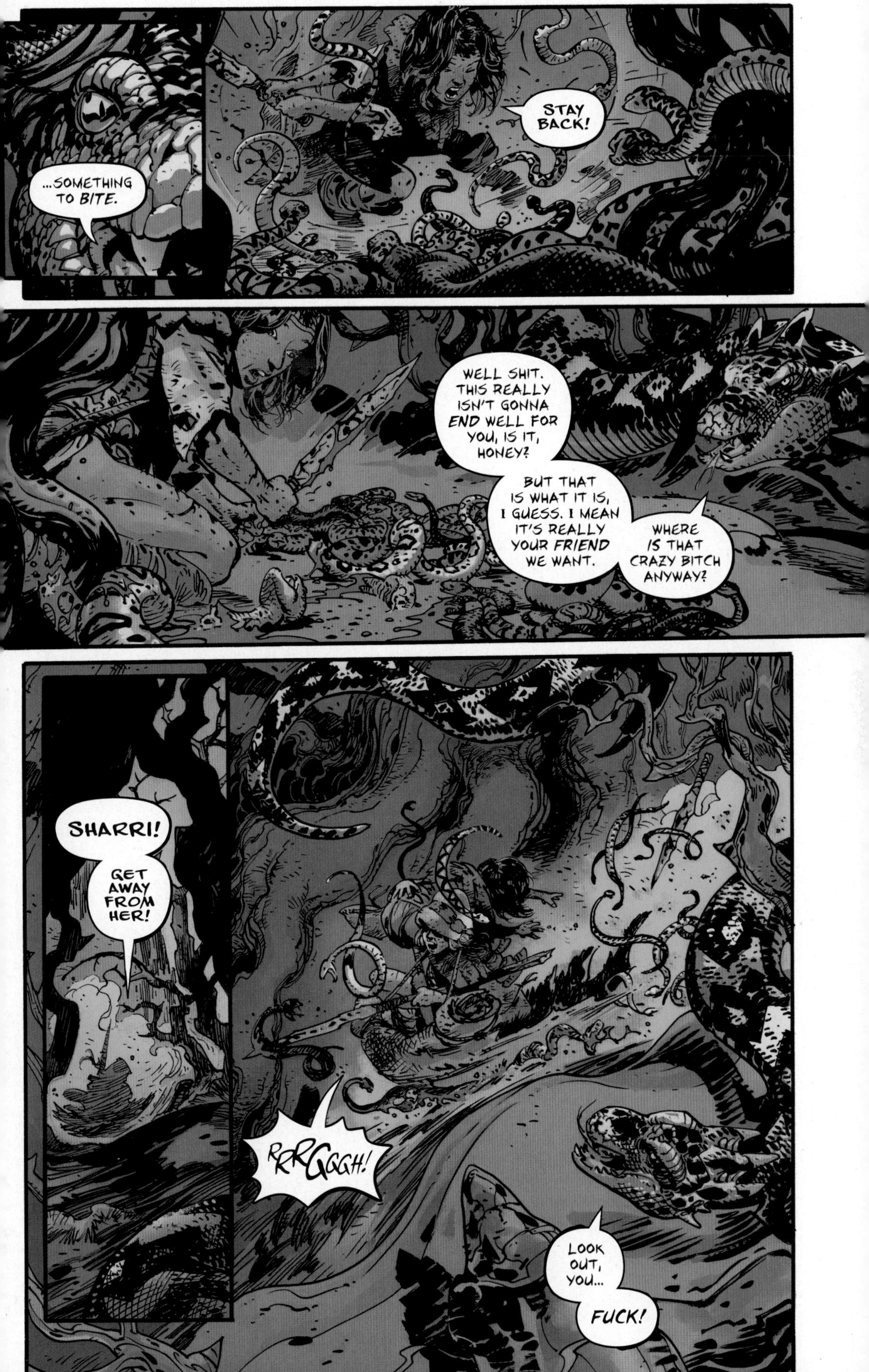

...SOMETHING TO BITE.
STAY BACK!
WELL SHIT. THIS REALLY ISN'T GONNA END WELL FOR YOU, IS IT, HONEY?
BUT THAT IS WHAT IT IS, I GUESS. I MEAN IT'S REALLY YOUR FRIEND WE WANT.
WHERE IS THAT CRAZY BITCH ANYWAY?
SHARRI!
GET AWAY FROM HER!
RRRGGGH!
LOOK OUT, YOU...
FUCK!

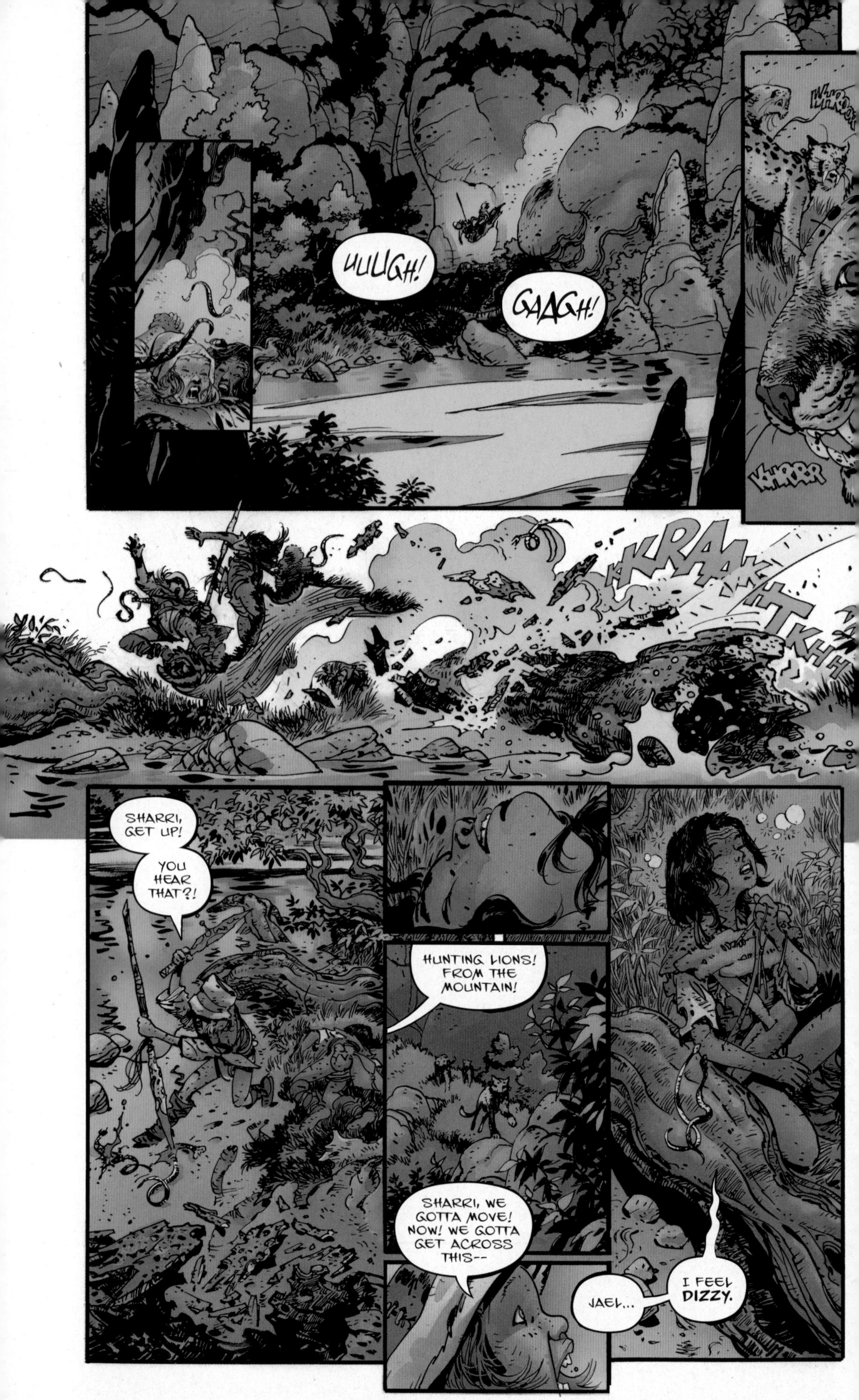

UUUGH!
GAAGH!
WHROOR
WHRRRR
KRAAK
TKHH
SHARRI, GET UP!
YOU HEAR THAT?!
HUNTING LIONS! FROM THE MOUNTAIN!
SHARRI, WE GOTTA MOVE! NOW! WE GOTTA GET ACROSS THIS--
JAEL...
I FEEL DIZZY.

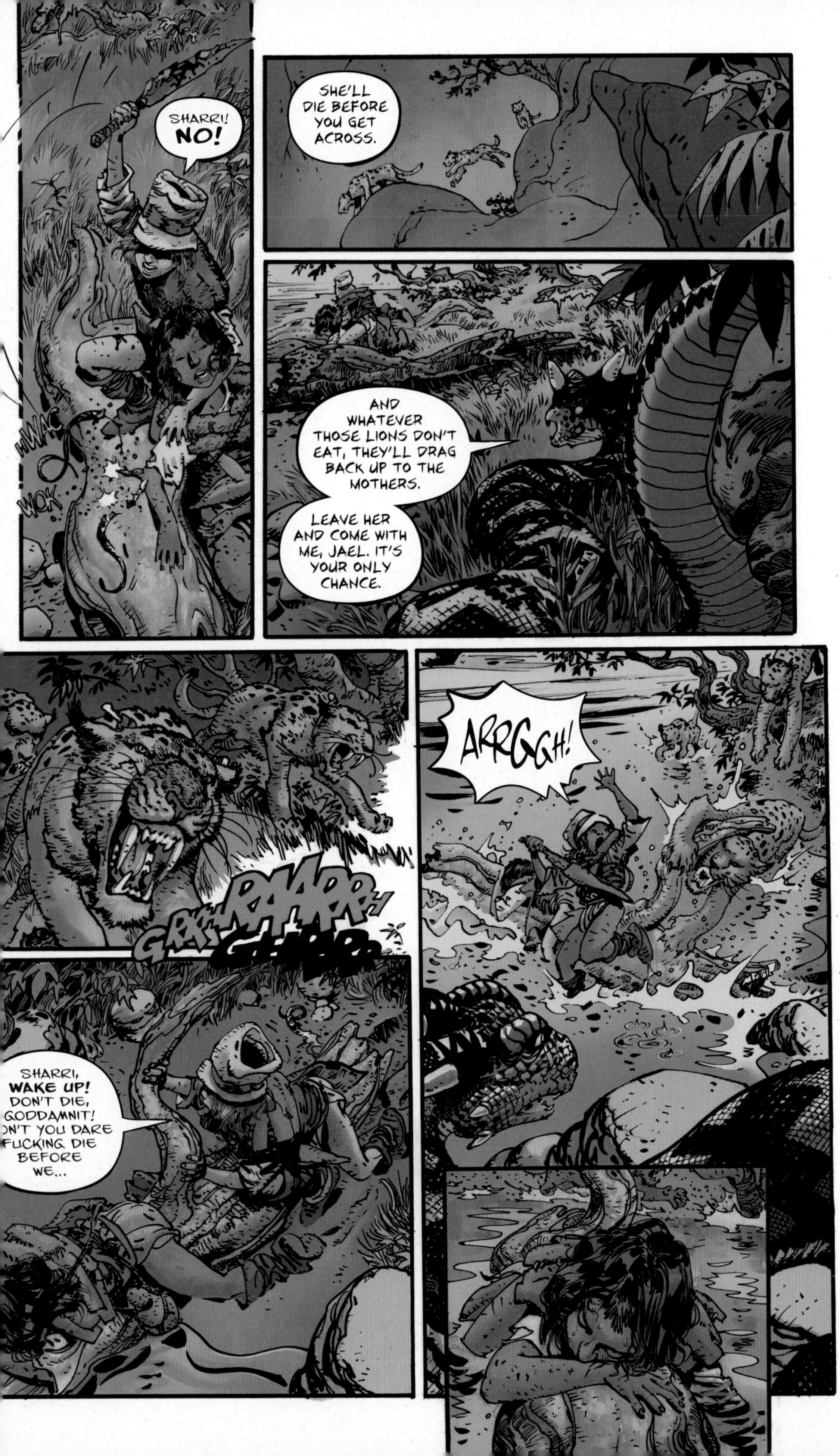
SHARRI! **NO!**
WWAC
WOK
SHE'LL DIE BEFORE YOU GET ACROSS.
AND WHATEVER THOSE LIONS DON'T EAT, THEY'LL DRAG BACK UP TO THE MOTHERS.
LEAVE HER AND COME WITH ME, JAEL. IT'S YOUR ONLY CHANCE.
ARRGGH!
SHARRI, **WAKE UP!** DON'T DIE, GODDAMNIT! DON'T YOU DARE FUCKING DIE BEFORE WE...

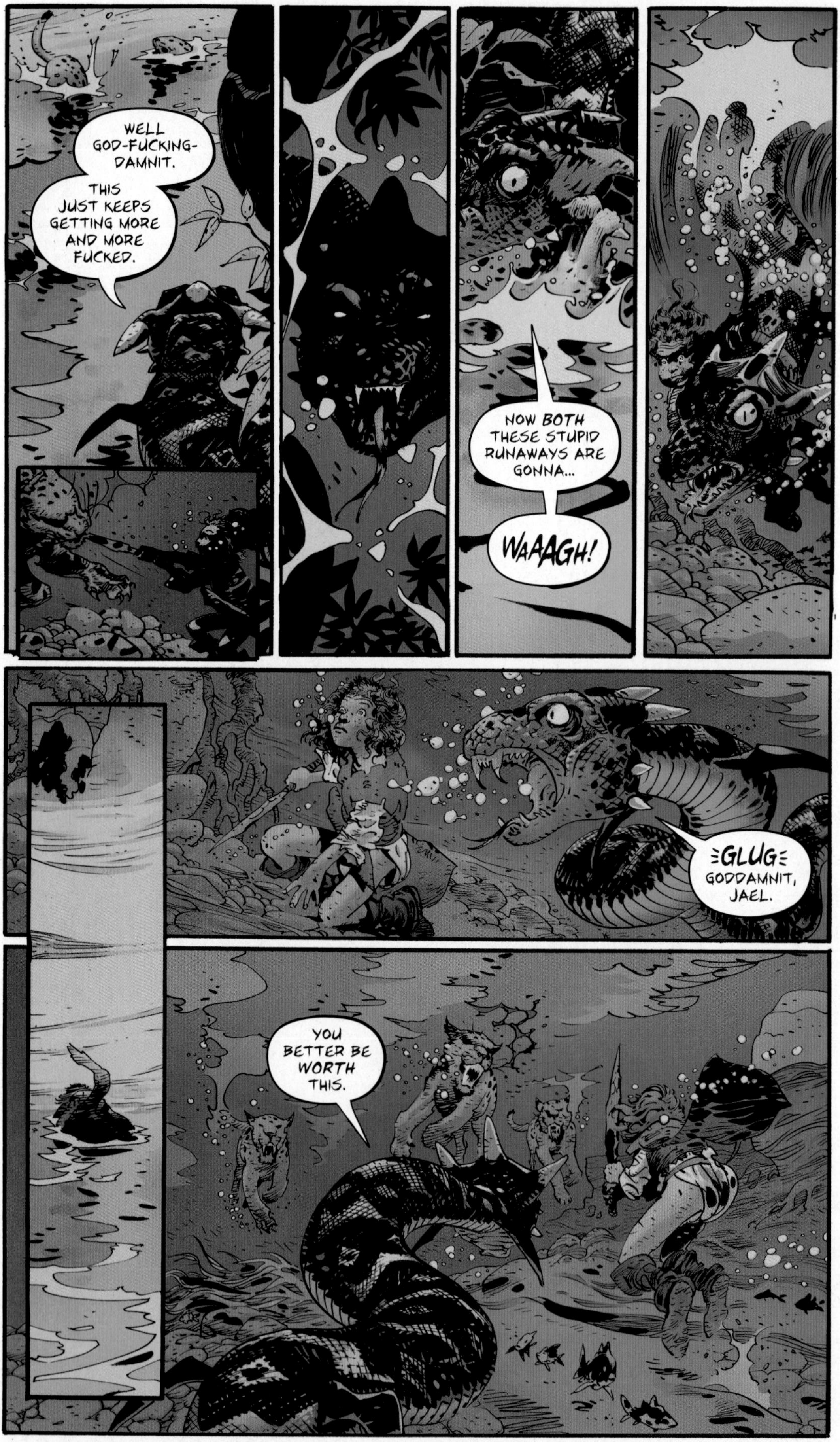
WELL GOD-FUCKING-DAMNIT.
THIS JUST KEEPS GETTING MORE AND MORE FUCKED.
NOW BOTH THESE STUPID RUNAWAYS ARE GONNA...
WAAAGH!
GLUG GODDAMNIT, JAEL.
YOU BETTER BE WORTH THIS.

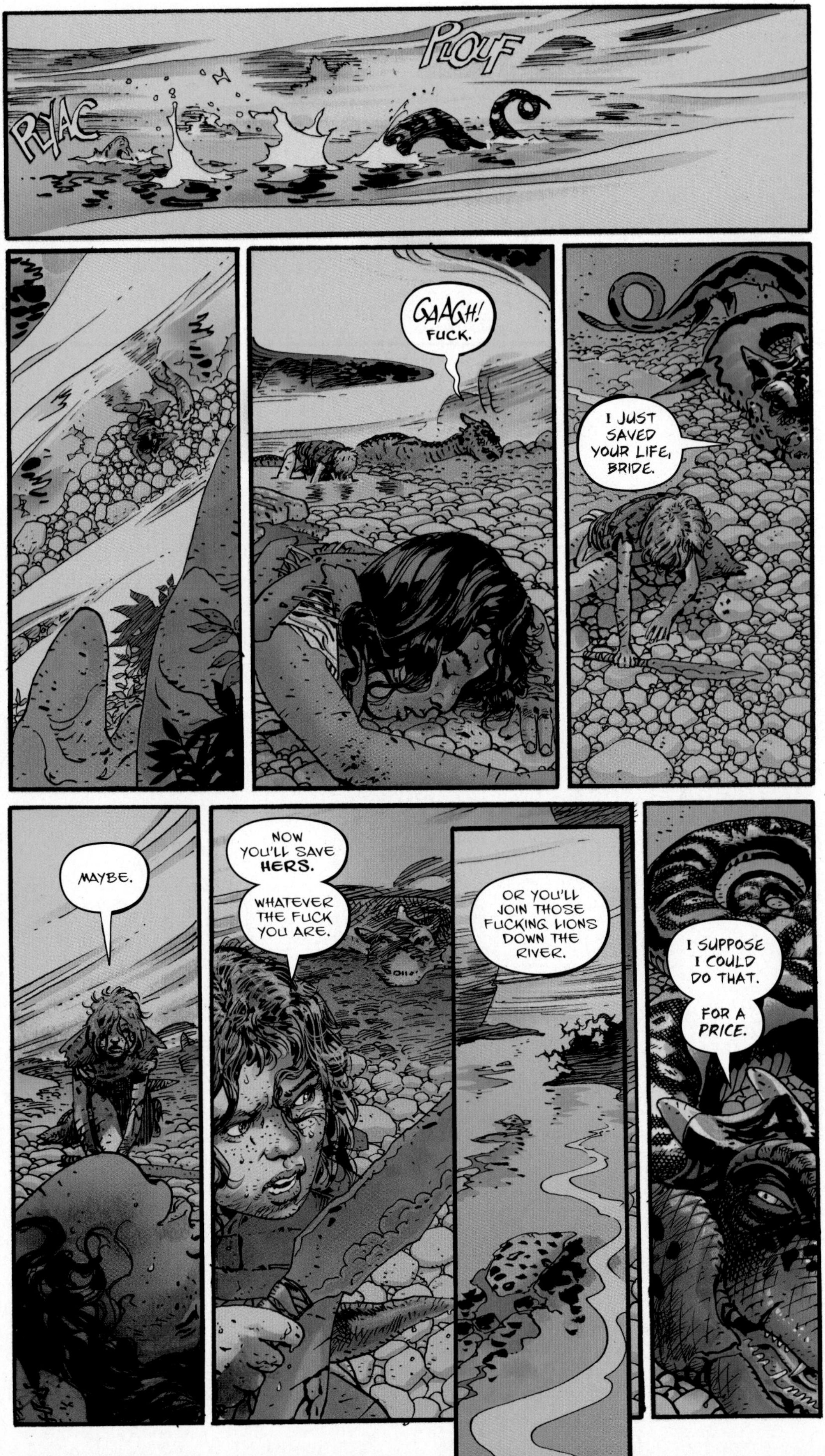
PLOUF
PLYAC
GAAGH! FUCK.
I JUST SAVED YOUR LIFE, BRIDE.
MAYBE.
NOW YOU'LL SAVE HERS.
WHATEVER THE FUCK YOU ARE.
OR YOU'LL JOIN THOSE FUCKING LIONS DOWN THE RIVER.
I SUPPOSE I COULD DO THAT.
FOR A PRICE.

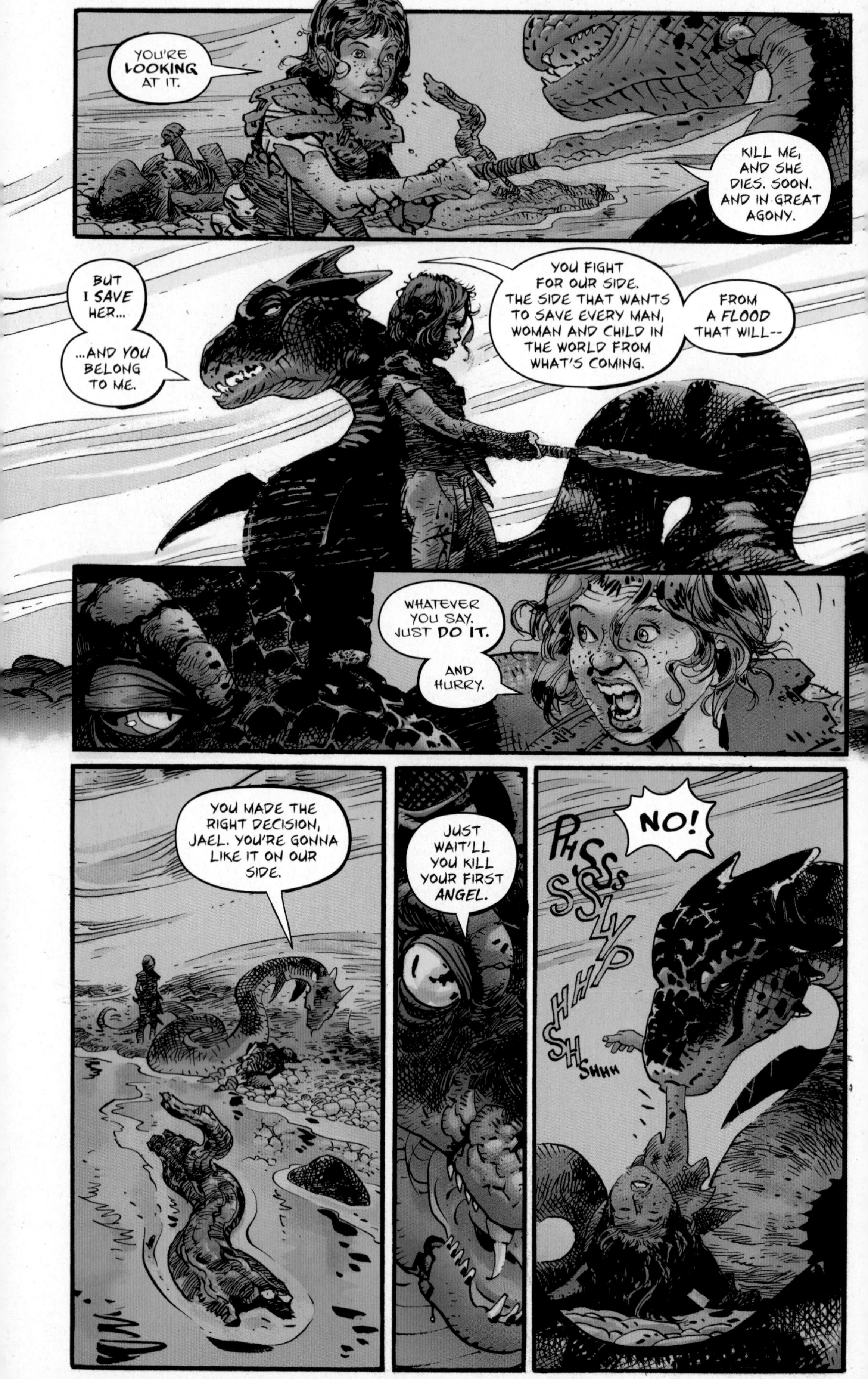

YOU'RE LOOKING AT IT.
KILL ME, AND SHE DIES. SOON. AND IN GREAT AGONY.
BUT I SAVE HER...
...AND YOU BELONG TO ME.
YOU FIGHT FOR OUR SIDE. THE SIDE THAT WANTS TO SAVE EVERY MAN, WOMAN AND CHILD IN THE WORLD FROM WHAT'S COMING.
FROM A FLOOD THAT WILL--
WHATEVER YOU SAY. JUST DO IT.
AND HURRY.
YOU MADE THE RIGHT DECISION, JAEL. YOU'RE GONNA LIKE IT ON OUR SIDE.
JUST WAIT'LL YOU KILL YOUR FIRST ANGEL.
NO!
PHSSSs
SSLYP
SHHH
SH SHHH

GET OFF HER! YOU BASTARD!

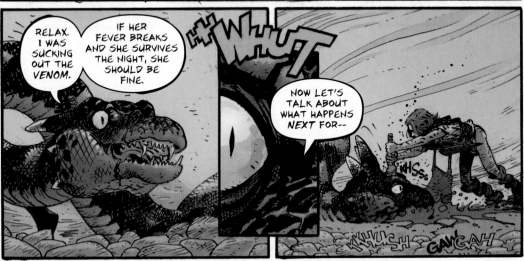

RELAX. I WAS SUCKING OUT THE VENOM.

IF HER FEVER BREAKS AND SHE SURVIVES THE NIGHT, SHE SHOULD BE FINE.

HHWHUT

NOW LET'S TALK ABOUT WHAT HAPPENS *NEXT* FOR--

KHSSs

KHUSH GAWGAH

YOU... LYING... LITTLE BITCH.

WE MADE A *DEAL*, JAEL. YOU CAN'T GO BACK ON THAT. YOU BELONG TO THE KINGDOM NOW.

DON'T BELONG TO ANYONE ANYMORE.

YOU TWO WILL NEVER MAKE IT. YOU DON'T EVEN KNOW WHERE YOU ARE.

THE LADIES OF THE MOUNTAIN WILL KILL YOU BOTH WHEN THEY CATCH YOU.

OR DRAG YOU BACK TO MEET YOUR GROOMS.

LIKE HELL THEY WILL.

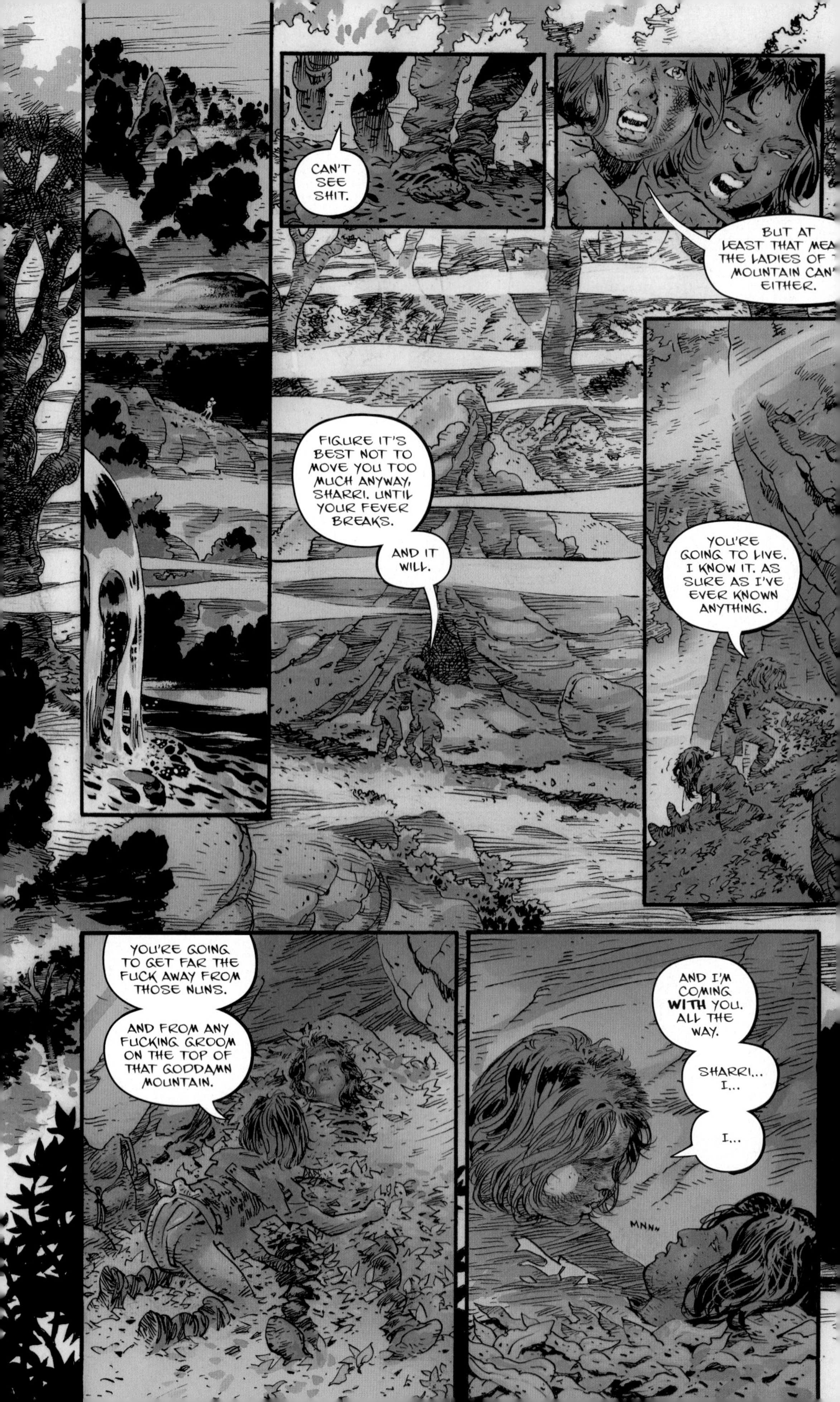
CAN'T SEE SHIT.
BUT AT LEAST THAT MEA THE LADIES OF T MOUNTAIN CAN EITHER.
FIGURE IT'S BEST NOT TO MOVE YOU TOO MUCH ANYWAY, SHARRI. UNTIL YOUR FEVER BREAKS.
AND IT WILL.
YOU'RE GOING TO LIVE. I KNOW IT. AS SURE AS I'VE EVER KNOWN ANYTHING.
YOU'RE GOING TO GET FAR THE FUCK AWAY FROM THOSE NUNS.
AND FROM ANY FUCKING GROOM ON THE TOP OF THAT GODDAMN MOUNTAIN.
AND I'M COMING **WITH** YOU. ALL THE WAY.
SHARRI... I...
I...
MNNN

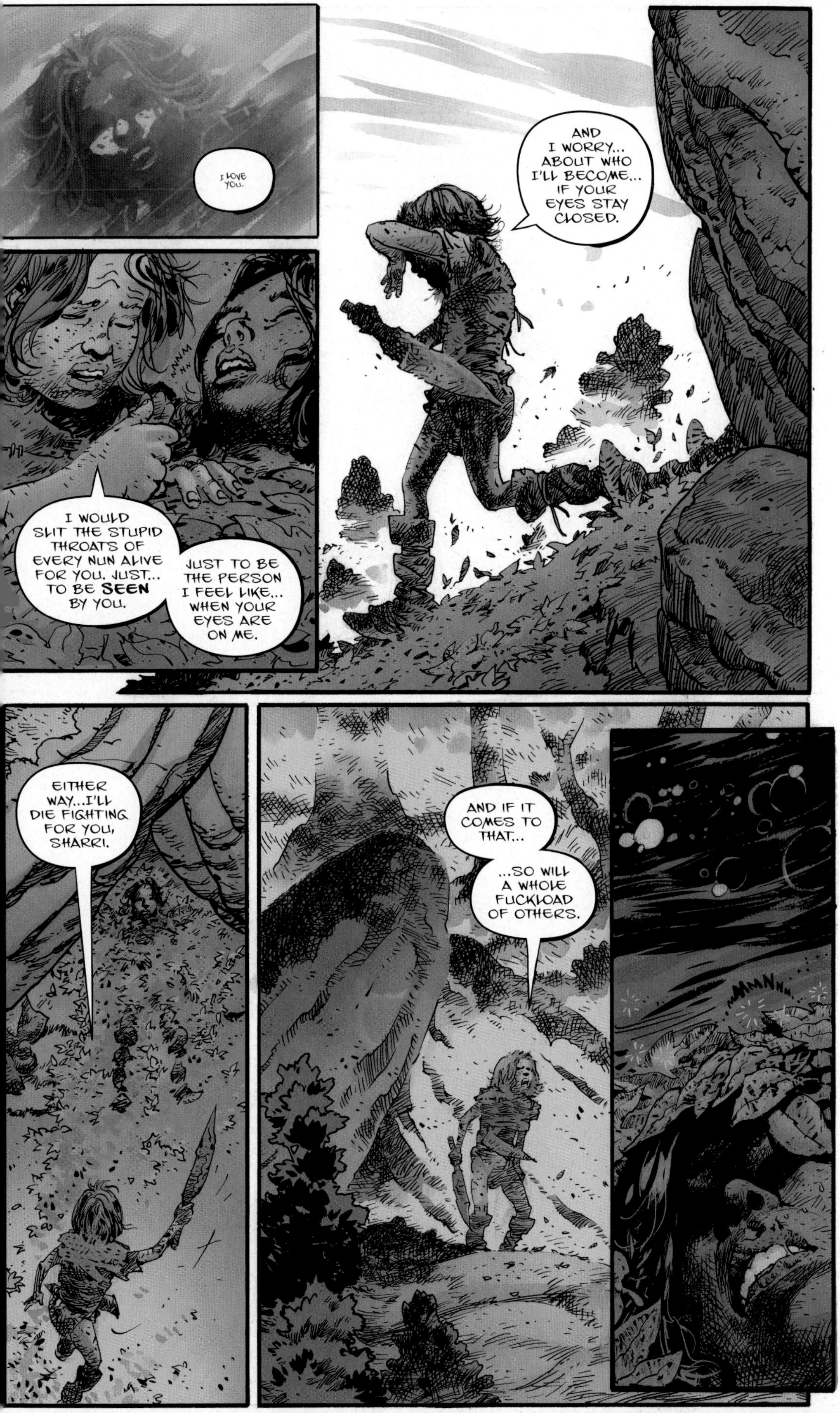
I LOVE YOU.
AND I WORRY... ABOUT WHO I'LL BECOME... IF YOUR EYES STAY CLOSED.
NNM NN
I WOULD SLIT THE STUPID THROATS OF EVERY NUN ALIVE FOR YOU. JUST... TO BE SEEN BY YOU.
JUST TO BE THE PERSON I FEEL LIKE... WHEN YOUR EYES ARE ON ME.
EITHER WAY...I'LL DIE FIGHTING FOR YOU, SHARRI.
AND IF IT COMES TO THAT...
...SO WILL A WHOLE FUCKLOAD OF OTHERS.
MMNN

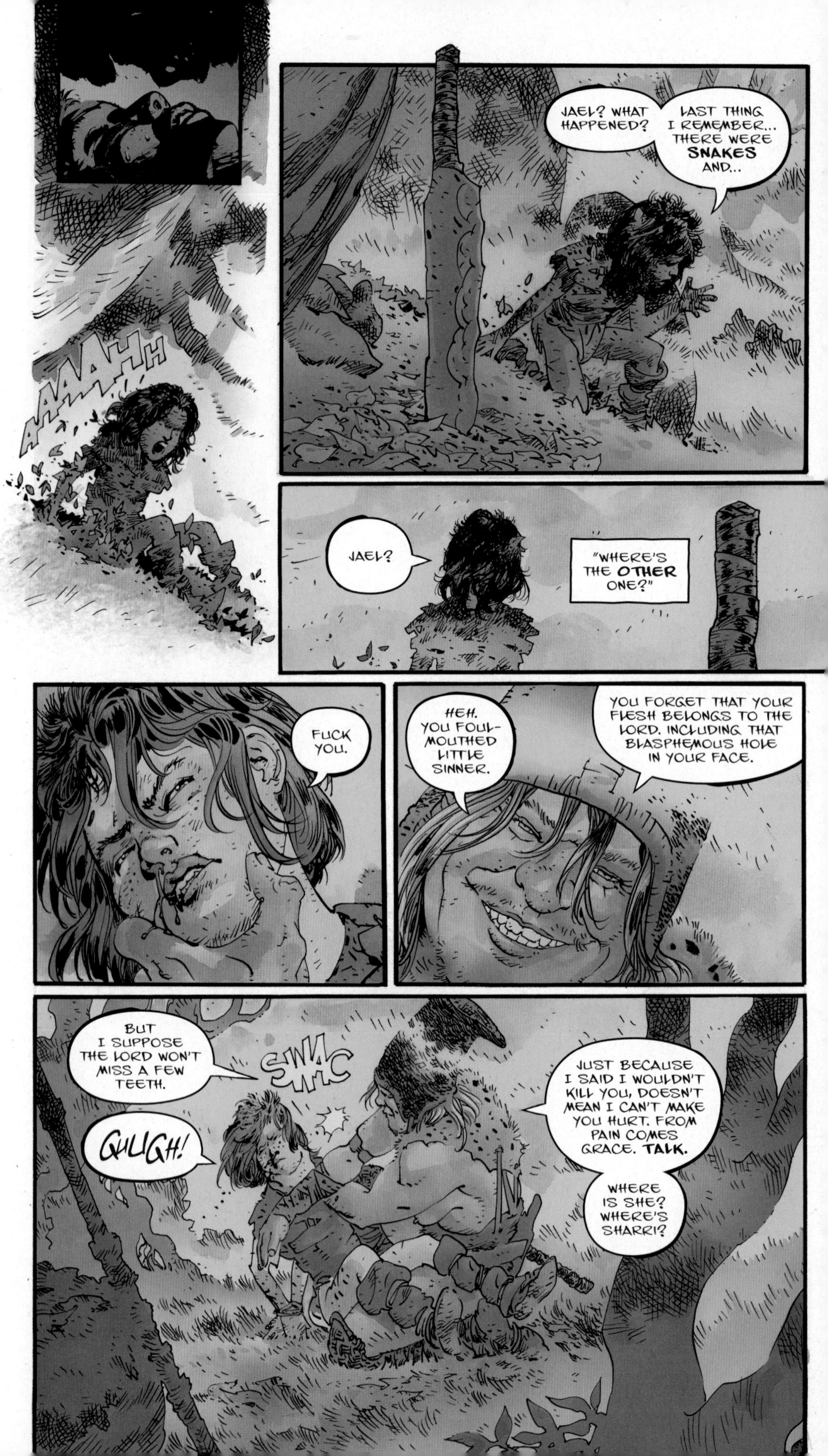
AAAAHH
JAEL? WHAT HAPPENED?
LAST THING I REMEMBER... THERE WERE SNAKES AND...
JAEL?
"WHERE'S THE OTHER ONE?"
FUCK YOU.
HEH. YOU FOUL-MOUTHED LITTLE SINNER.
YOU FORGET THAT YOUR FLESH BELONGS TO THE LORD. INCLUDING THAT BLASPHEMOUS HOLE IN YOUR FACE.
BUT I SUPPOSE THE LORD WON'T MISS A FEW TEETH.
SWAC
QULGH!
JUST BECAUSE I SAID I WOULDN'T KILL YOU, DOESN'T MEAN I CAN'T MAKE YOU HURT. FROM PAIN COMES GRACE. TALK.
WHERE IS SHE? WHERE'S SHARRI?

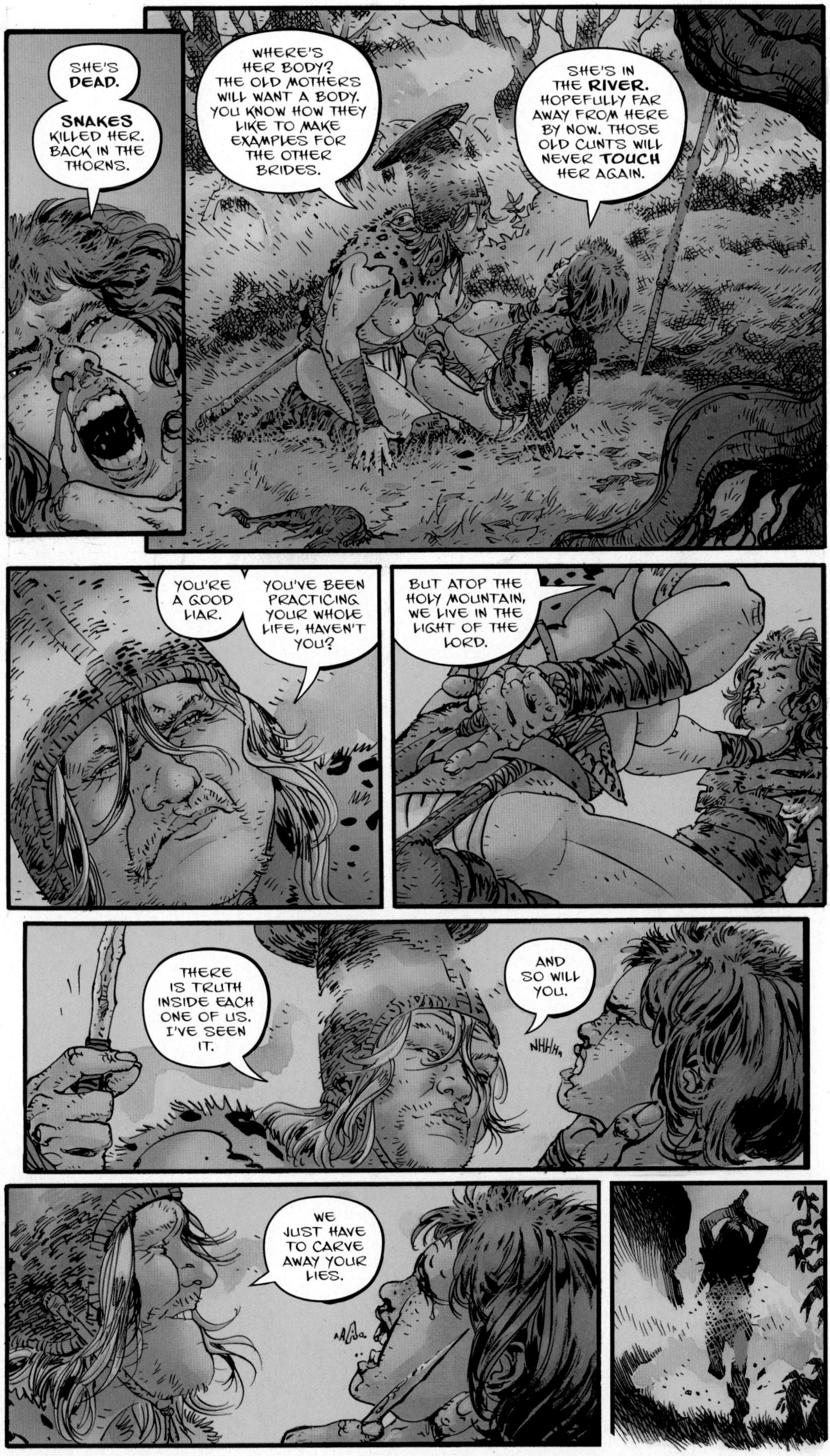
SHE'S **DEAD.**
**SNAKES** KILLED HER. BACK IN THE THORNS.
WHERE'S HER BODY? THE OLD MOTHERS WILL WANT A BODY. YOU KNOW HOW THEY LIKE TO MAKE EXAMPLES FOR THE OTHER BRIDES.
SHE'S IN THE **RIVER.** HOPEFULLY FAR AWAY FROM HERE BY NOW. THOSE OLD CUNTS WILL NEVER **TOUCH** HER AGAIN.
YOU'RE A GOOD LIAR.
YOU'VE BEEN PRACTICING YOUR WHOLE LIFE, HAVEN'T YOU?
BUT ATOP THE HOLY MOUNTAIN, WE LIVE IN THE LIGHT OF THE LORD.
THERE IS TRUTH INSIDE EACH ONE OF US. I'VE SEEN IT.
AND SO WILL YOU.
NHHH..
WE JUST HAVE TO CARVE AWAY YOUR LIES.

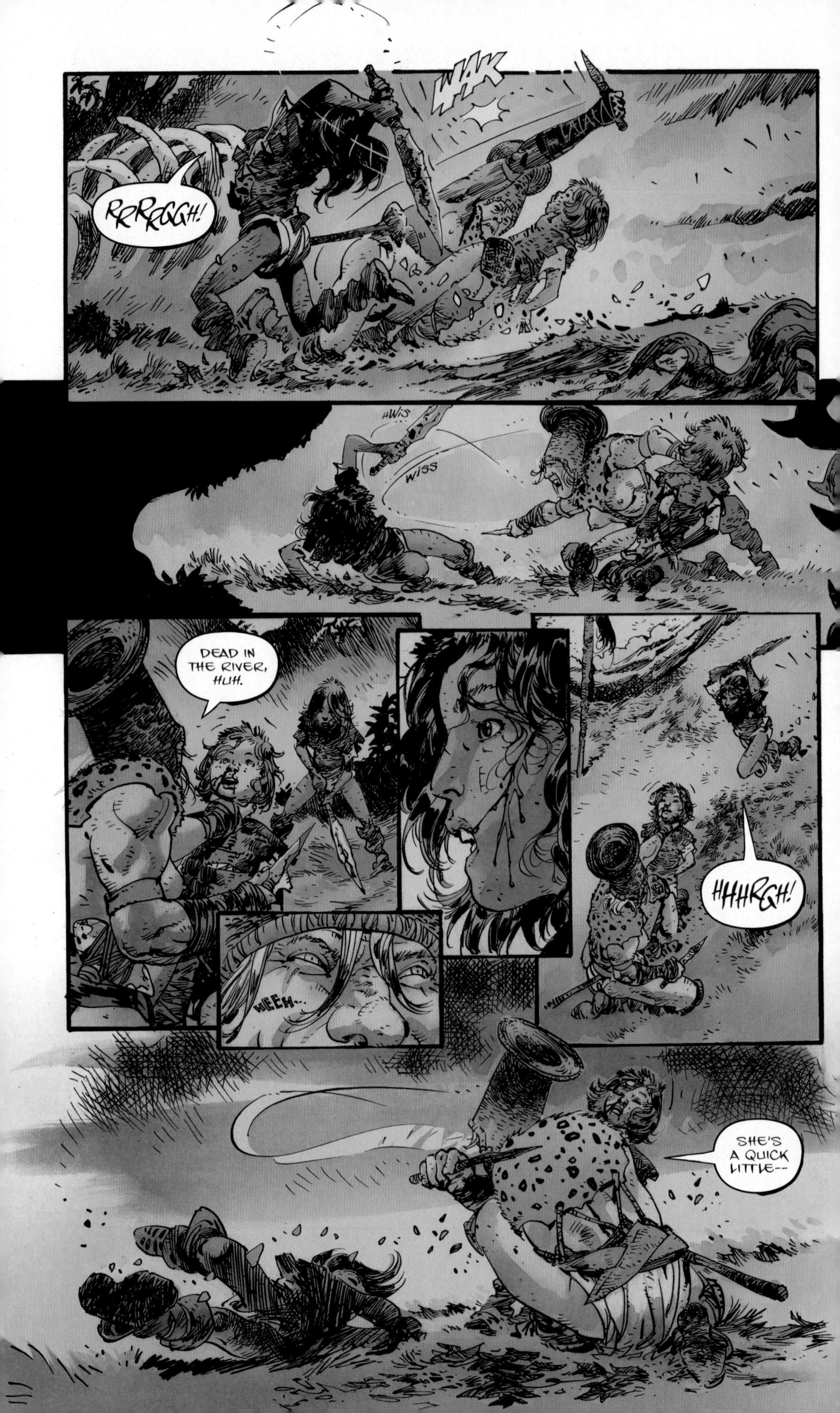
WAK
RRRRGGH!
HWiS
WISS
DEAD IN THE RIVER, HUH.
WEEEH...
HHHRGH!
SHE'S A QUICK LITTLE--

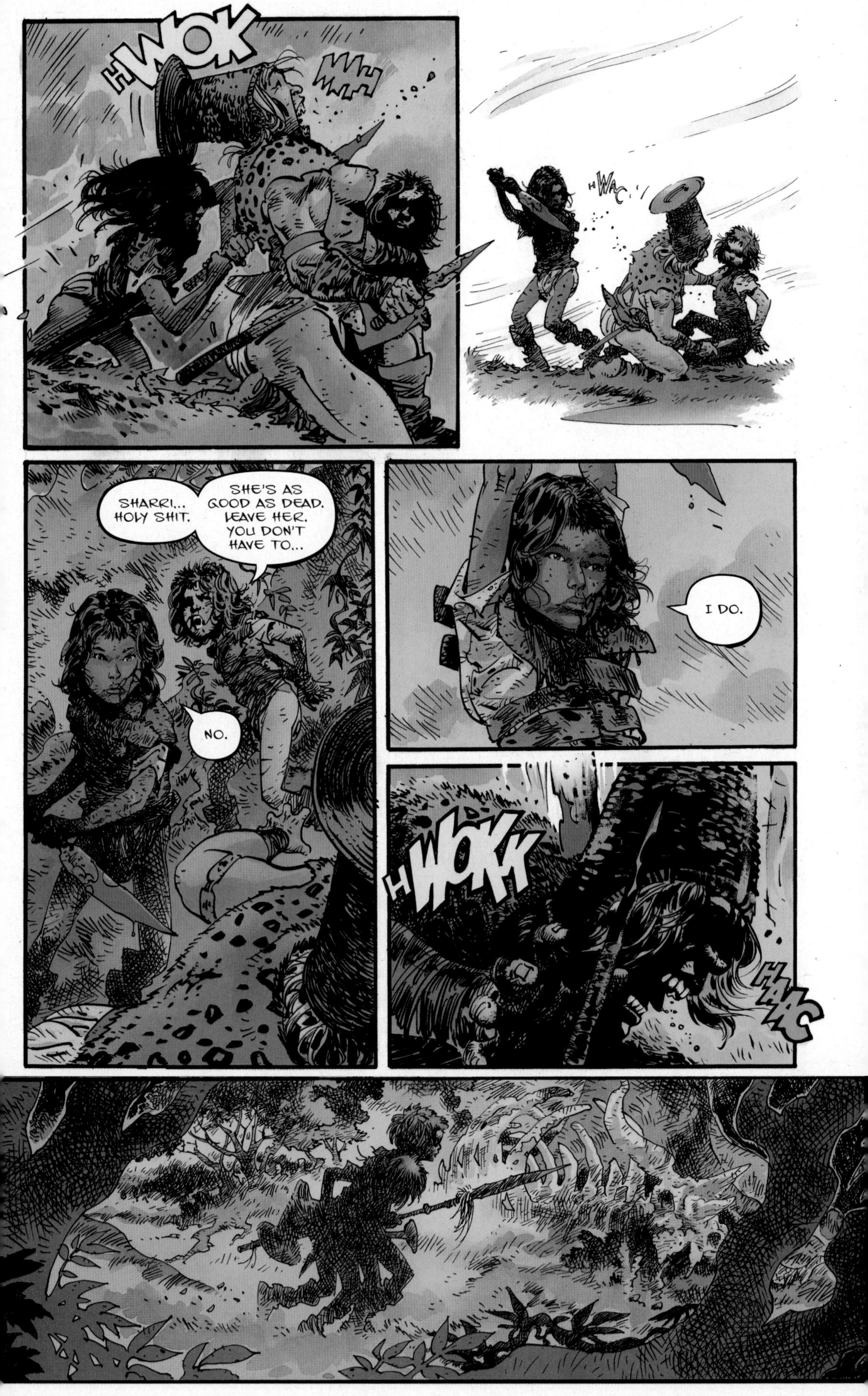
HWOK
WAH
HWAC
SHARRI... HOLY SHIT.
SHE'S AS GOOD AS DEAD. LEAVE HER. YOU DON'T HAVE TO...
NO.
I DO.
HWOKK
HWAC

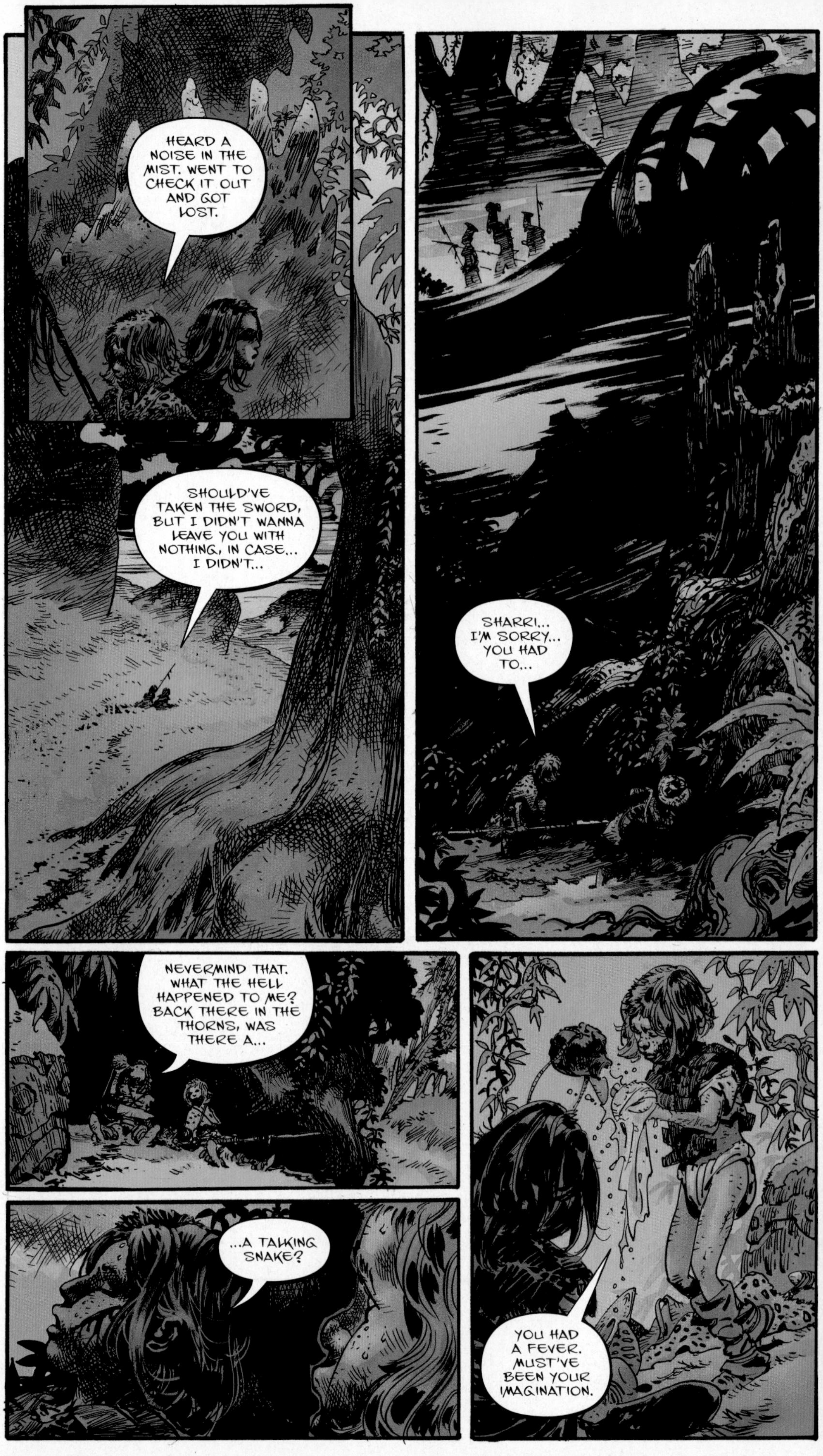
HEARD A NOISE IN THE MIST. WENT TO CHECK IT OUT AND GOT LOST.
SHOULD'VE TAKEN THE SWORD, BUT I DIDN'T WANNA LEAVE YOU WITH NOTHING, IN CASE... I DIDN'T...
SHARRI... I'M SORRY... YOU HAD TO...
NEVERMIND THAT. WHAT THE HELL HAPPENED TO ME? BACK THERE IN THE THORNS, WAS THERE A...
...A TALKING SNAKE?
YOU HAD A FEVER. MUST'VE BEEN YOUR IMAGINATION.

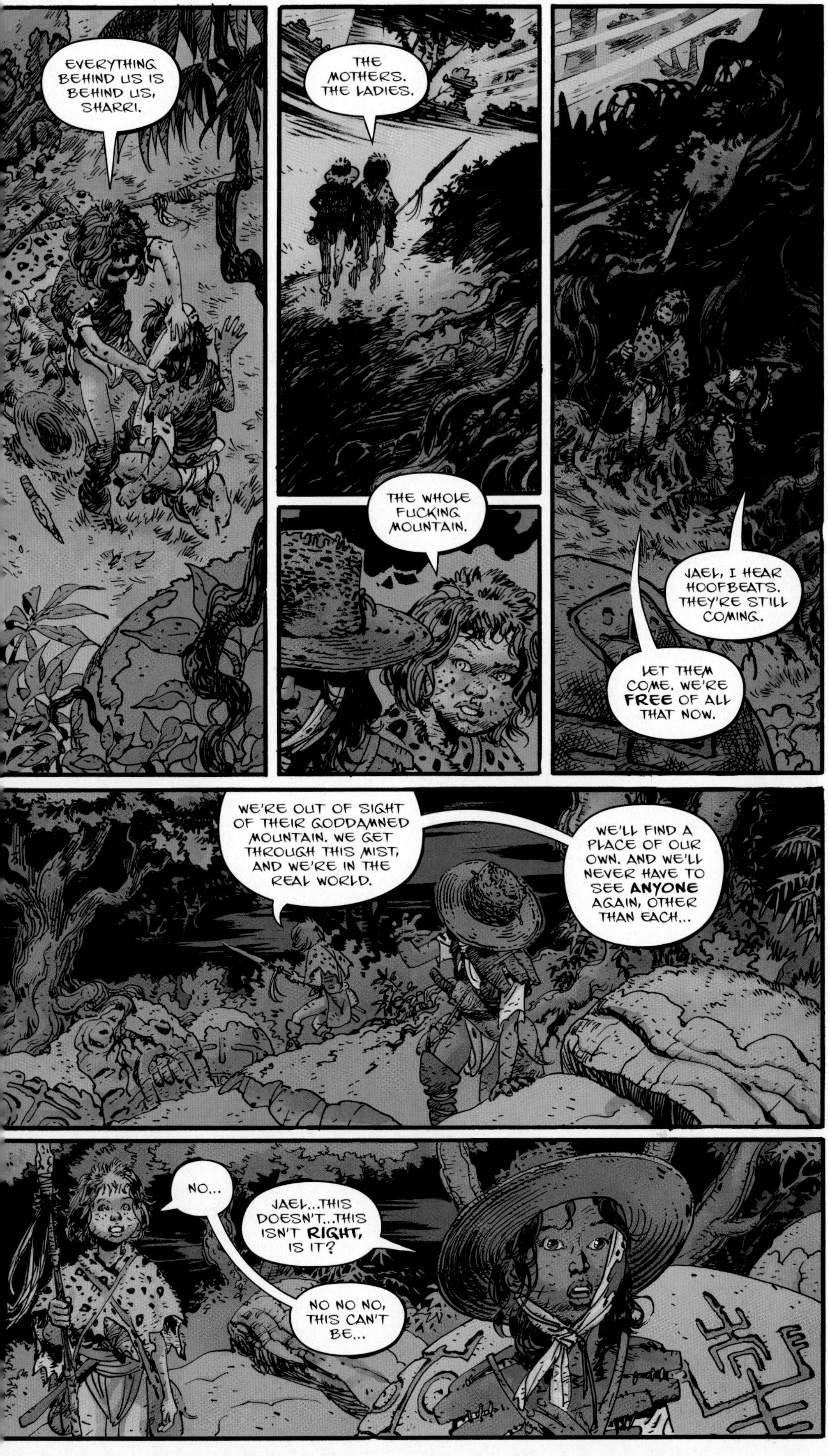

EVERYTHING BEHIND US IS BEHIND US, SHARRI.
THE MOTHERS. THE LADIES.
THE WHOLE FUCKING MOUNTAIN.
JAEL, I HEAR HOOFBEATS. THEY'RE STILL COMING.
LET THEM COME. WE'RE **FREE** OF ALL THAT NOW.
WE'RE OUT OF SIGHT OF THEIR GODDAMNED MOUNTAIN. WE GET THROUGH THIS MIST, AND WE'RE IN THE REAL WORLD.
WE'LL FIND A PLACE OF OUR OWN. AND WE'LL NEVER HAVE TO SEE **ANYONE** AGAIN, OTHER THAN EACH...
NO...
JAEL...THIS DOESN'T...THIS ISN'T **RIGHT,** IS IT?
NO NO NO, THIS CAN'T BE...

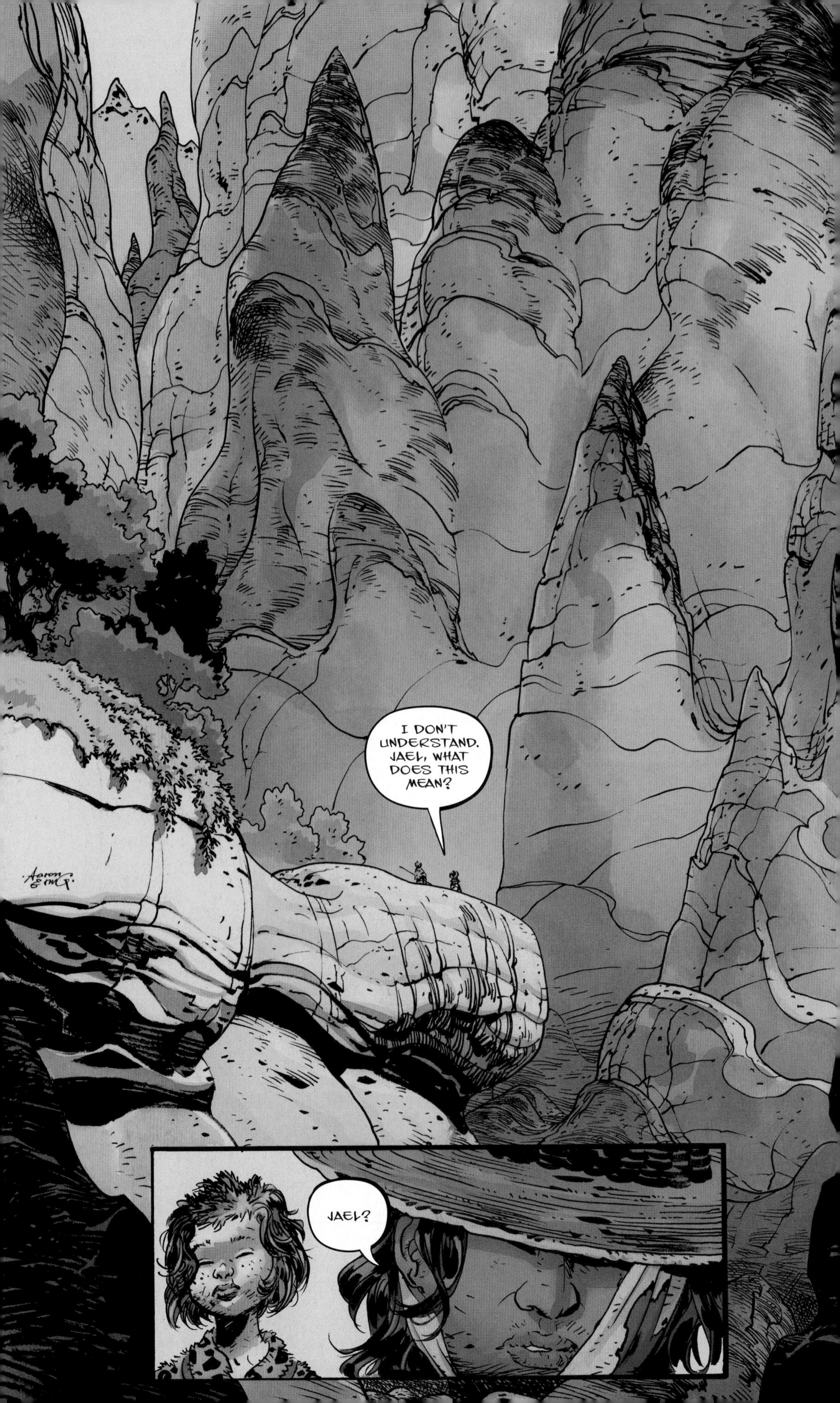
I DON'T UNDERSTAND. JAEL, WHAT DOES THIS MEAN?
JAEL?

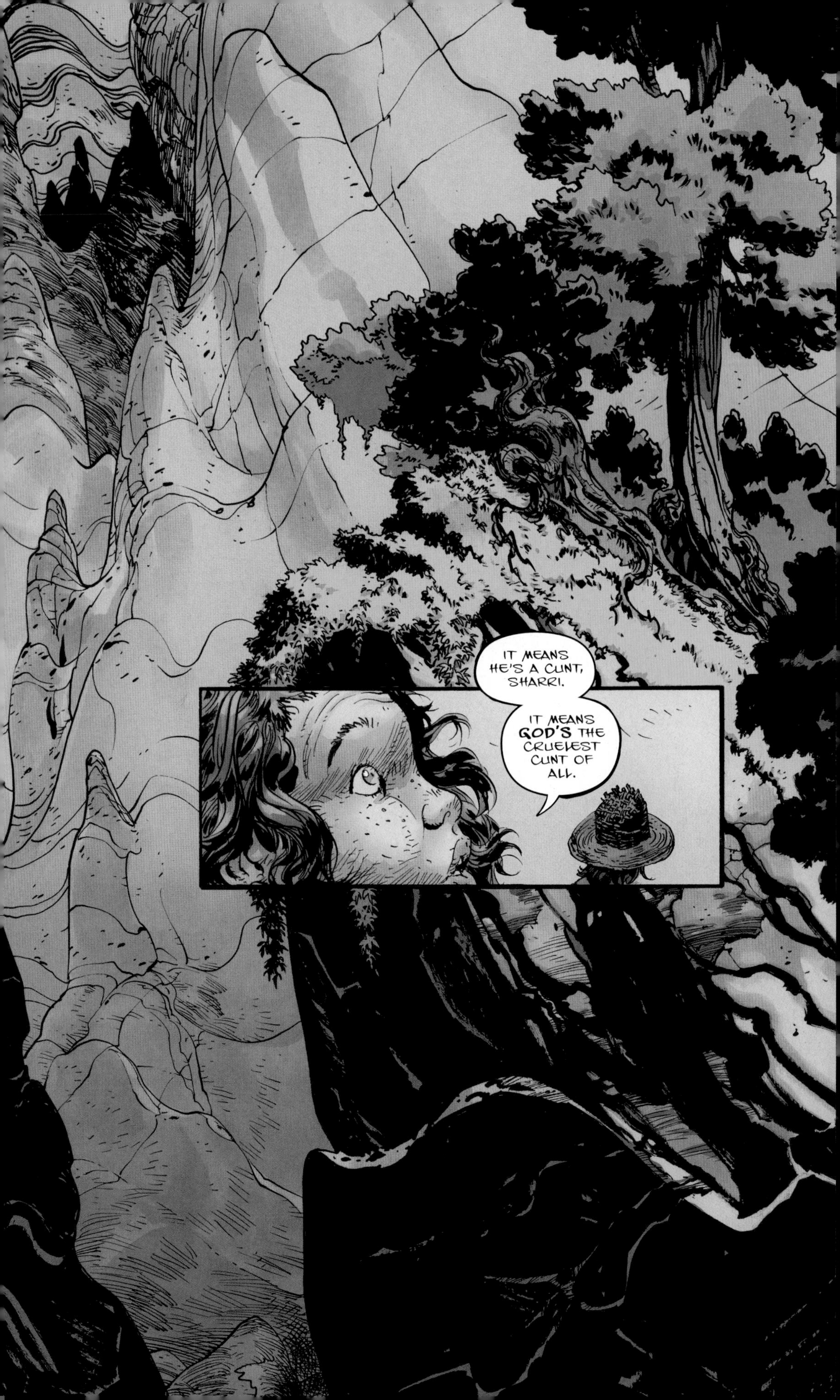
IT MEANS HE'S A CUNT, SHARRI.
IT MEANS GOD'S THE CRUELEST CUNT OF ALL.

# Chapter Four

## "The Mount of the Lord"

Escape for thy life;
look not behind thee,
neither stay thou in all the plain;
escape to the mountain,
lest thou be consumed.

--Genesis 19:17

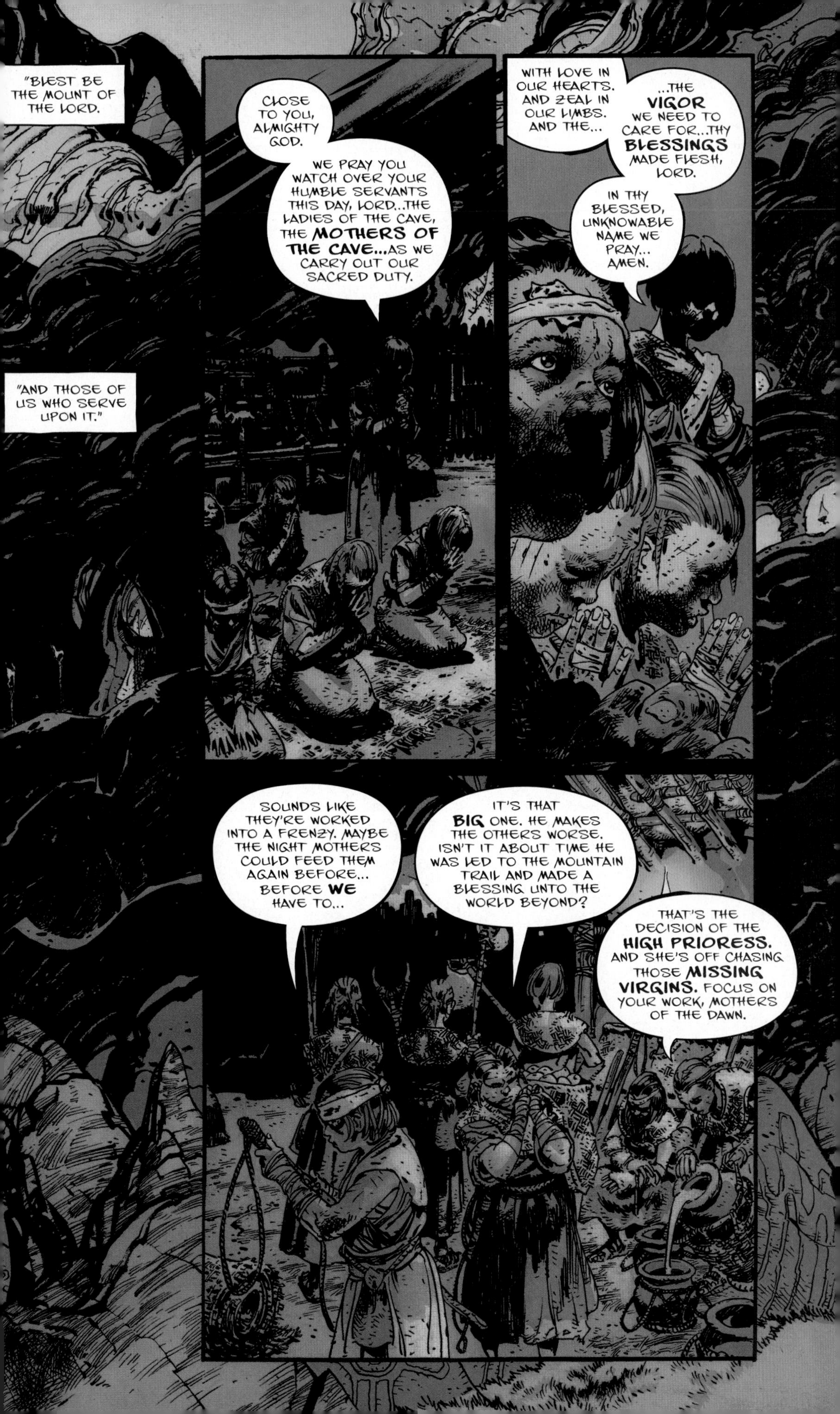
"BLEST BE THE MOUNT OF THE LORD.
CLOSE TO YOU, ALMIGHTY GOD.
WE PRAY YOU WATCH OVER YOUR HUMBLE SERVANTS THIS DAY, LORD...THE LADIES OF THE CAVE, THE MOTHERS OF THE CAVE...AS WE CARRY OUT OUR SACRED DUTY.
WITH LOVE IN OUR HEARTS. AND ZEAL IN OUR LIMBS. AND THE...
...THE VIGOR WE NEED TO CARE FOR...THY BLESSINGS MADE FLESH, LORD.
IN THY BLESSED, UNKNOWABLE NAME WE PRAY... AMEN.
"AND THOSE OF US WHO SERVE UPON IT."
SOUNDS LIKE THEY'RE WORKED INTO A FRENZY. MAYBE THE NIGHT MOTHERS COULD FEED THEM AGAIN BEFORE... BEFORE WE HAVE TO...
IT'S THAT BIG ONE. HE MAKES THE OTHERS WORSE. ISN'T IT ABOUT TIME HE WAS LED TO THE MOUNTAIN TRAIL AND MADE A BLESSING UNTO THE WORLD BEYOND?
THAT'S THE DECISION OF THE HIGH PRIORESS. AND SHE'S OFF CHASING THOSE MISSING VIRGINS. FOCUS ON YOUR WORK, MOTHERS OF THE DAWN.

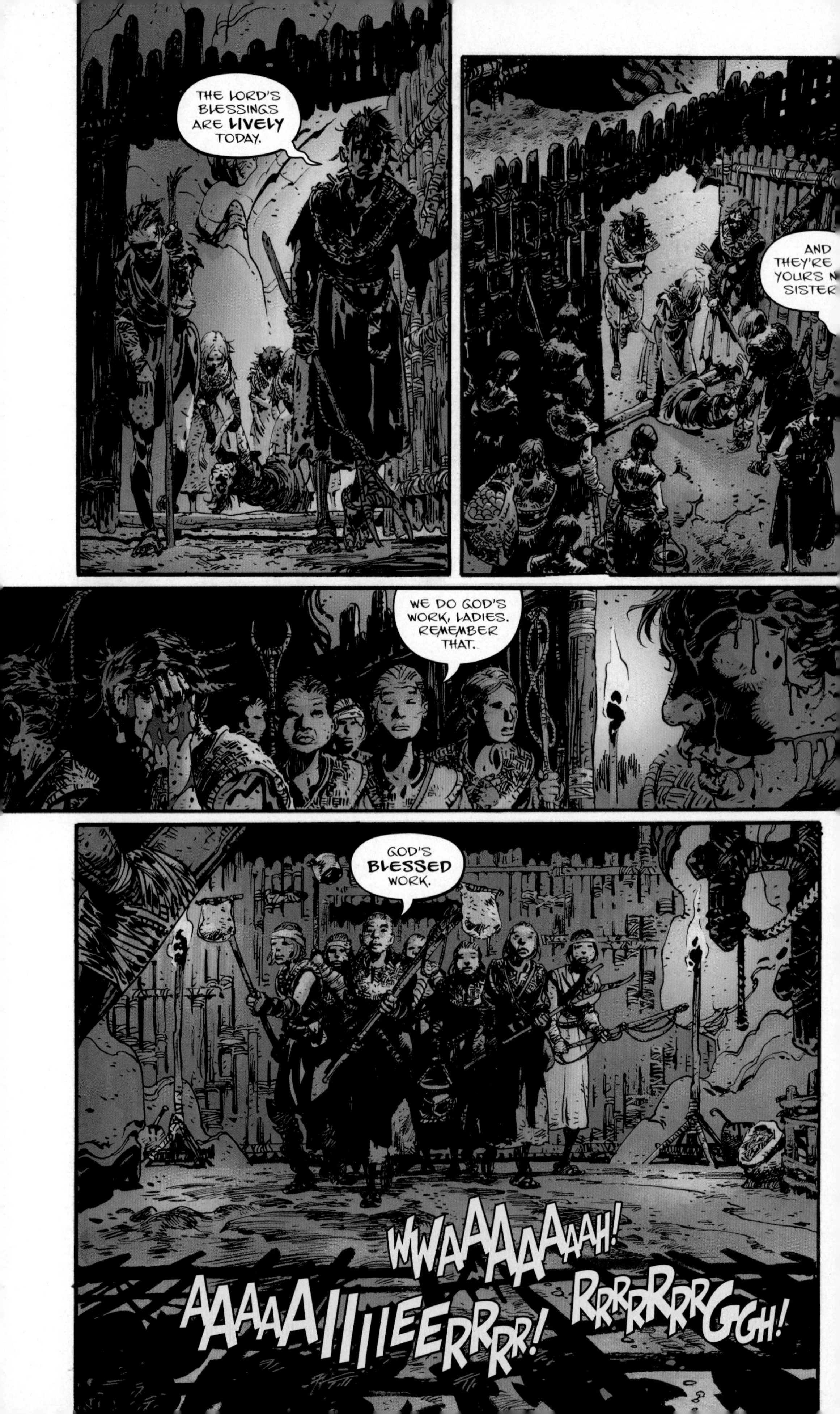
THE LORD'S BLESSINGS ARE LIVELY TODAY.
AND THEY'RE YOURS SISTER
WE DO GOD'S WORK, LADIES. REMEMBER THAT.
GOD'S BLESSED WORK.
WWAAAAAAAAH!
AAAAAIIIIIEERRRRR!
RRRRRRRRGGH!

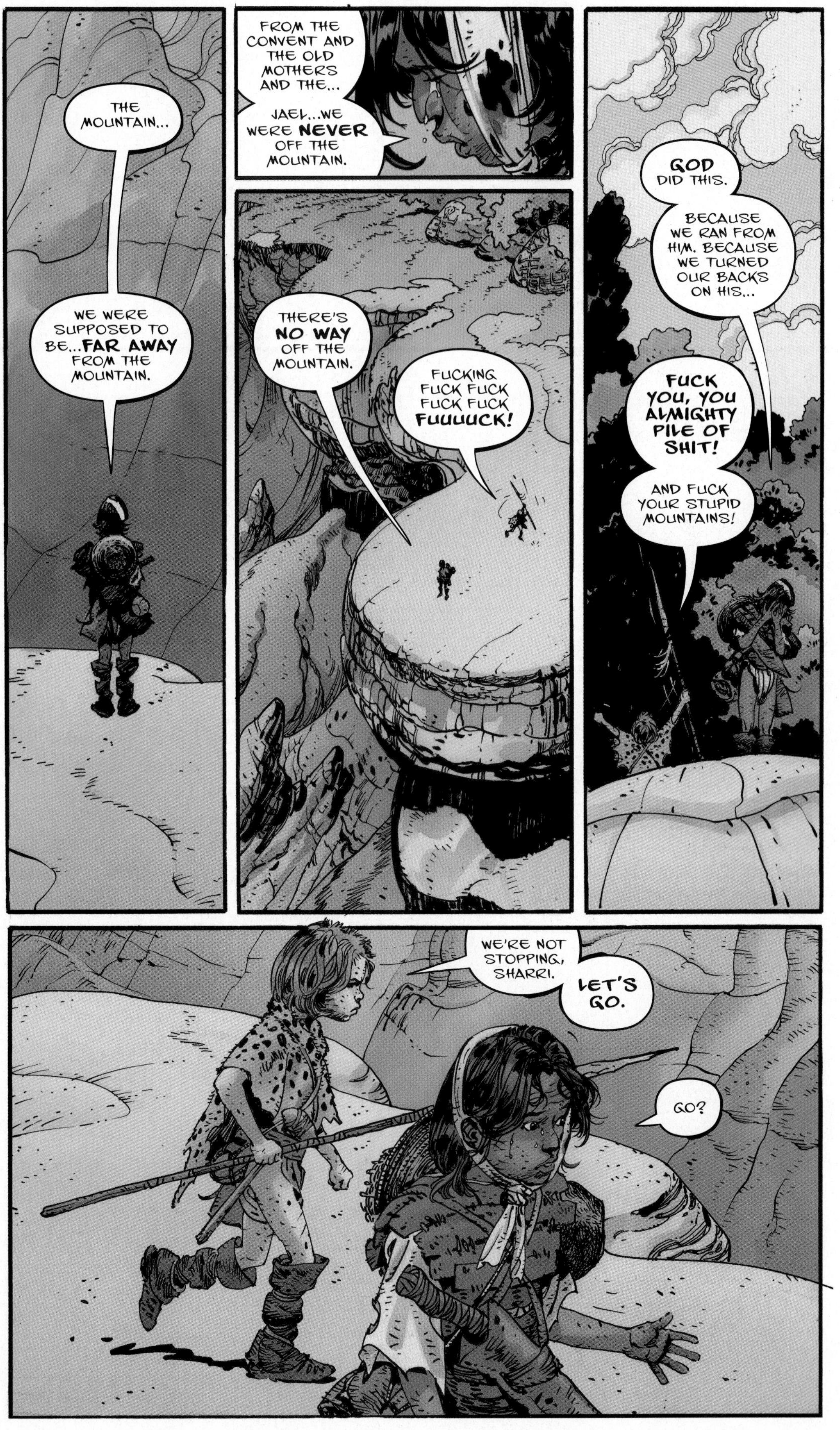
THE MOUNTAIN...
WE WERE SUPPOSED TO BE...FAR AWAY FROM THE MOUNTAIN.
FROM THE CONVENT AND THE OLD MOTHERS AND THE...
JAEL...WE WERE NEVER OFF THE MOUNTAIN.
THERE'S NO WAY OFF THE MOUNTAIN.
FUCKING FUCK FUCK FUCK FUCK FUUUUCK!
GOD DID THIS.
BECAUSE WE RAN FROM HIM. BECAUSE WE TURNED OUR BACKS ON HIS...
FUCK YOU, YOU ALMIGHTY PILE OF SHIT!
AND FUCK YOUR STUPID MOUNTAINS!
WE'RE NOT STOPPING, SHARRI.
LET'S GO.
GO?

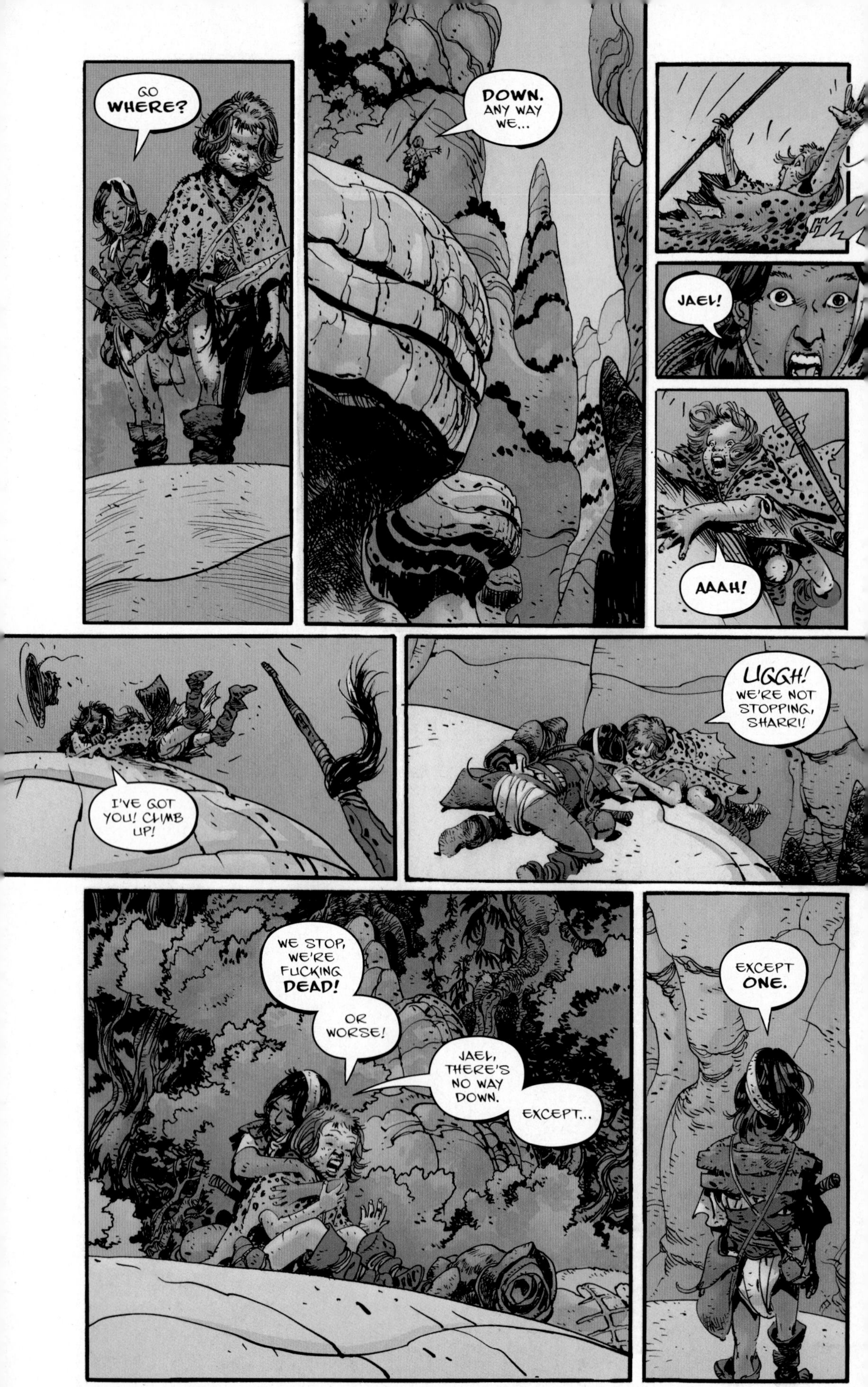
GO WHERE?
DOWN. ANY WAY WE...
JAEL!
AAAH!
I'VE GOT YOU! CLIMB UP!
UGGH! WE'RE NOT STOPPING, SHARRI!
WE STOP, WE'RE FUCKING DEAD!
OR WORSE!
JAEL, THERE'S NO WAY DOWN.
EXCEPT...
EXCEPT ONE.

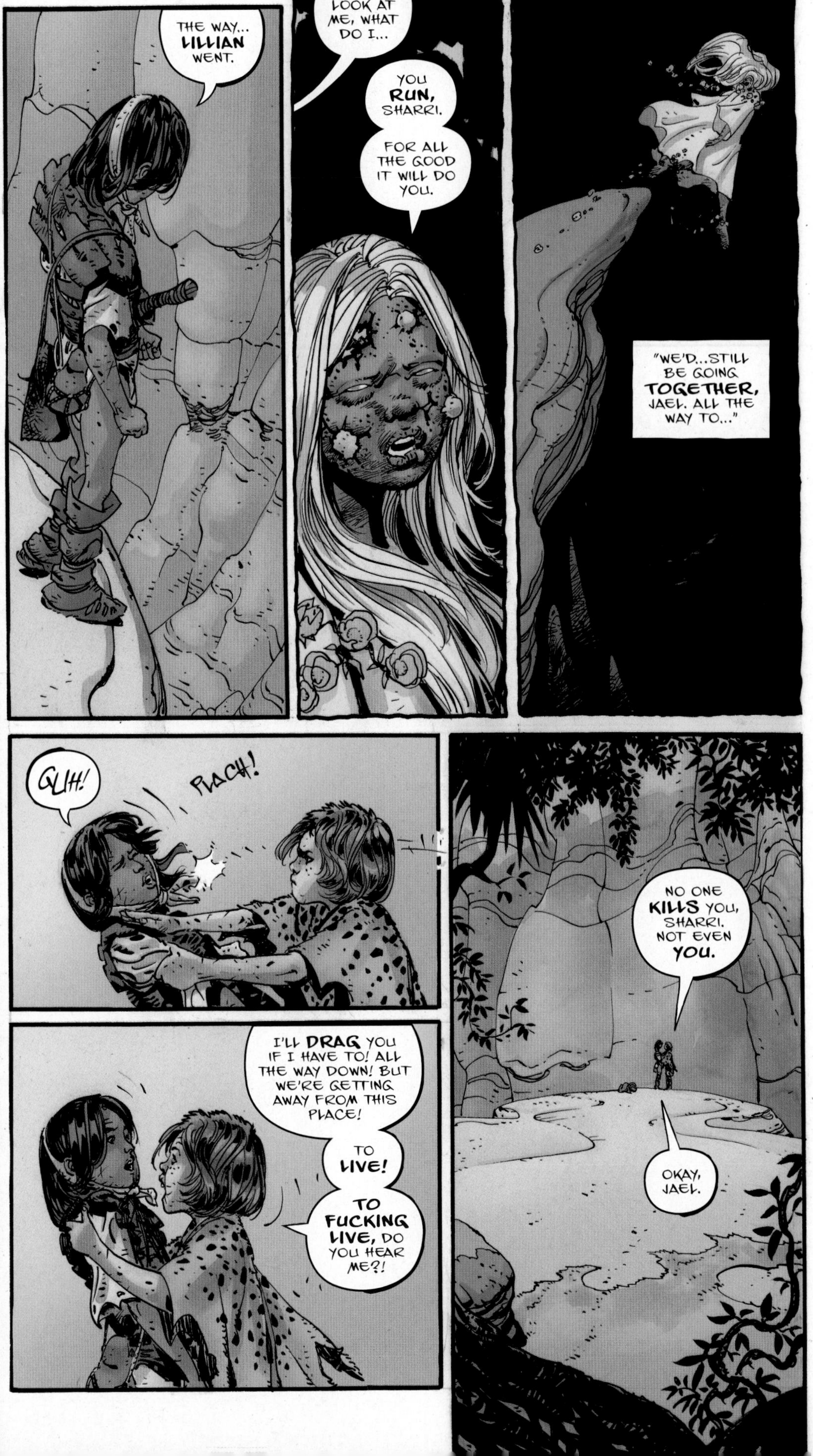
THE WAY... LILLIAN WENT.
LILLIAN, LOOK AT ME, WHAT DO I...
YOU RUN, SHARRI.
FOR ALL THE GOOD IT WILL DO YOU.
"WE'D...STILL BE GOING TOGETHER, JAEL. ALL THE WAY TO..."
GUH!
PLACH!
I'LL DRAG YOU IF I HAVE TO! ALL THE WAY DOWN! BUT WE'RE GETTING AWAY FROM THIS PLACE!
TO LIVE!
TO FUCKING LIVE, DO YOU HEAR ME?!
NO ONE KILLS YOU, SHARRI. NOT EVEN YOU.
OKAY, JAEL.

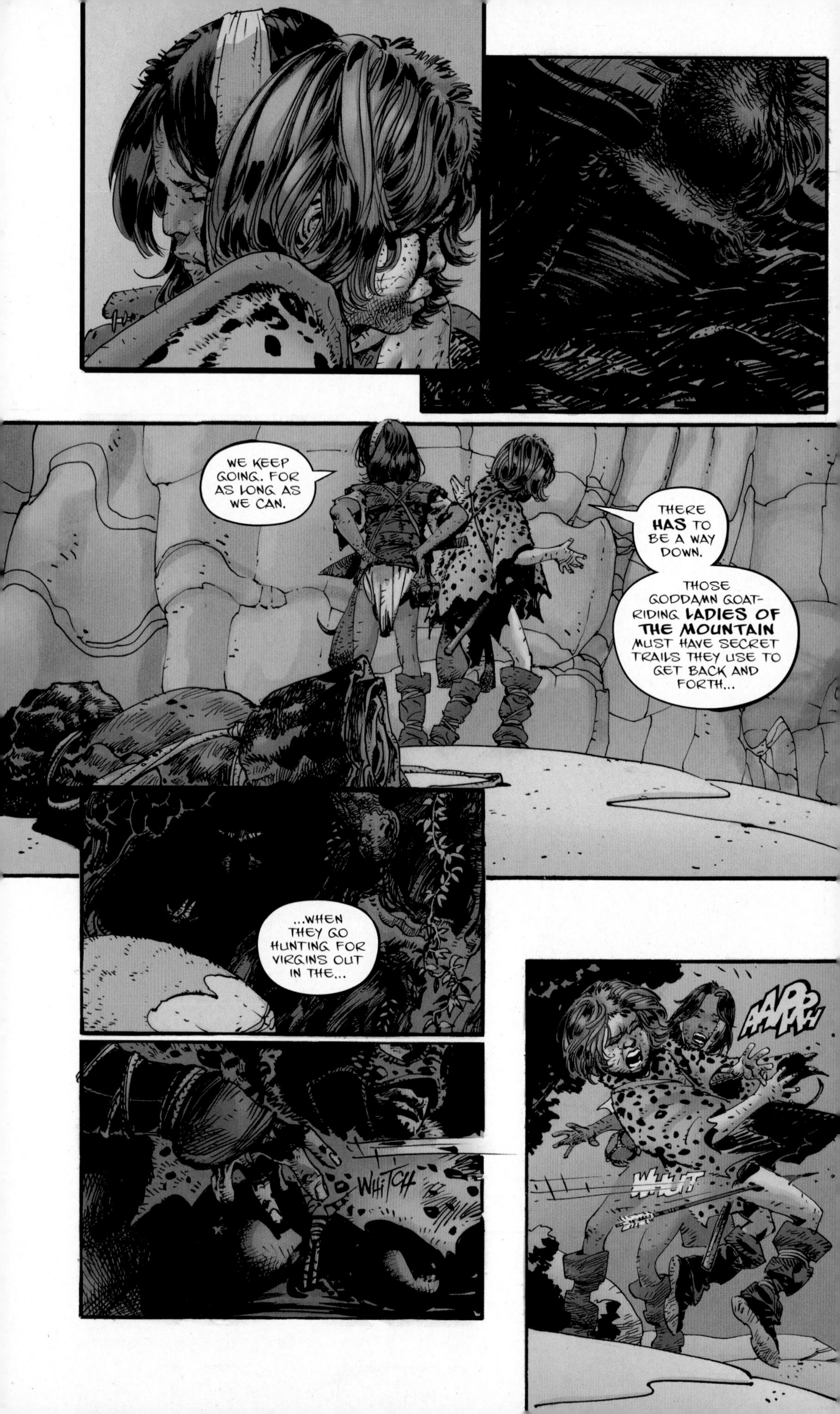
WE KEEP GOING. FOR AS LONG AS WE CAN.
THERE HAS TO BE A WAY DOWN.
THOSE GODDAMN GOAT-RIDING LADIES OF THE MOUNTAIN MUST HAVE SECRET TRAILS THEY USE TO GET BACK AND FORTH...
...WHEN THEY GO HUNTING FOR VIRGINS OUT IN THE...
WHITCH
AAAHH
WHUT

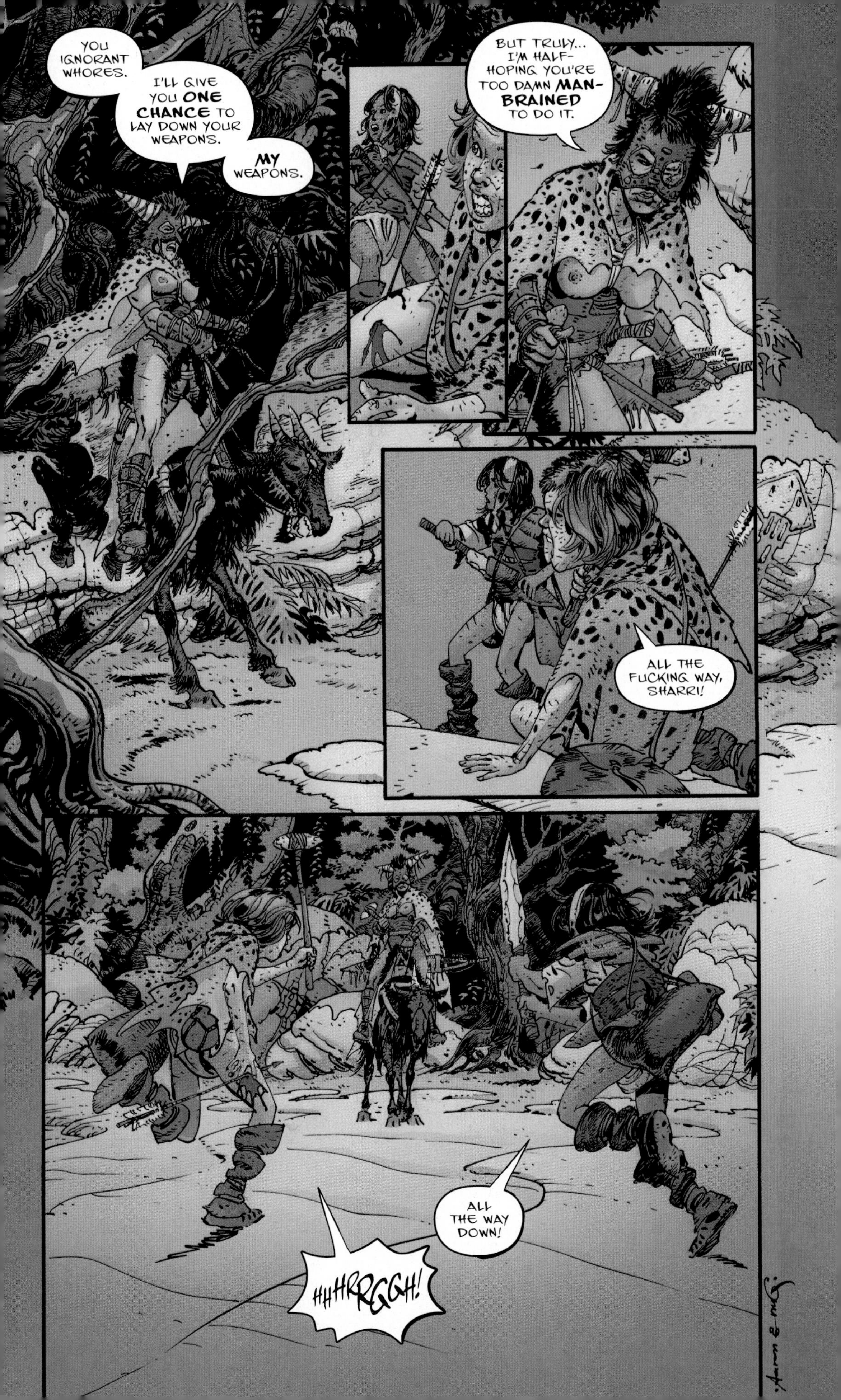

YOU IGNORANT WHORES.
I'LL GIVE YOU **ONE CHANCE** TO LAY DOWN YOUR WEAPONS.
**MY** WEAPONS.
BUT TRULY... I'M HALF-HOPING YOU'RE TOO DAMN **MAN-BRAINED** TO DO IT.
ALL THE FUCKING WAY, SHARRI!
ALL THE WAY DOWN!
HHHRRGGH!

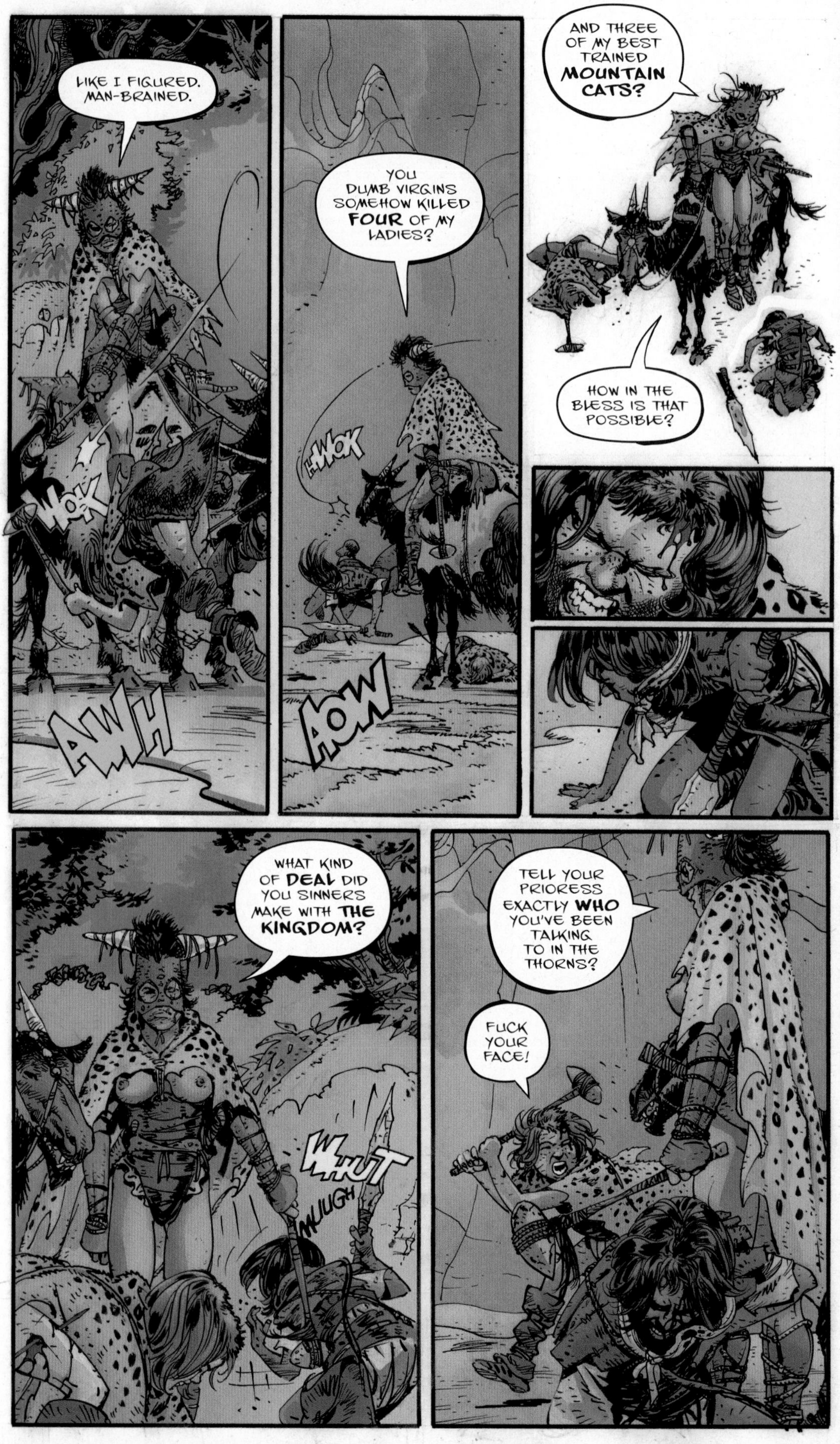

LIKE I FIGURED. MAN-BRAINED.
WOK
AWH
YOU DUMB VIRGINS SOMEHOW KILLED FOUR OF MY LADIES?
THWOK
AOW
AND THREE OF MY BEST TRAINED MOUNTAIN CATS?
HOW IN THE BLESS IS THAT POSSIBLE?
WHAT KIND OF DEAL DID YOU SINNERS MAKE WITH THE KINGDOM?
WHUT
MUUGH
TELL YOUR PRIORESS EXACTLY WHO YOU'VE BEEN TALKING TO IN THE THORNS?
FUCK YOUR FACE!

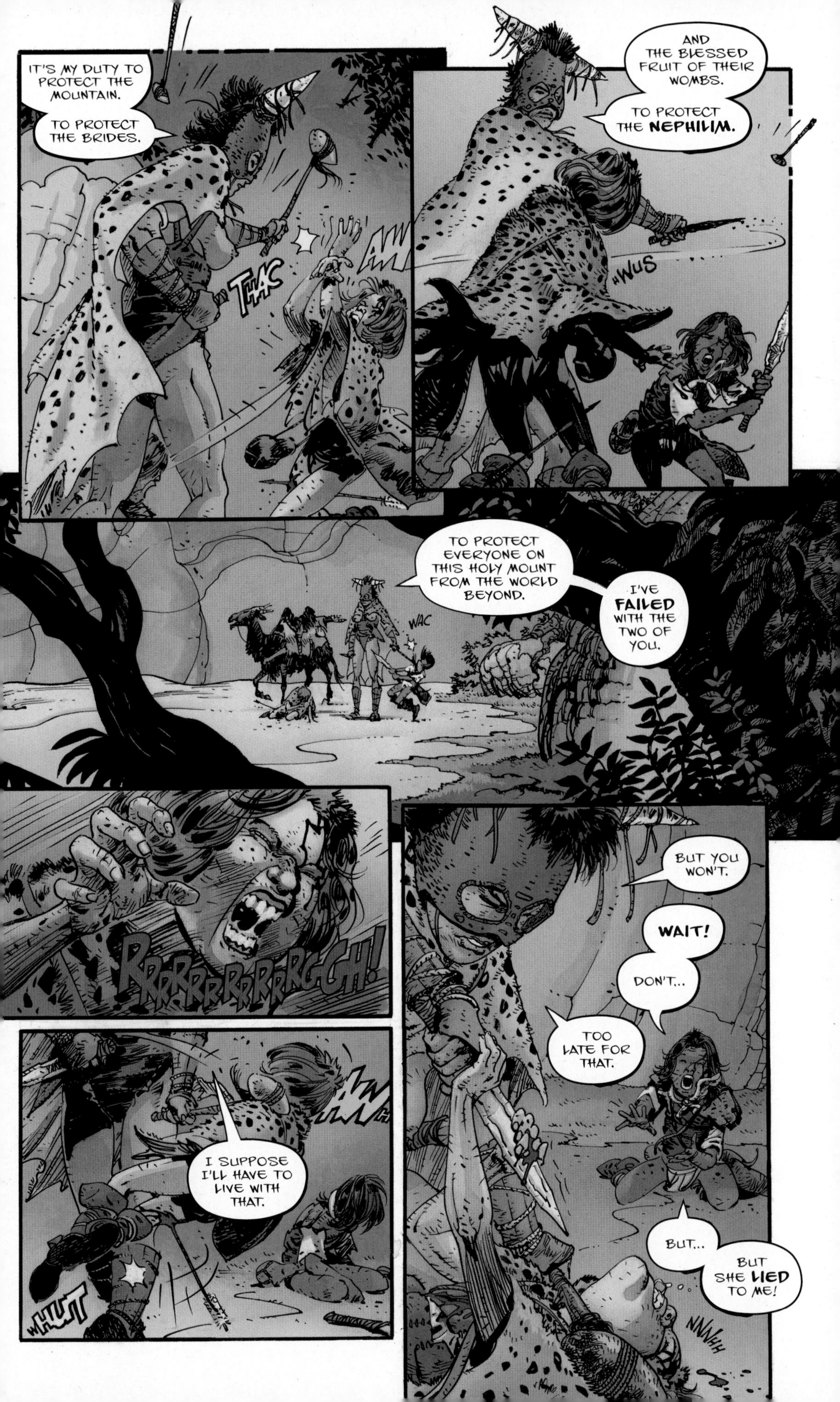

IT'S MY DUTY TO PROTECT THE MOUNTAIN.
TO PROTECT THE BRIDES.
THAC
AND THE BLESSED FRUIT OF THEIR WOMBS.
TO PROTECT THE NEPHILIM.
WUS
TO PROTECT EVERYONE ON THIS HOLY MOUNT FROM THE WORLD BEYOND.
I'VE FAILED WITH THE TWO OF YOU.
WAC
RRRRRRRRRRRRGGH!
I SUPPOSE I'LL HAVE TO LIVE WITH THAT.
WHUT
BUT YOU WON'T.
WAIT!
DON'T...
TOO LATE FOR THAT.
BUT...
BUT SHE LIED TO ME!
NNNHH

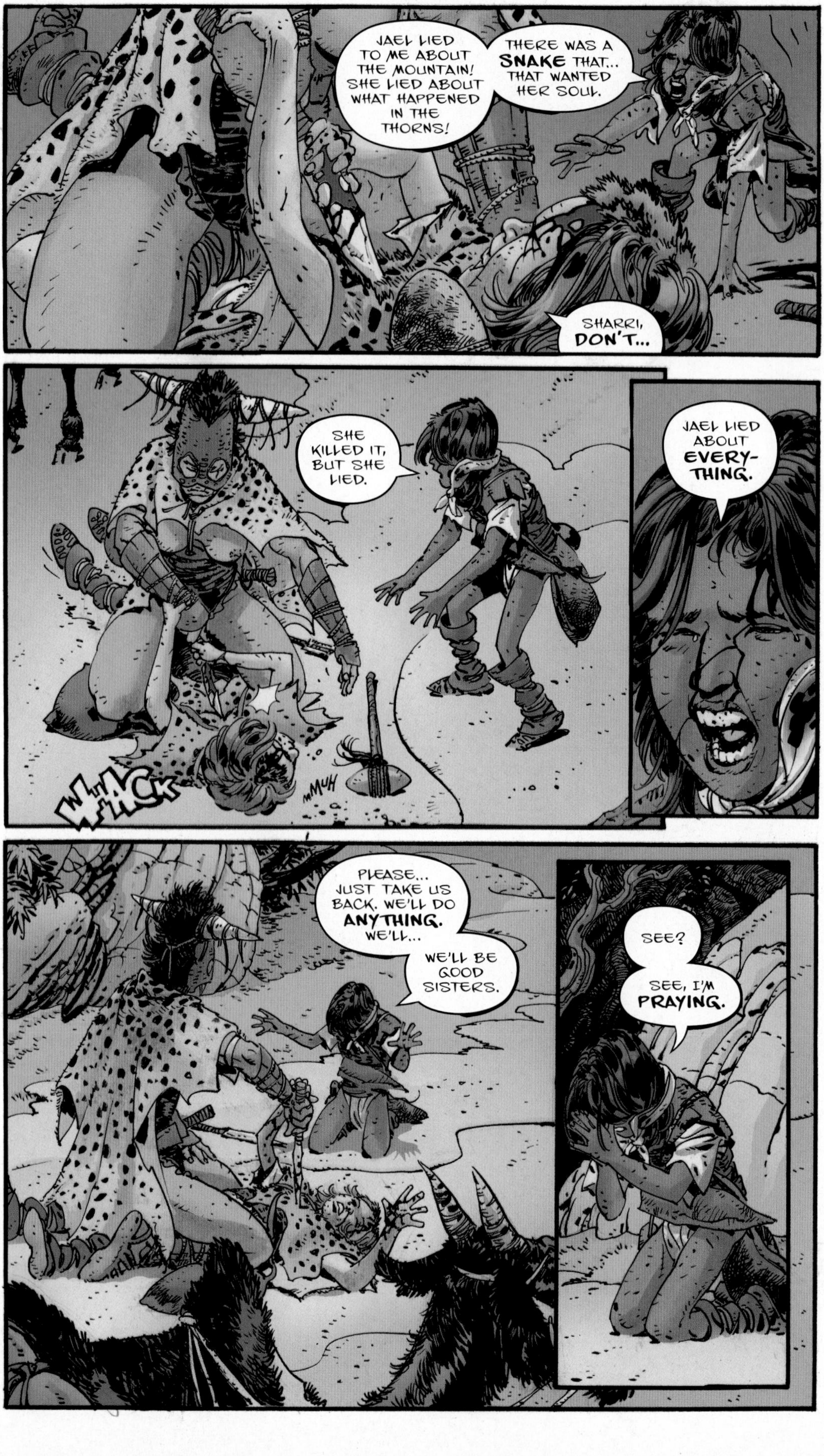
JAEL LIED TO ME ABOUT THE MOUNTAIN! SHE LIED ABOUT WHAT HAPPENED IN THE THORNS!
THERE WAS A SNAKE THAT... THAT WANTED HER SOUL.
SHARRI, DON'T...
SHE KILLED IT, BUT SHE LIED.
WHACK
MMUH
JAEL LIED ABOUT EVERY-THING.
PLEASE... JUST TAKE US BACK. WE'LL DO ANYTHING. WE'LL...
WE'LL BE GOOD SISTERS.
SEE?
SEE, I'M PRAYING.

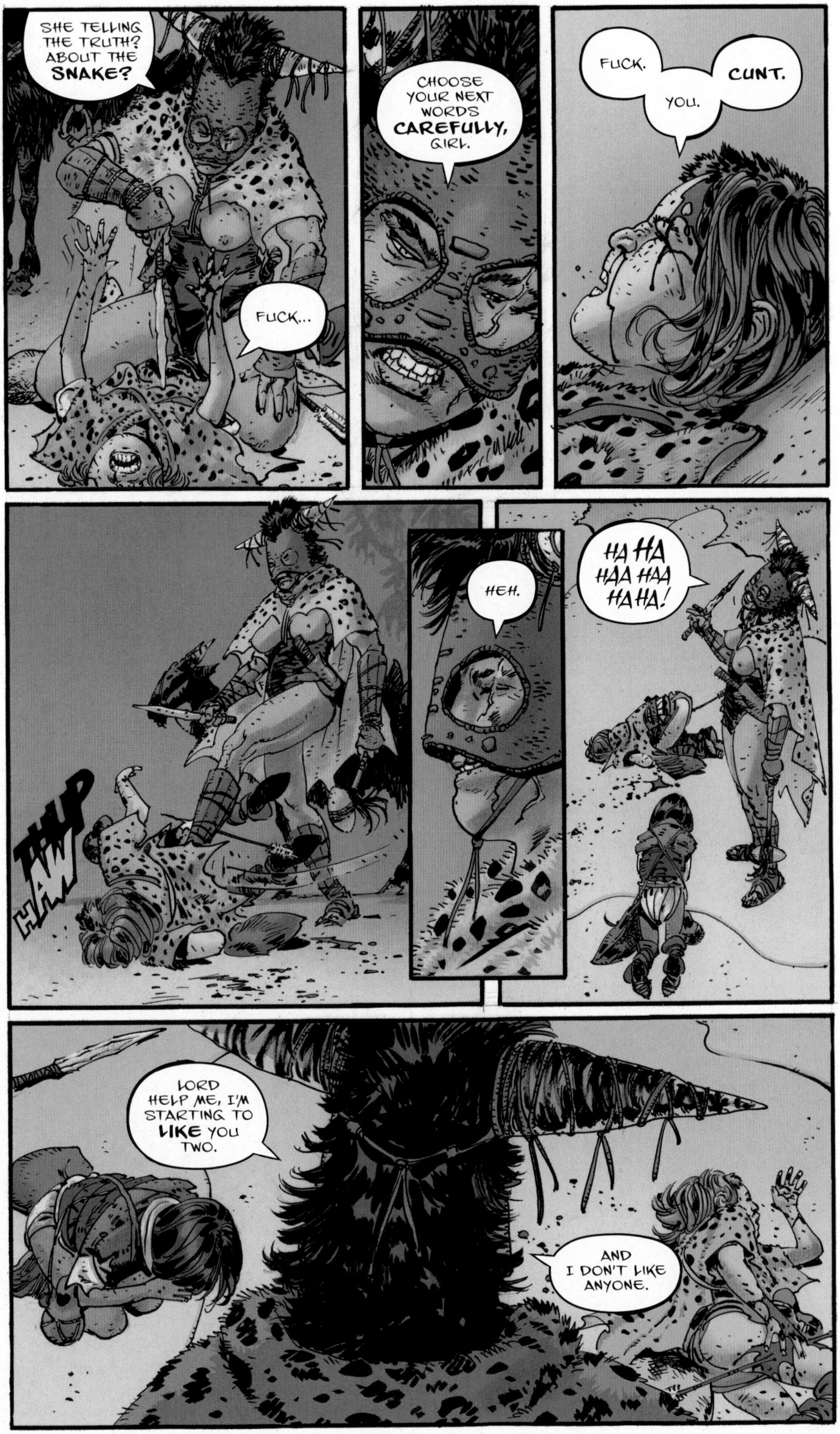
SHE TELLING THE TRUTH? ABOUT THE SNAKE?
FUCK...
CHOOSE YOUR NEXT WORDS CAREFULLY, GIRL.
FUCK.
YOU.
CUNT.
THUP
HAW
HEH.
HA HA HAA HAA HAHA!
LORD HELP ME, I'M STARTING TO LIKE YOU TWO.
AND I DON'T LIKE ANYONE.

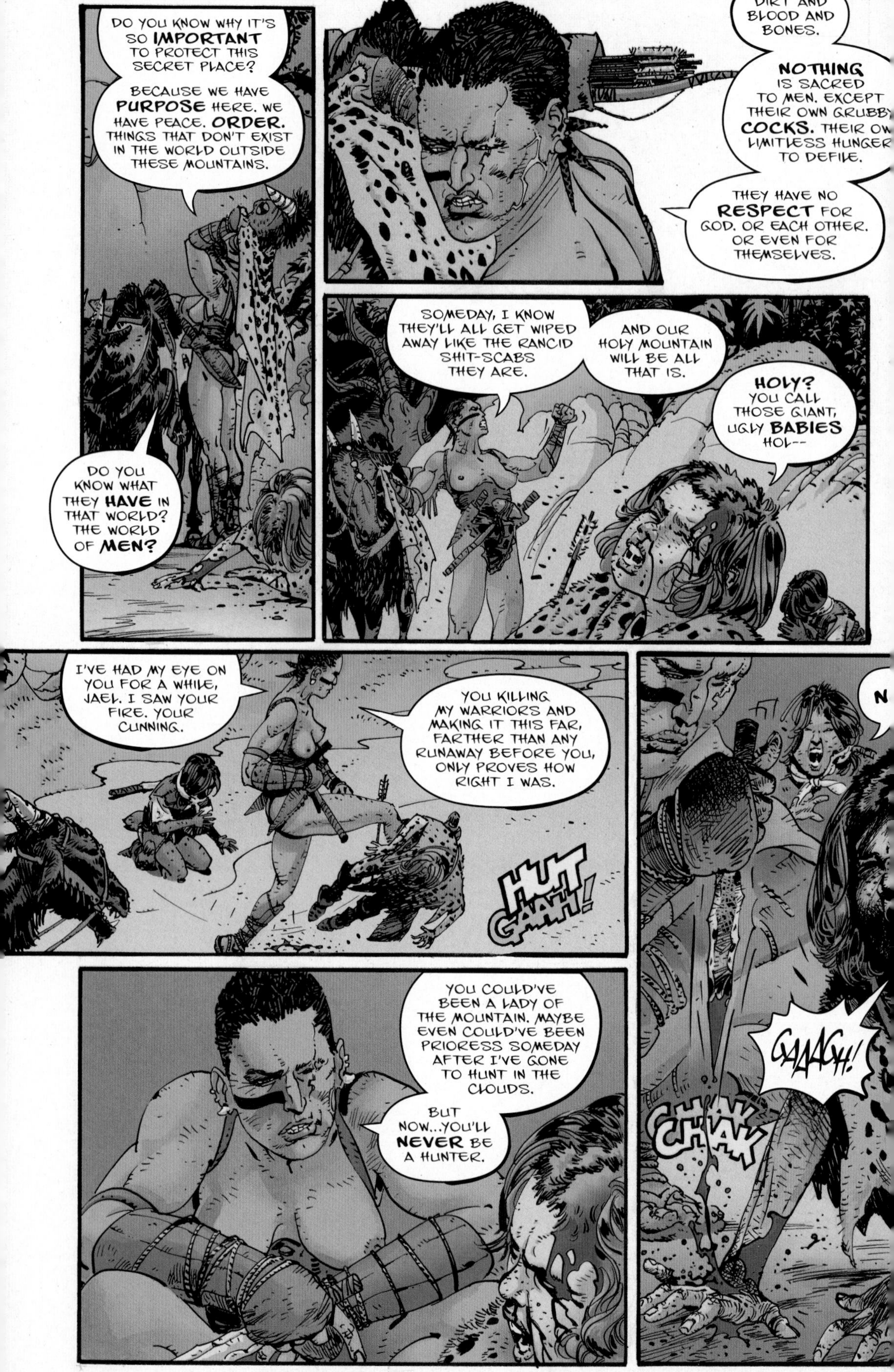

DO YOU KNOW WHY IT'S SO IMPORTANT TO PROTECT THIS SECRET PLACE?
BECAUSE WE HAVE PURPOSE HERE. WE HAVE PEACE. ORDER. THINGS THAT DON'T EXIST IN THE WORLD OUTSIDE THESE MOUNTAINS.
DO YOU KNOW WHAT THEY HAVE IN THAT WORLD? THE WORLD OF MEN?
DIRT AND BLOOD AND BONES.
NOTHING IS SACRED TO MEN. EXCEPT THEIR OWN GRUBBY COCKS. THEIR OWN LIMITLESS HUNGER TO DEFILE.
THEY HAVE NO RESPECT FOR GOD. OR EACH OTHER. OR EVEN FOR THEMSELVES.
SOMEDAY, I KNOW THEY'LL ALL GET WIPED AWAY LIKE THE RANCID SHIT-SCABS THEY ARE.
AND OUR HOLY MOUNTAIN WILL BE ALL THAT IS.
HOLY? YOU CALL THOSE GIANT, UGLY BABIES HOL--
I'VE HAD MY EYE ON YOU FOR A WHILE, JAEL. I SAW YOUR FIRE. YOUR CUNNING.
YOU KILLING MY WARRIORS AND MAKING IT THIS FAR, FARTHER THAN ANY RUNAWAY BEFORE YOU, ONLY PROVES HOW RIGHT I WAS.
HUT GAAH!
YOU COULD'VE BEEN A LADY OF THE MOUNTAIN. MAYBE EVEN COULD'VE BEEN PRIORESS SOMEDAY AFTER I'VE GONE TO HUNT IN THE CLOUDS.
BUT NOW...YOU'LL NEVER BE A HUNTER.
N
GAAAGH!
CHAK

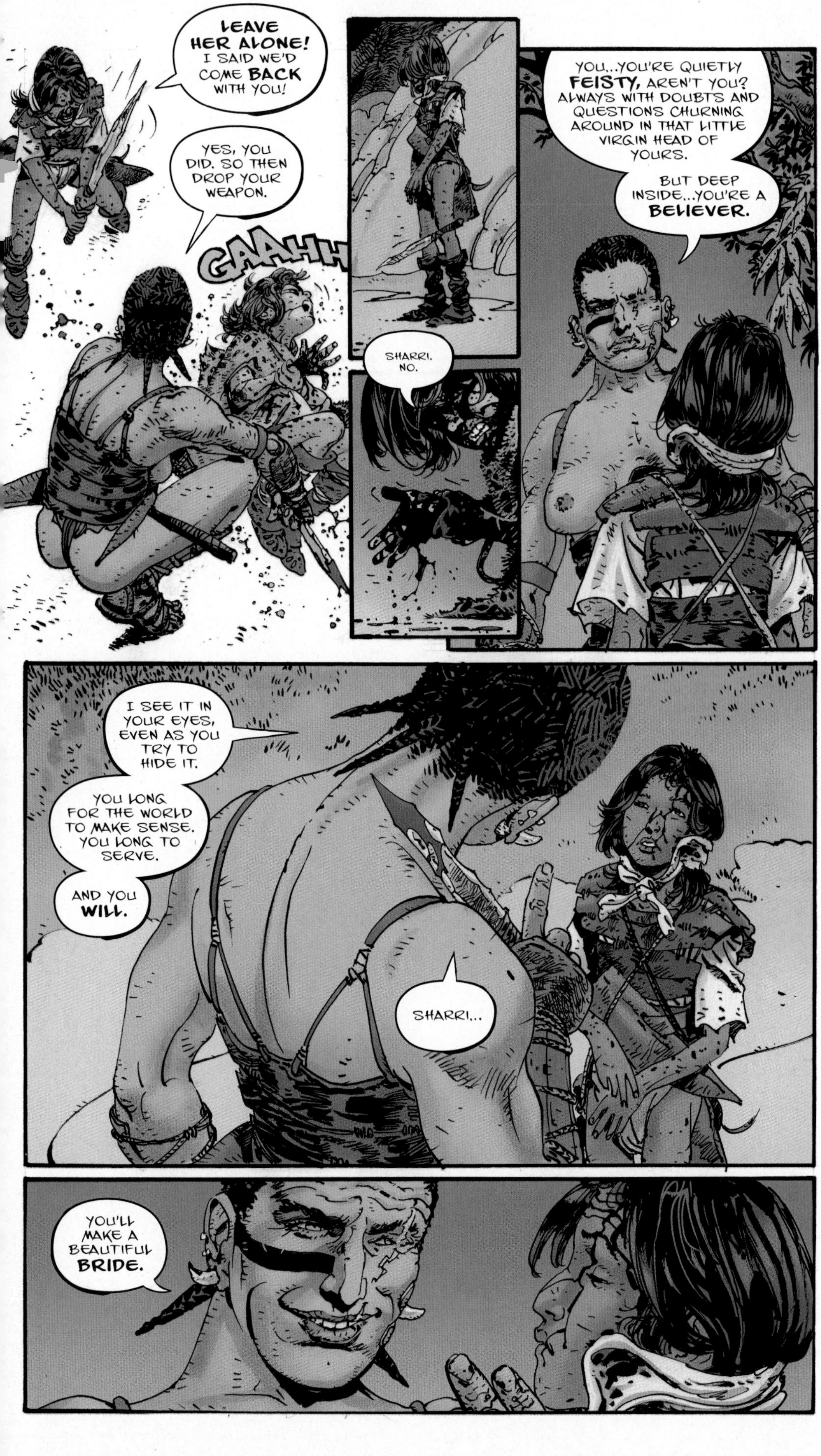
LEAVE HER ALONE! I SAID WE'D COME BACK WITH YOU!
YES, YOU DID. SO THEN DROP YOUR WEAPON.
GAAHH
SHARRI. NO.
YOU...YOU'RE QUIETLY FEISTY, AREN'T YOU? ALWAYS WITH DOUBTS AND QUESTIONS CHURNING AROUND IN THAT LITTLE VIRGIN HEAD OF YOURS.
BUT DEEP INSIDE...YOU'RE A BELIEVER.
I SEE IT IN YOUR EYES, EVEN AS YOU TRY TO HIDE IT.
YOU LONG FOR THE WORLD TO MAKE SENSE. YOU LONG TO SERVE.
AND YOU WILL.
SHARRI...
YOU'LL MAKE A BEAUTIFUL BRIDE.

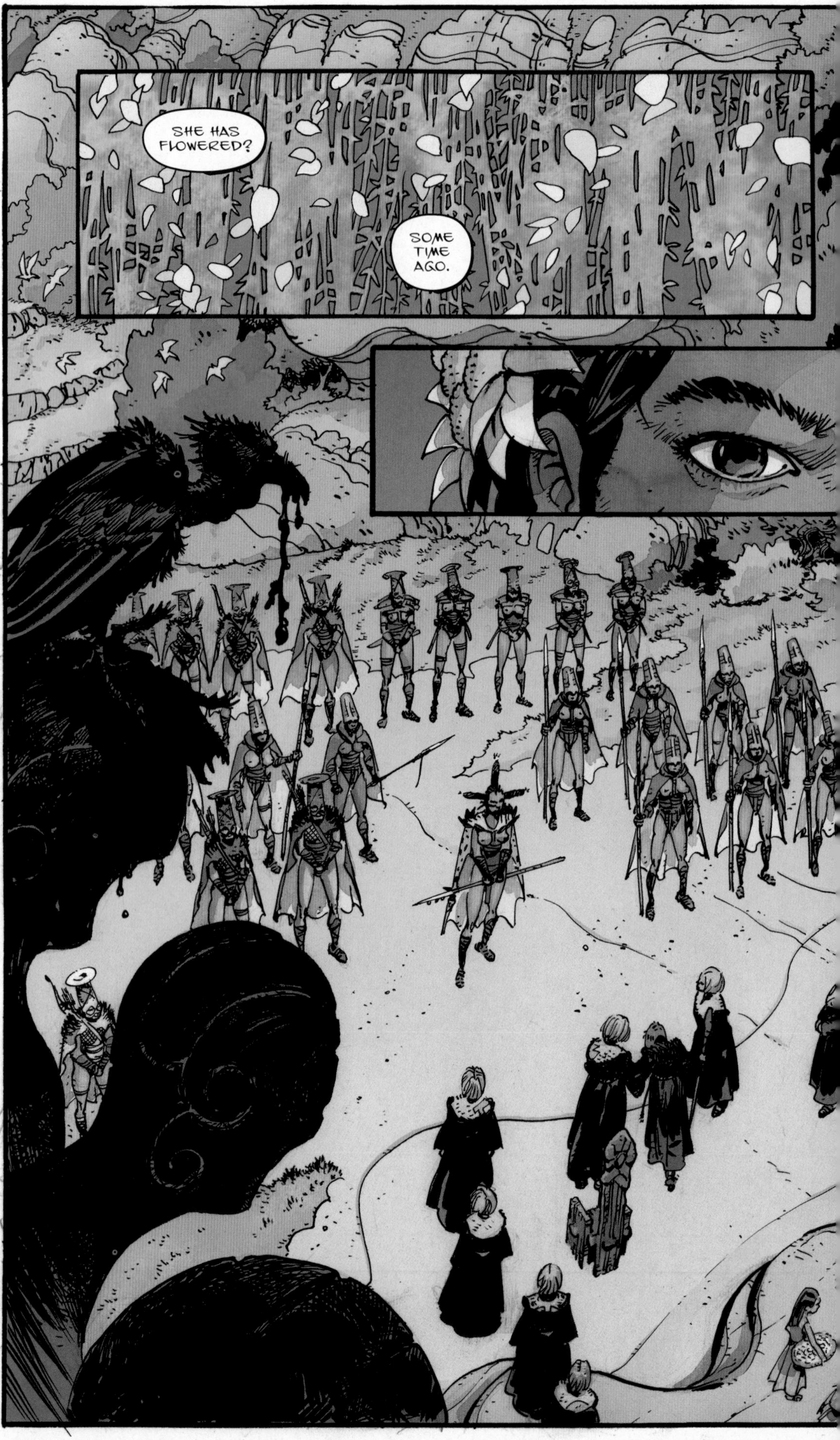
SHE HAS FLOWERED?
SOME TIME AGO.

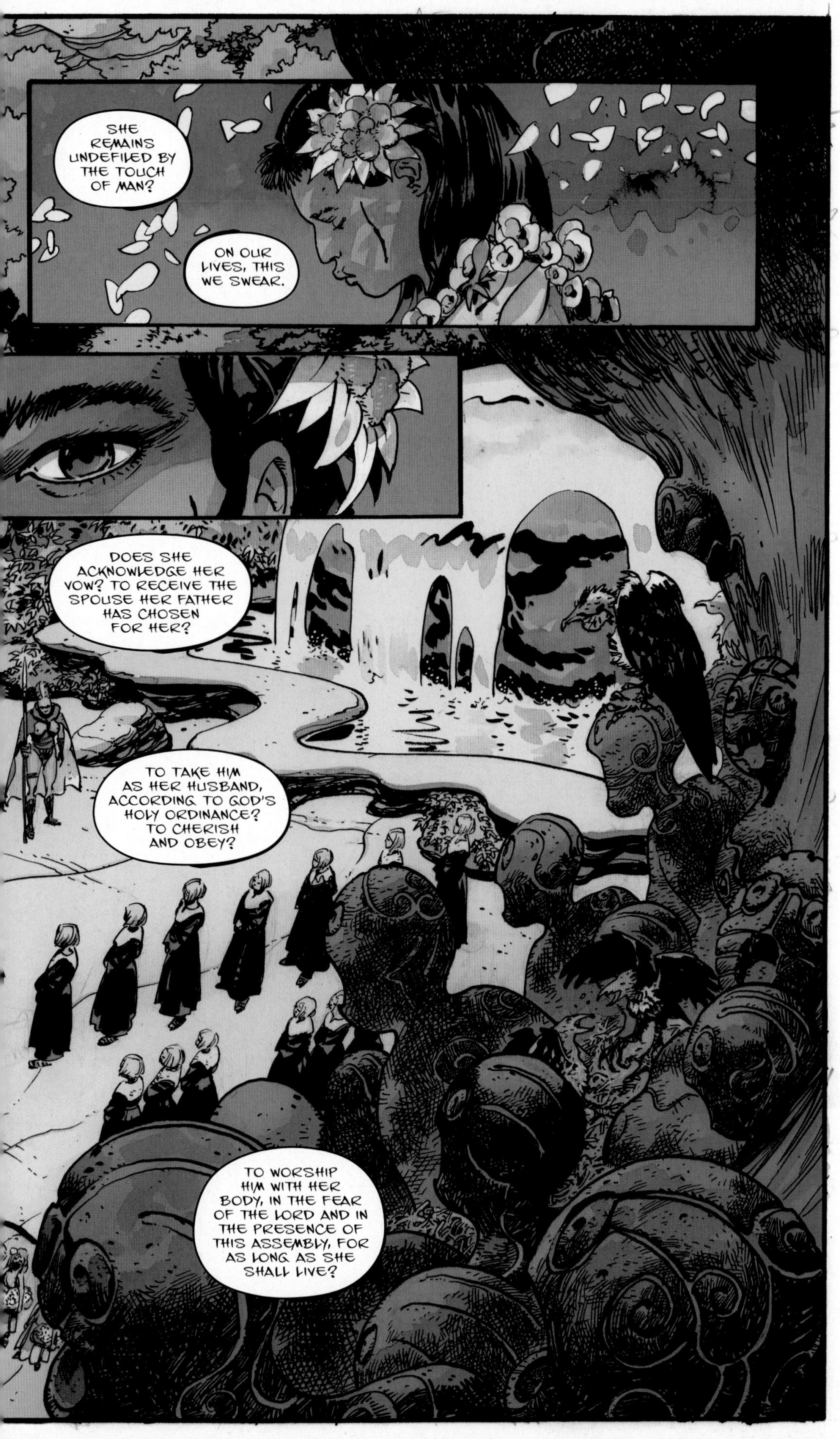
SHE REMAINS UNDEFILED BY THE TOUCH OF MAN?
ON OUR LIVES, THIS WE SWEAR.
DOES SHE ACKNOWLEDGE HER VOW? TO RECEIVE THE SPOUSE HER FATHER HAS CHOSEN FOR HER?
TO TAKE HIM AS HER HUSBAND, ACCORDING TO GOD'S HOLY ORDINANCE? TO CHERISH AND OBEY?
TO WORSHIP HIM WITH HER BODY, IN THE FEAR OF THE LORD AND IN THE PRESENCE OF THIS ASSEMBLY, FOR AS LONG AS SHE SHALL LIVE?

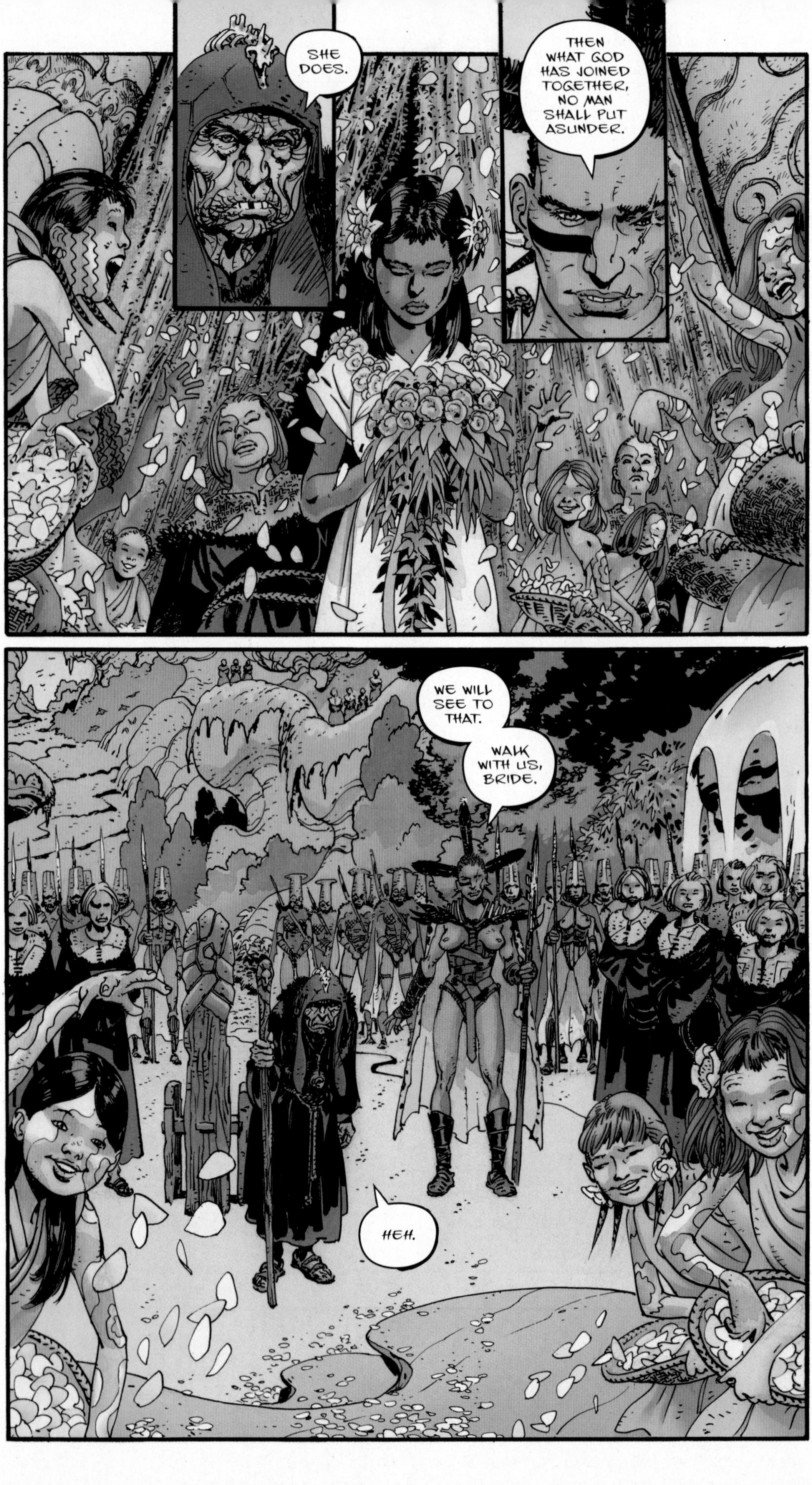
SHE DOES.
THEN WHAT GOD HAS JOINED TOGETHER, NO MAN SHALL PUT ASUNDER.
WE WILL SEE TO THAT.
WALK WITH US, BRIDE.
HEH.

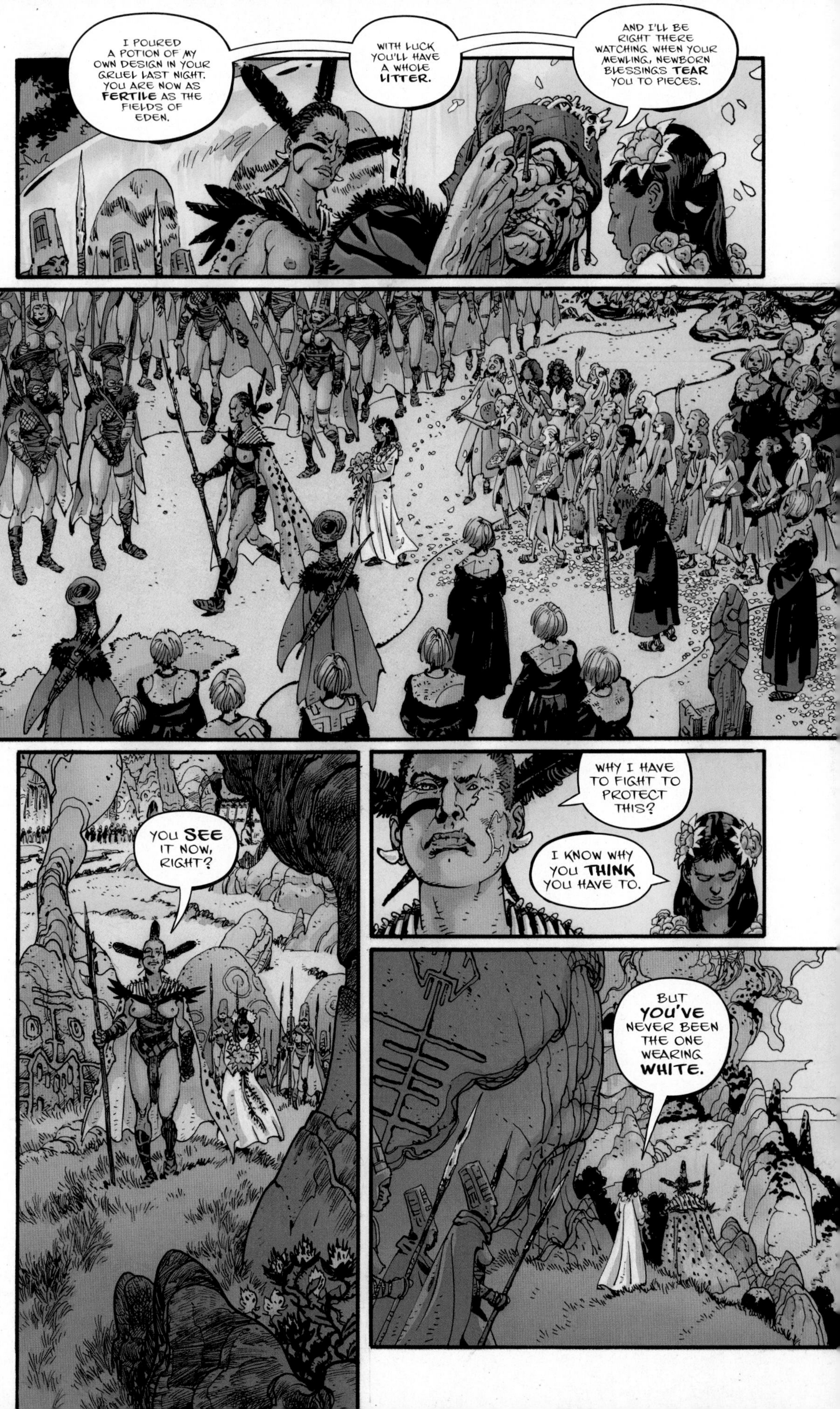
I POURED A POTION OF MY OWN DESIGN IN YOUR GRUEL LAST NIGHT. YOU ARE NOW AS FERTILE AS THE FIELDS OF EDEN.
WITH LUCK YOU'LL HAVE A WHOLE LITTER.
AND I'LL BE RIGHT THERE WATCHING WHEN YOUR MEWLING, NEWBORN BLESSINGS TEAR YOU TO PIECES.
YOU SEE IT NOW, RIGHT?
WHY I HAVE TO FIGHT TO PROTECT THIS?
I KNOW WHY YOU THINK YOU HAVE TO.
BUT YOU'VE NEVER BEEN THE ONE WEARING WHITE.

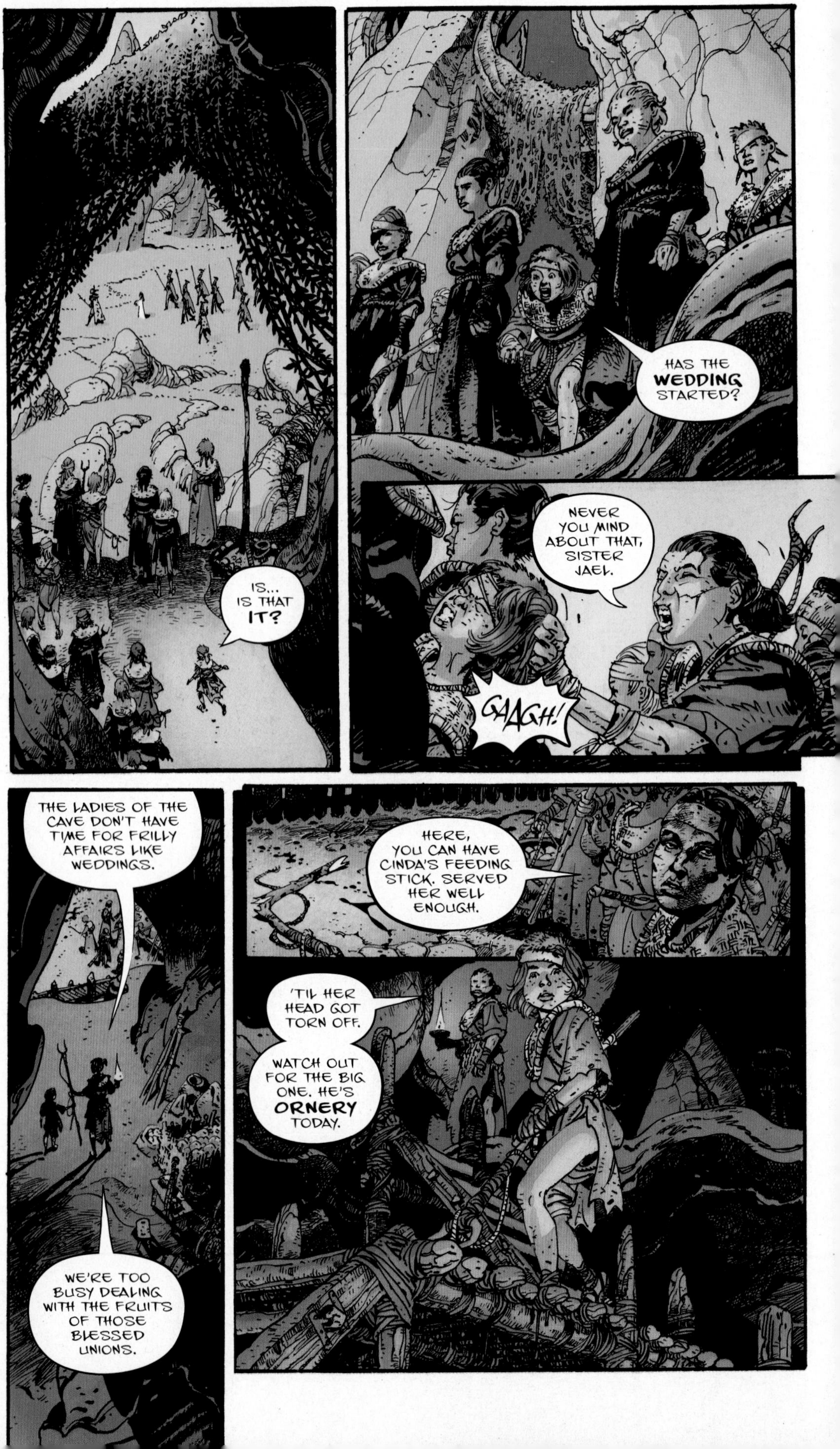
IS... IS THAT IT?
HAS THE WEDDING STARTED?
NEVER YOU MIND ABOUT THAT, SISTER JAEL.
GAAGH!
THE LADIES OF THE CAVE DON'T HAVE TIME FOR FRILLY AFFAIRS LIKE WEDDINGS.
WE'RE TOO BUSY DEALING WITH THE FRUITS OF THOSE BLESSED UNIONS.
HERE, YOU CAN HAVE CINDA'S FEEDING STICK. SERVED HER WELL ENOUGH.
'TIL HER HEAD GOT TORN OFF.
WATCH OUT FOR THE BIG ONE. HE'S ORNERY TODAY.

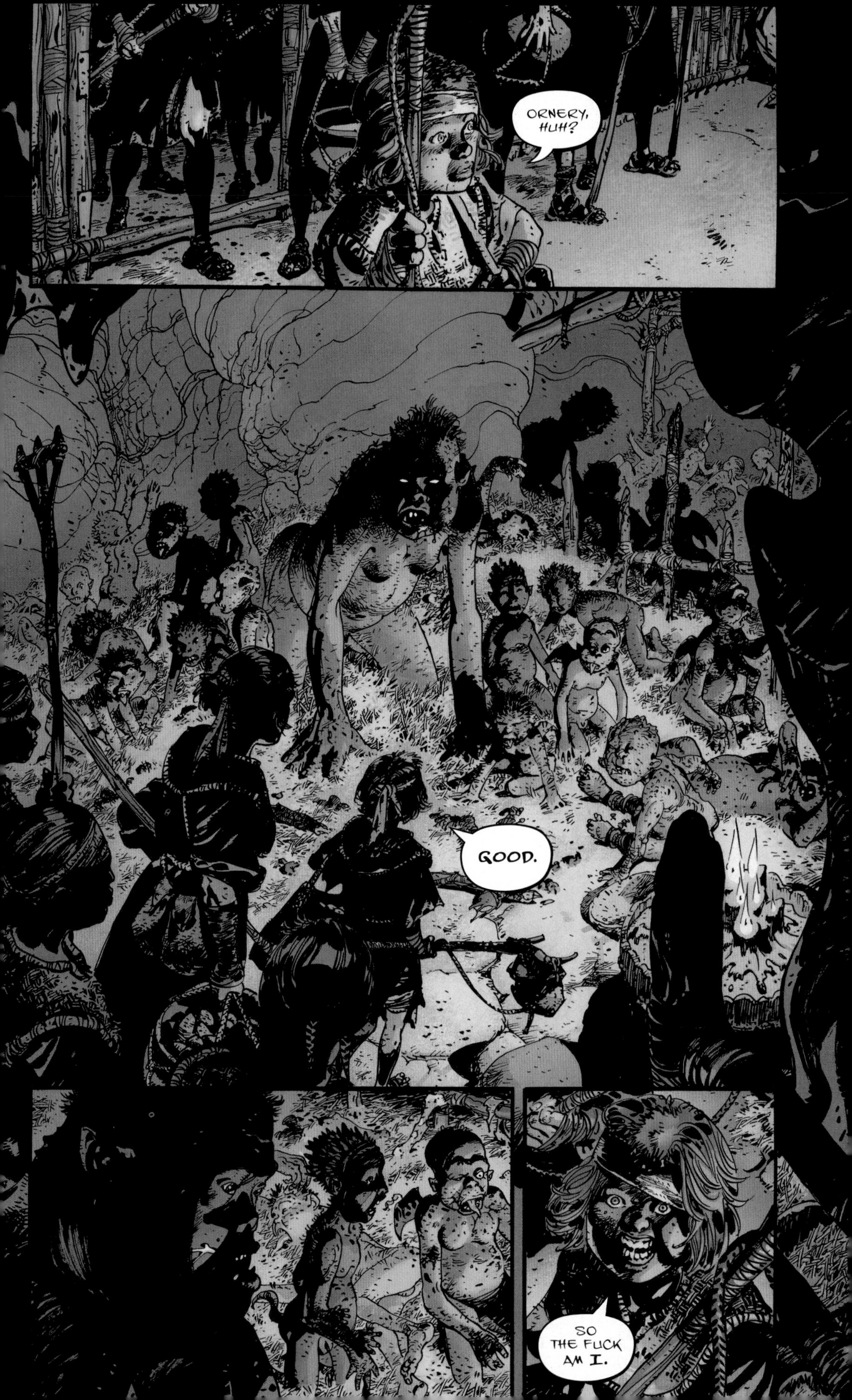

ORNERY, HUH?
GOOD.
SO THE FUCK AM I.

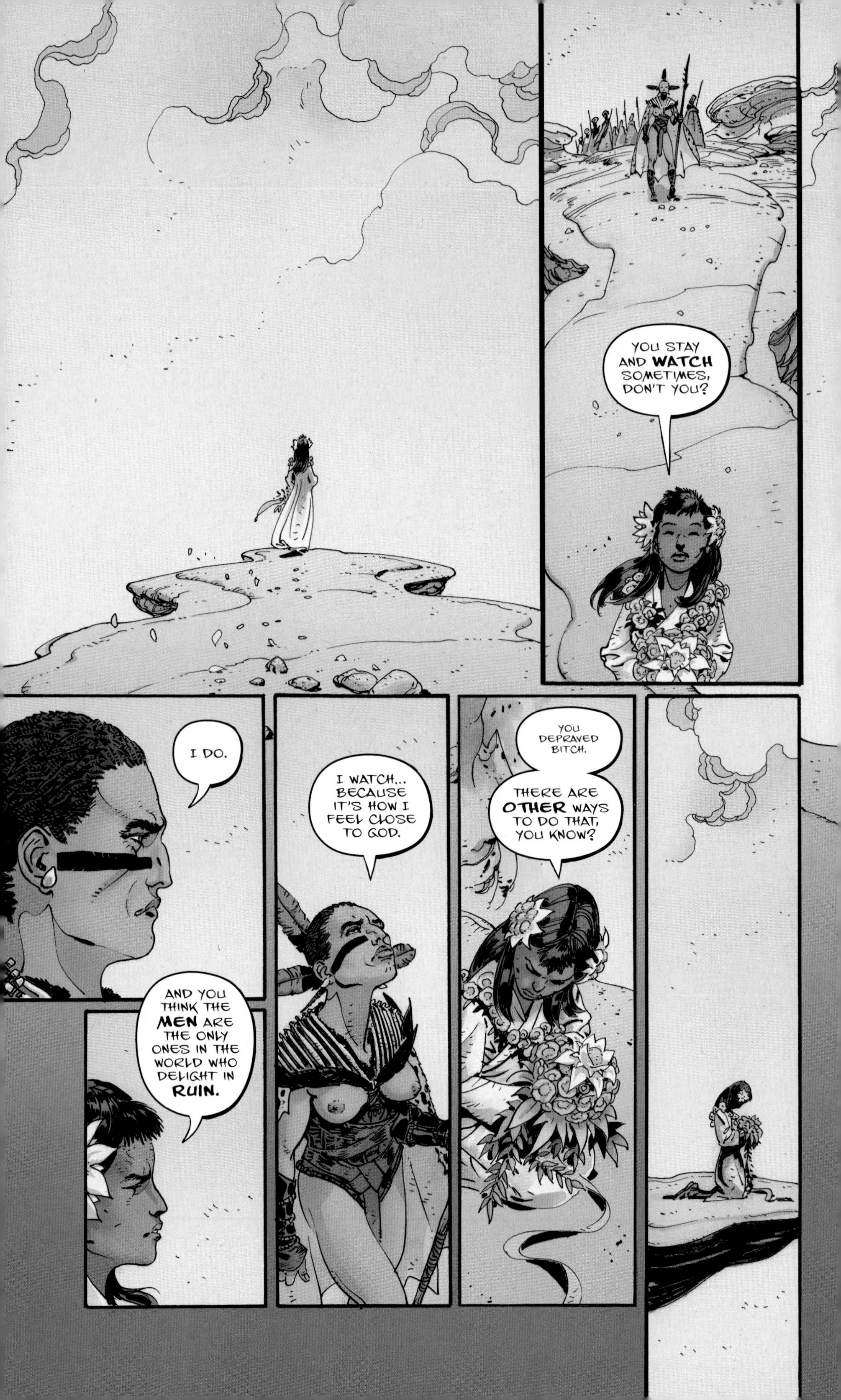

YOU STAY AND WATCH SOMETIMES, DON'T YOU?
I DO.
AND YOU THINK THE MEN ARE THE ONLY ONES IN THE WORLD WHO DELIGHT IN RUIN.
I WATCH... BECAUSE IT'S HOW I FEEL CLOSE TO GOD.
YOU DEPRAVED BITCH.
THERE ARE OTHER WAYS TO DO THAT, YOU KNOW?

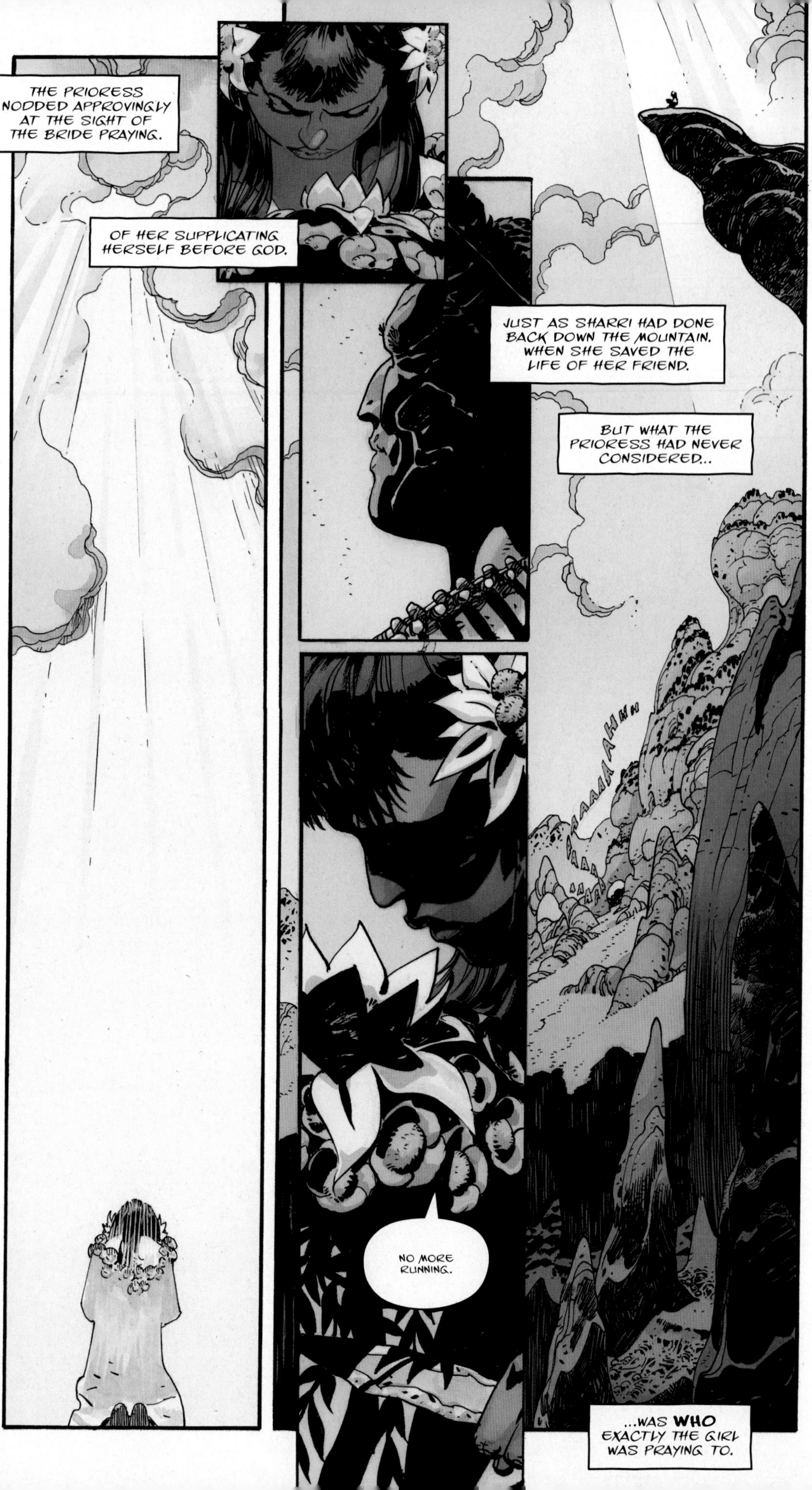
THE PRIORESS NODDED APPROVINGLY AT THE SIGHT OF THE BRIDE PRAYING.
OF HER SUPPLICATING HERSELF BEFORE GOD.
JUST AS SHARRI HAD DONE BACK DOWN THE MOUNTAIN. WHEN SHE SAVED THE LIFE OF HER FRIEND.
BUT WHAT THE PRIORESS HAD NEVER CONSIDERED...
AAAAAAAAAAAAAAAHHH
NO MORE RUNNING.
...WAS WHO EXACTLY THE GIRL WAS PRAYING TO.

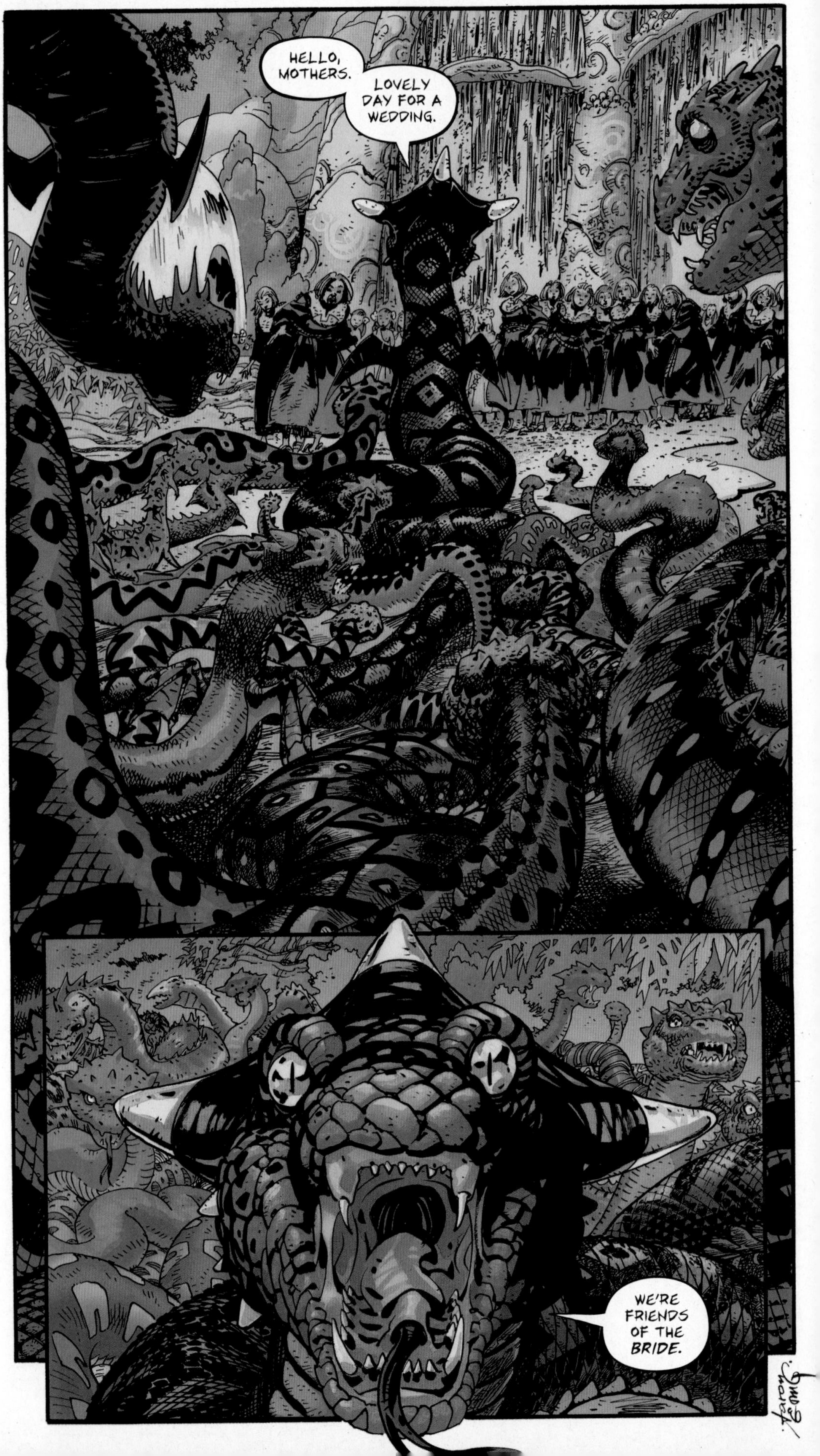
HELLO, MOTHERS.
LOVELY DAY FOR A WEDDING.
WE'RE FRIENDS OF THE BRIDE.

# Chapter Five

## "What Therefore God Hath Joined Together"

**W**HAT THEREFORE GOD
HATH JOINED TOGETHER,
LET NOT MAN PUT ASUNDER.

--MARK 10:9

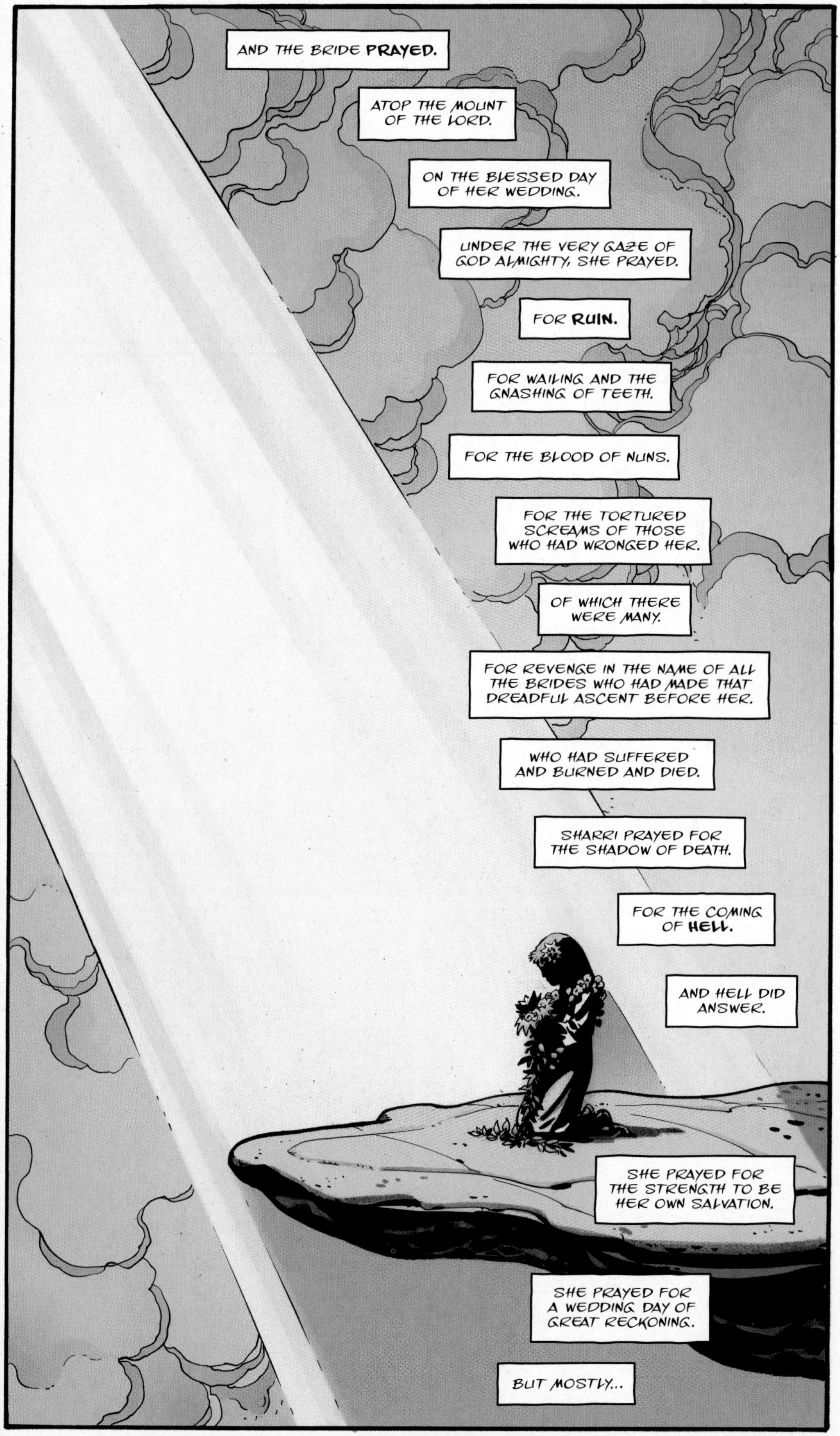
AND THE BRIDE PRAYED.
ATOP THE MOUNT OF THE LORD.
ON THE BLESSED DAY OF HER WEDDING.
UNDER THE VERY GAZE OF GOD ALMIGHTY, SHE PRAYED.
FOR RUIN.
FOR WAILING AND THE GNASHING OF TEETH.
FOR THE BLOOD OF NUNS.
FOR THE TORTURED SCREAMS OF THOSE WHO HAD WRONGED HER.
OF WHICH THERE WERE MANY.
FOR REVENGE IN THE NAME OF ALL THE BRIDES WHO HAD MADE THAT DREADFUL ASCENT BEFORE HER.
WHO HAD SUFFERED AND BURNED AND DIED.
SHARRI PRAYED FOR THE SHADOW OF DEATH.
FOR THE COMING OF HELL.
AND HELL DID ANSWER.
SHE PRAYED FOR THE STRENGTH TO BE HER OWN SALVATION.
SHE PRAYED FOR A WEDDING DAY OF GREAT RECKONING.
BUT MOSTLY...

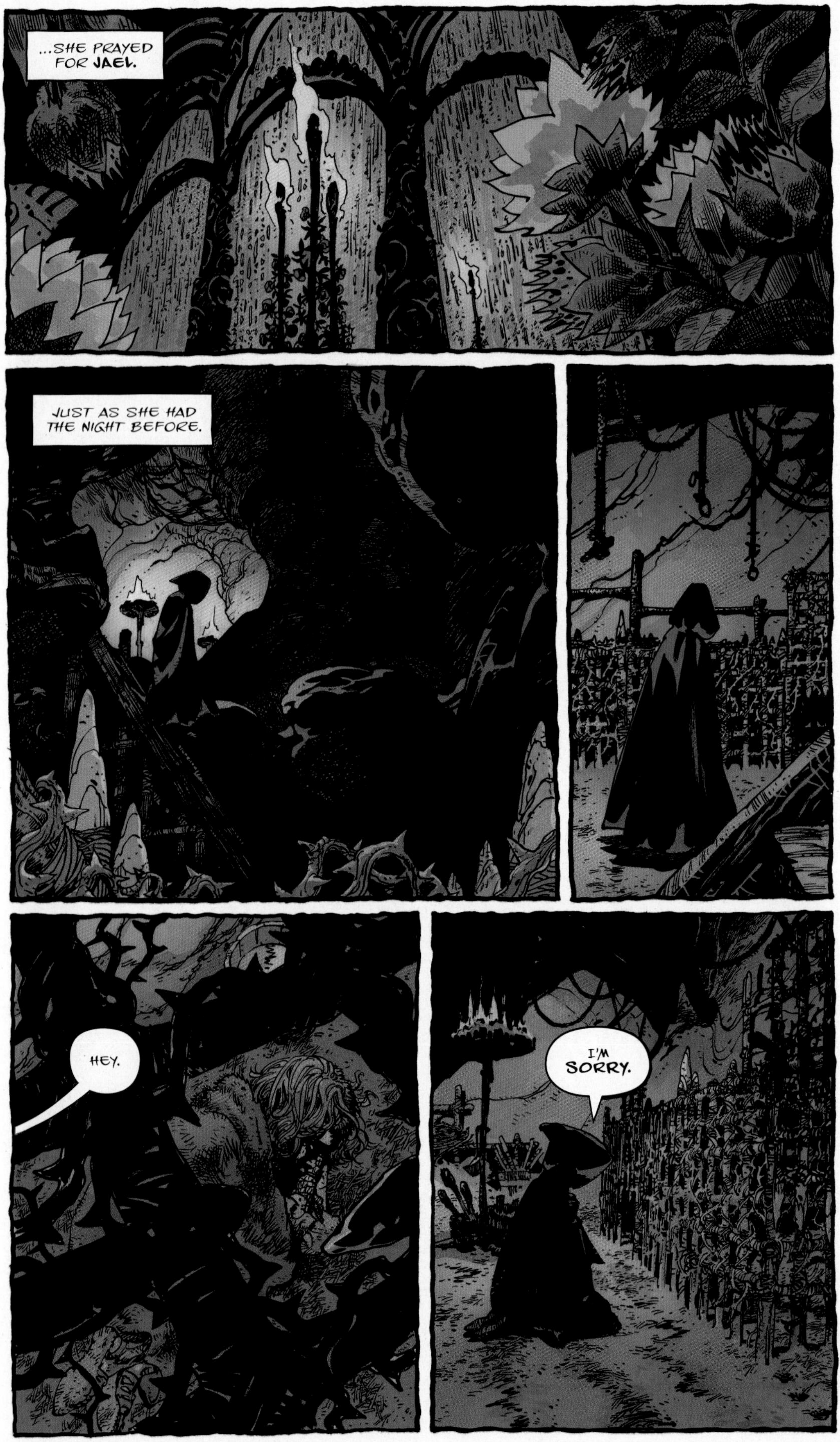
...SHE PRAYED FOR JAEL.
JUST AS SHE HAD THE NIGHT BEFORE.
HEY.
I'M SORRY.

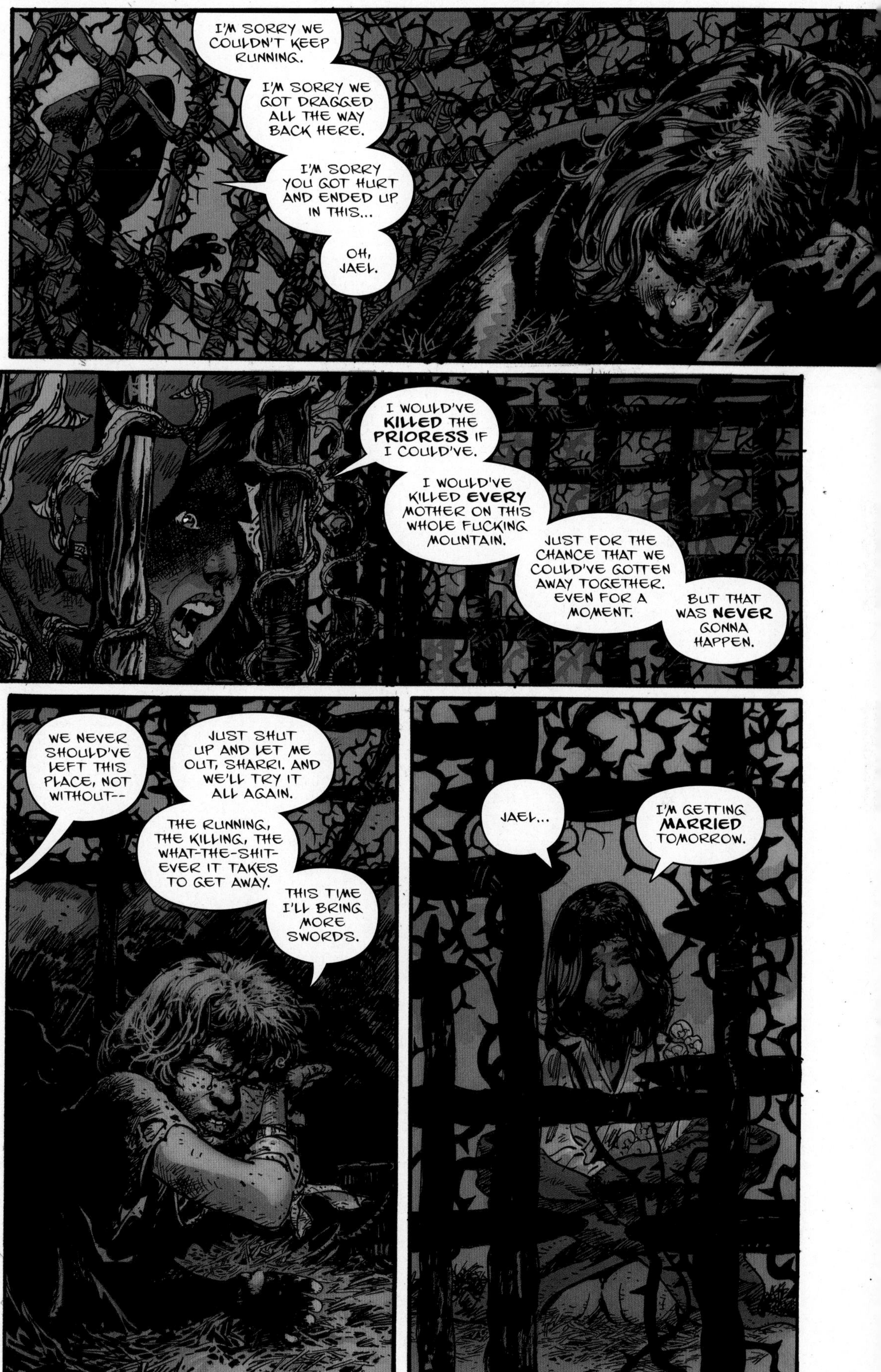
I'M SORRY WE COULDN'T KEEP RUNNING.
I'M SORRY WE GOT DRAGGED ALL THE WAY BACK HERE.
I'M SORRY YOU GOT HURT AND ENDED UP IN THIS...
OH, JAEL.
I WOULD'VE KILLED THE PRIORESS IF I COULD'VE.
I WOULD'VE KILLED EVERY MOTHER ON THIS WHOLE FUCKING MOUNTAIN.
JUST FOR THE CHANCE THAT WE COULD'VE GOTTEN AWAY TOGETHER. EVEN FOR A MOMENT.
BUT THAT WAS NEVER GONNA HAPPEN.
WE NEVER SHOULD'VE LEFT THIS PLACE, NOT WITHOUT--
JUST SHUT UP AND LET ME OUT, SHARRI. AND WE'LL TRY IT ALL AGAIN.
THE RUNNING, THE KILLING, THE WHAT-THE-SHIT-EVER IT TAKES TO GET AWAY.
THIS TIME I'LL BRING MORE SWORDS.
JAEL...
I'M GETTING MARRIED TOMORROW.

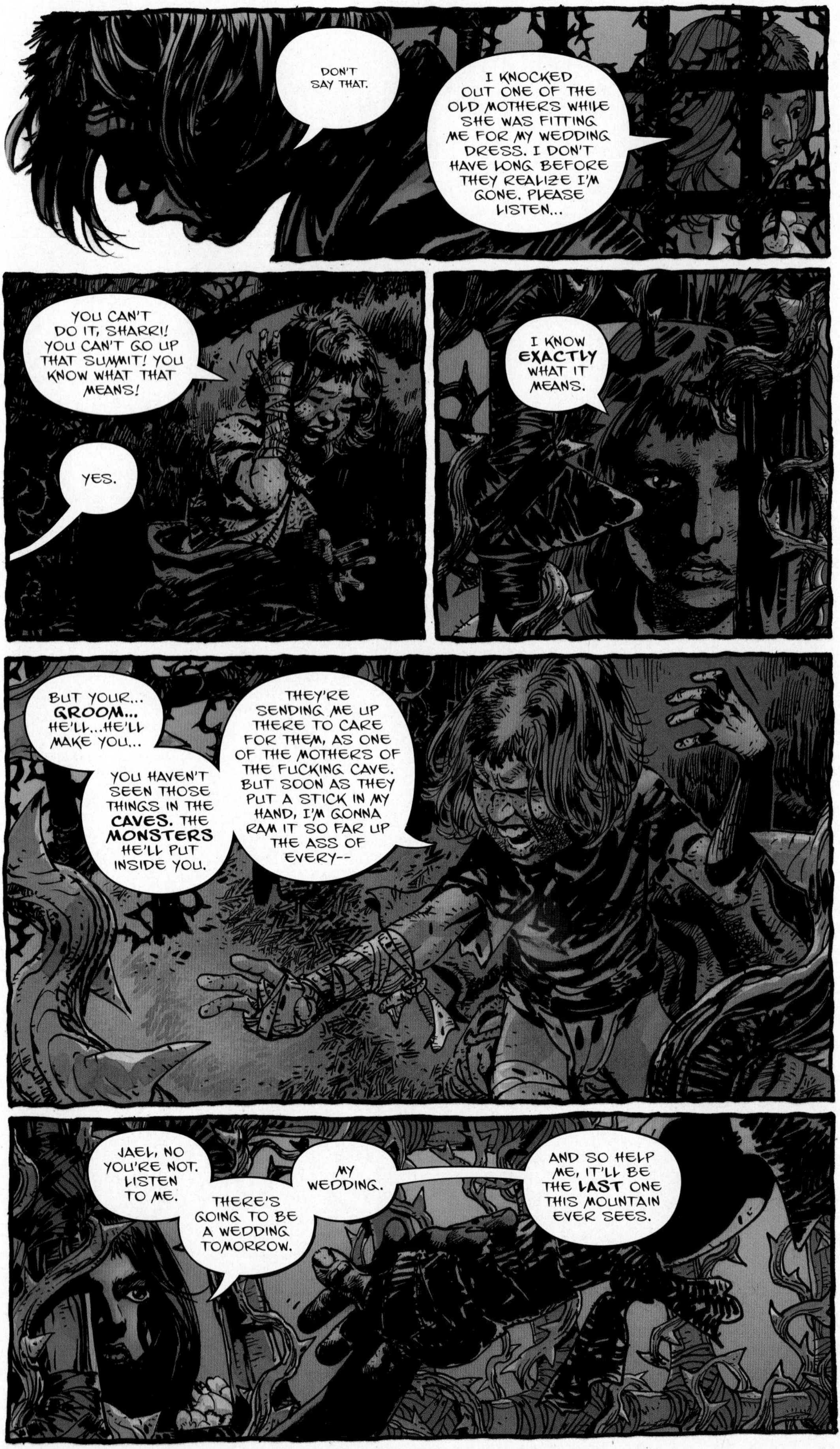
DON'T SAY THAT.
I KNOCKED OUT ONE OF THE OLD MOTHERS WHILE SHE WAS FITTING ME FOR MY WEDDING DRESS. I DON'T HAVE LONG BEFORE THEY REALIZE I'M GONE. PLEASE LISTEN...
YOU CAN'T DO IT, SHARRI! YOU CAN'T GO UP THAT SUMMIT! YOU KNOW WHAT THAT MEANS!
YES.
I KNOW EXACTLY WHAT IT MEANS.
BUT YOUR... GROOM... HE'LL...HE'LL MAKE YOU...
YOU HAVEN'T SEEN THOSE THINGS IN THE CAVES. THE MONSTERS HE'LL PUT INSIDE YOU.
THEY'RE SENDING ME UP THERE TO CARE FOR THEM, AS ONE OF THE MOTHERS OF THE FUCKING CAVE. BUT SOON AS THEY PUT A STICK IN MY HAND, I'M GONNA RAM IT SO FAR UP THE ASS OF EVERY--
JAEL, NO YOU'RE NOT. LISTEN TO ME.
THERE'S GOING TO BE A WEDDING TOMORROW.
MY WEDDING.
AND SO HELP ME, IT'LL BE THE LAST ONE THIS MOUNTAIN EVER SEES.

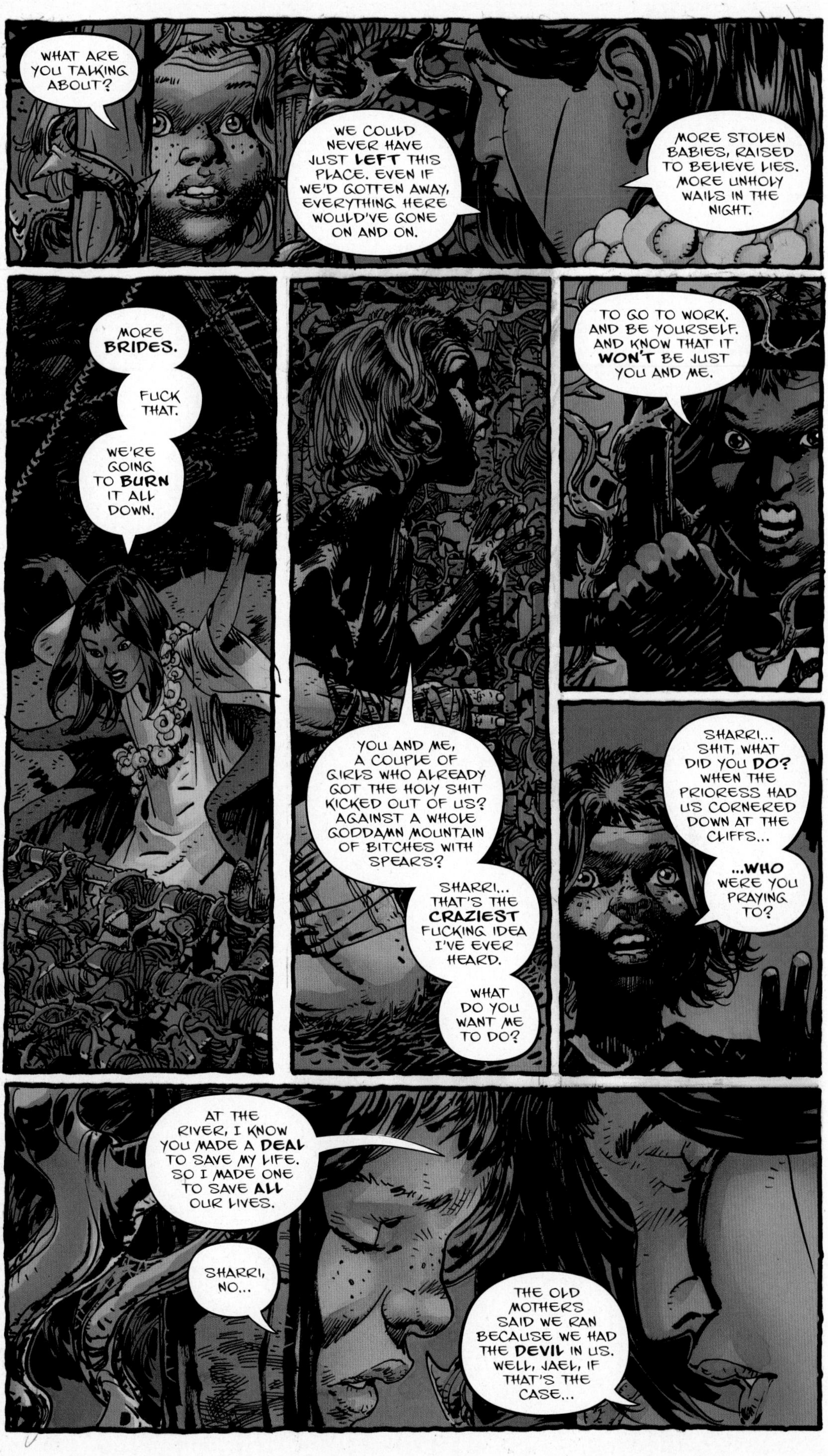
WHAT ARE YOU TALKING ABOUT?
WE COULD NEVER HAVE JUST LEFT THIS PLACE. EVEN IF WE'D GOTTEN AWAY, EVERYTHING HERE WOULD'VE GONE ON AND ON.
MORE STOLEN BABIES, RAISED TO BELIEVE LIES. MORE UNHOLY WAILS IN THE NIGHT.
MORE BRIDES.
FUCK THAT.
WE'RE GOING TO BURN IT ALL DOWN.
YOU AND ME, A COUPLE OF GIRLS WHO ALREADY GOT THE HOLY SHIT KICKED OUT OF US? AGAINST A WHOLE GODDAMN MOUNTAIN OF BITCHES WITH SPEARS?
SHARRI... THAT'S THE CRAZIEST FUCKING IDEA I'VE EVER HEARD.
WHAT DO YOU WANT ME TO DO?
TO GO TO WORK. AND BE YOURSELF. AND KNOW THAT IT WON'T BE JUST YOU AND ME.
SHARRI... SHIT, WHAT DID YOU DO? WHEN THE PRIORESS HAD US CORNERED DOWN AT THE CLIFFS...
...WHO WERE YOU PRAYING TO?
AT THE RIVER, I KNOW YOU MADE A DEAL TO SAVE MY LIFE. SO I MADE ONE TO SAVE ALL OUR LIVES.
SHARRI, NO...
THE OLD MOTHERS SAID WE RAN BECAUSE WE HAD THE DEVIL IN US. WELL, JAEL, IF THAT'S THE CASE...

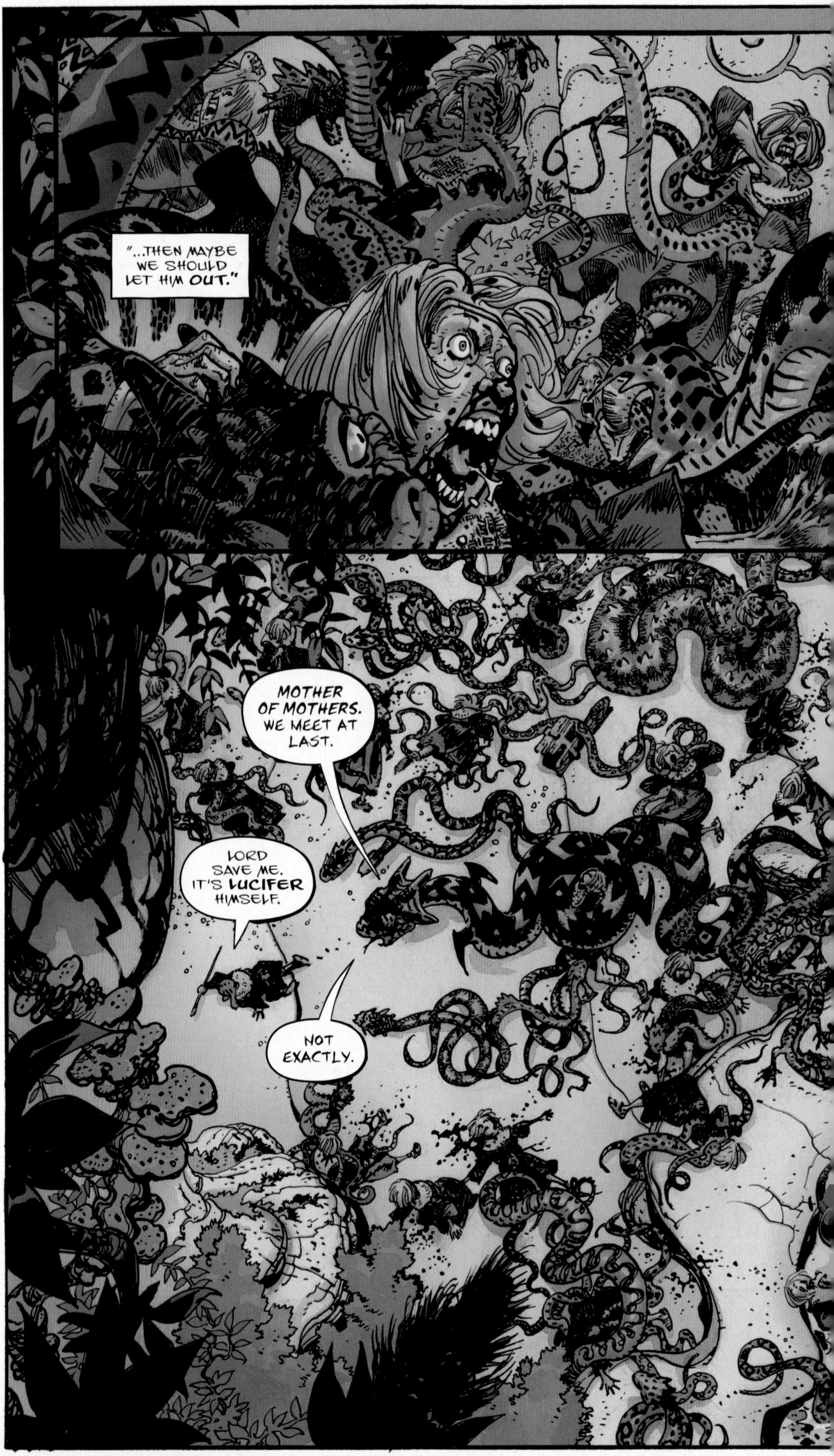
"...THEN MAYBE WE SHOULD LET HIM OUT."
MOTHER OF MOTHERS. WE MEET AT LAST.
LORD SAVE ME. IT'S LUCIFER HIMSELF.
NOT EXACTLY.

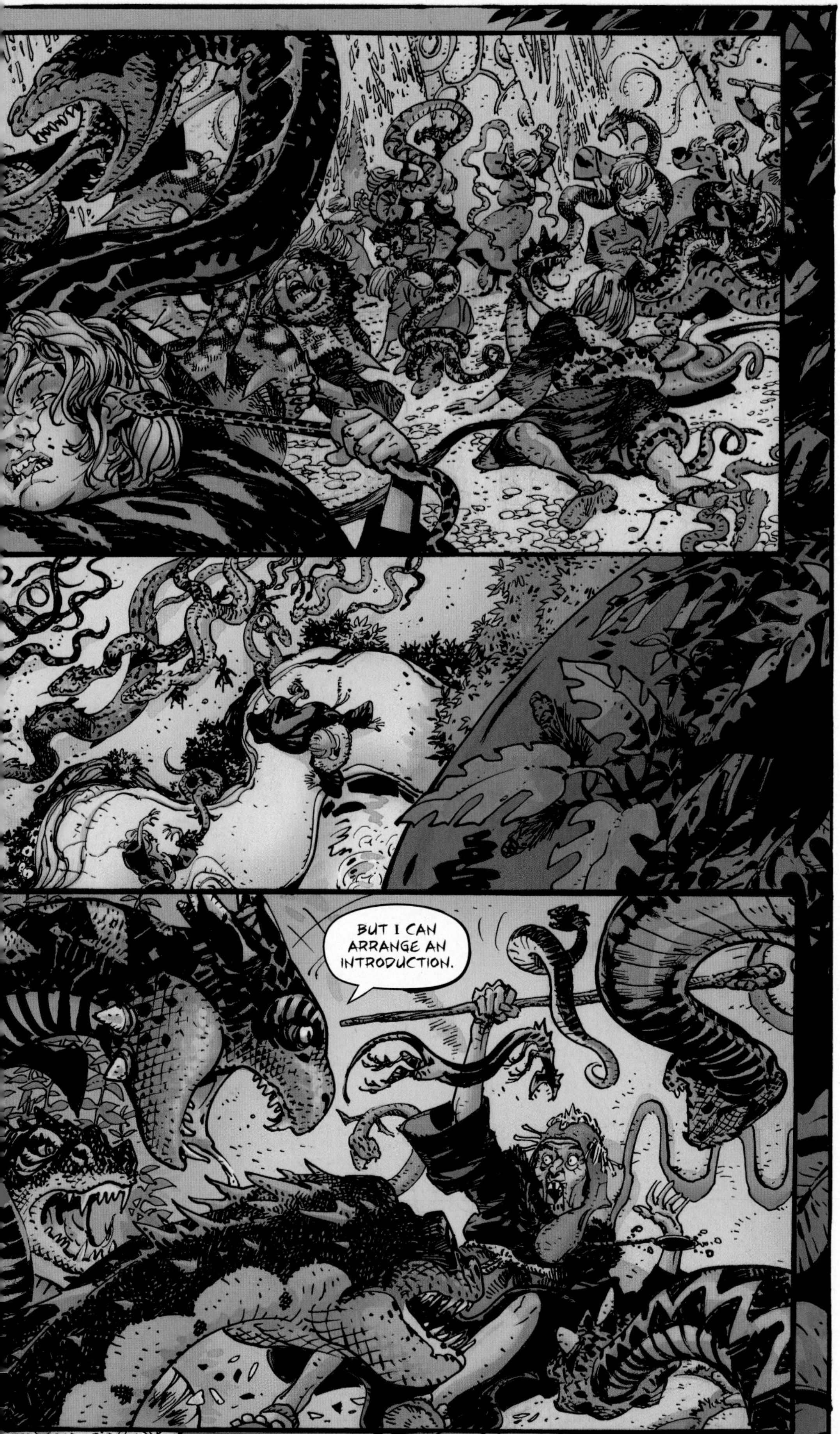
BUT I CAN ARRANGE AN INTRODUCTION.

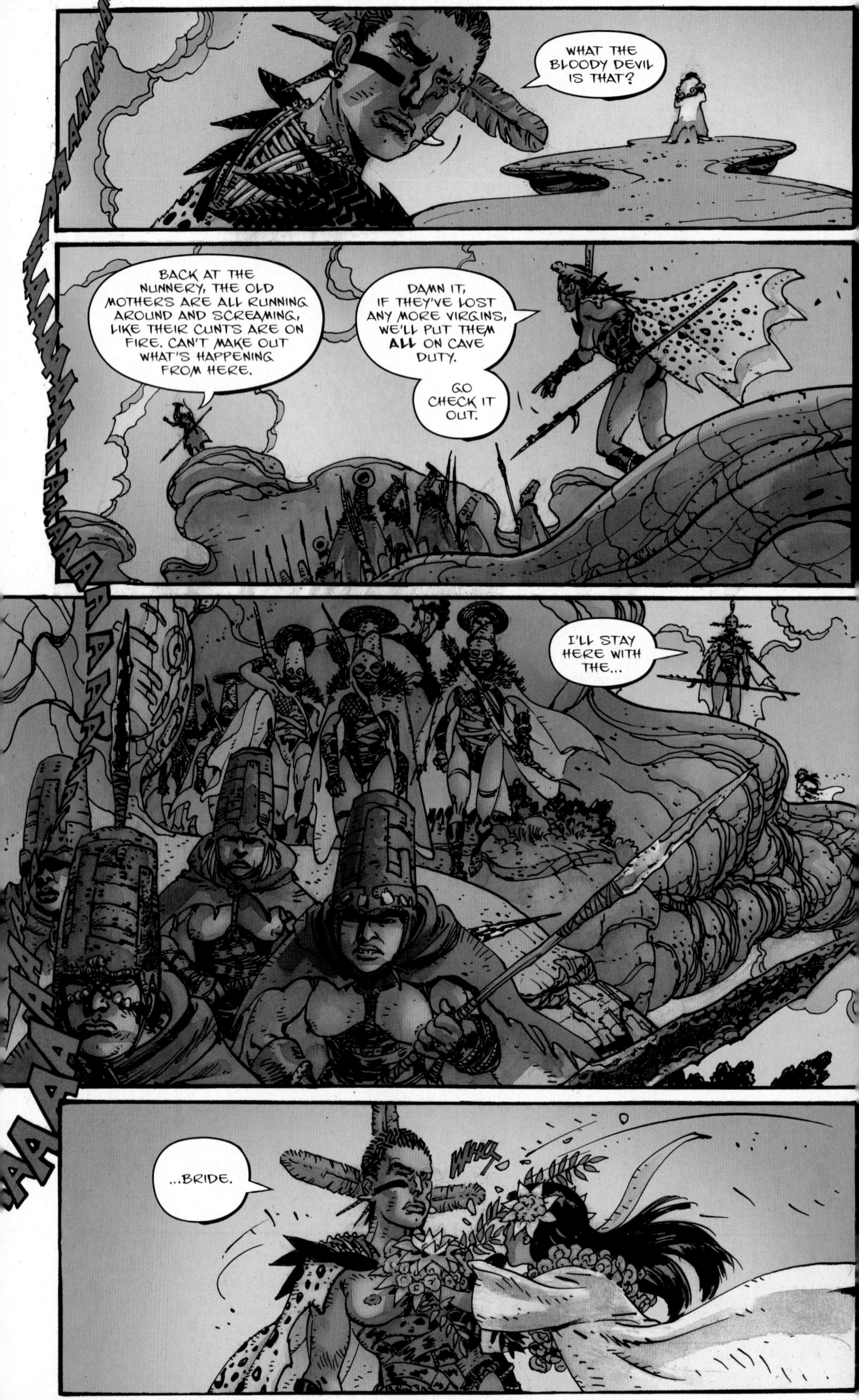

WHAT THE BLOODY DEVIL IS THAT?
BACK AT THE NUNNERY, THE OLD MOTHERS ARE ALL RUNNING AROUND AND SCREAMING, LIKE THEIR CUNTS ARE ON FIRE. CAN'T MAKE OUT WHAT'S HAPPENING FROM HERE.
DAMN IT, IF THEY'VE LOST ANY MORE VIRGINS, WE'LL PUT THEM **ALL** ON CAVE DUTY.
GO CHECK IT OUT.
I'LL STAY HERE WITH THE...
...BRIDE.

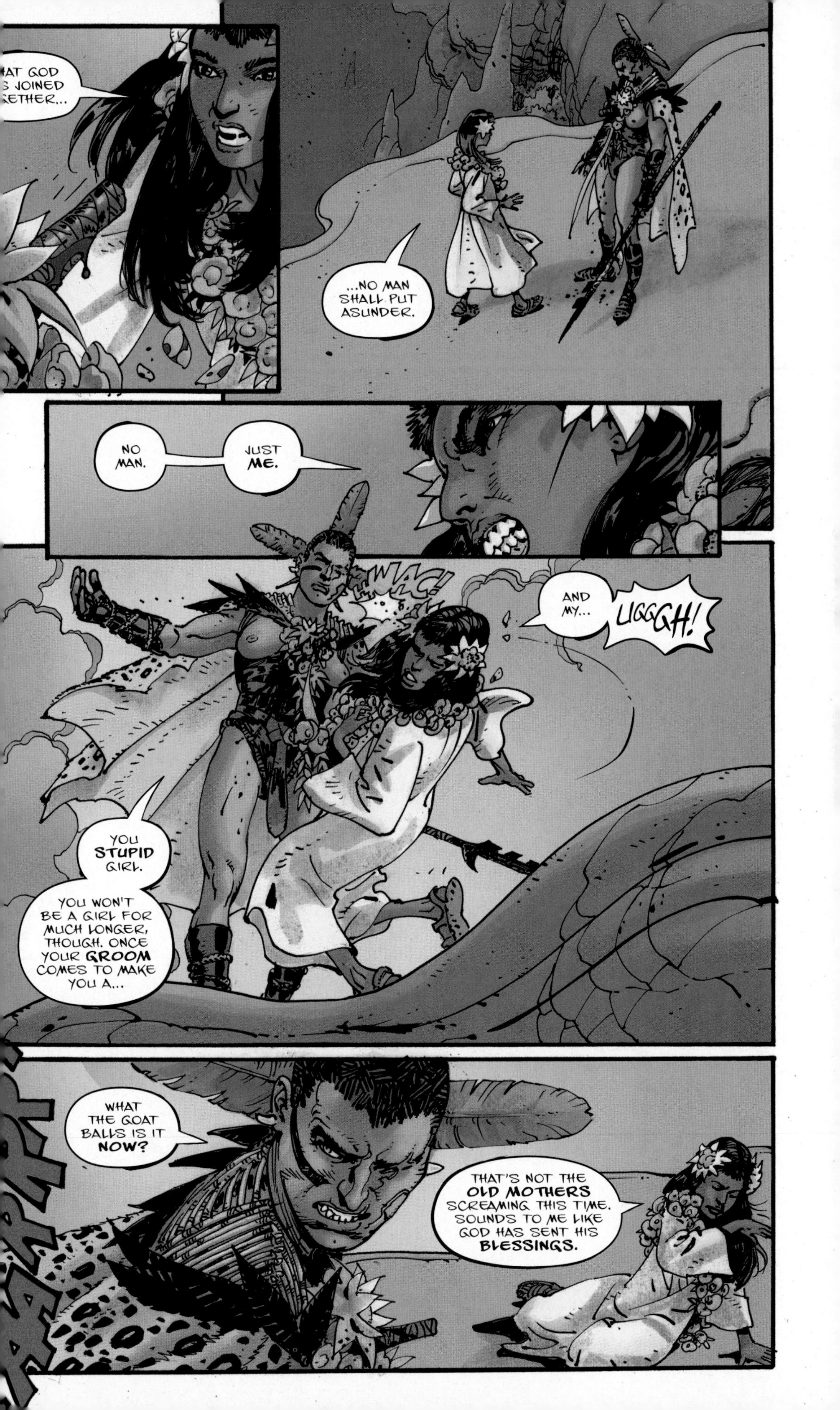
AT GOD S JOINED ETHER...
...NO MAN SHALL PUT ASUNDER.
NO MAN.
JUST ME.
WAC!
AND MY...
UGGGH!
YOU STUPID GIRL.
YOU WON'T BE A GIRL FOR MUCH LONGER, THOUGH. ONCE YOUR GROOM COMES TO MAKE YOU A...
WHAT THE GOAT BALLS IS IT NOW?
THAT'S NOT THE OLD MOTHERS SCREAMING THIS TIME. SOUNDS TO ME LIKE GOD HAS SENT HIS BLESSINGS.

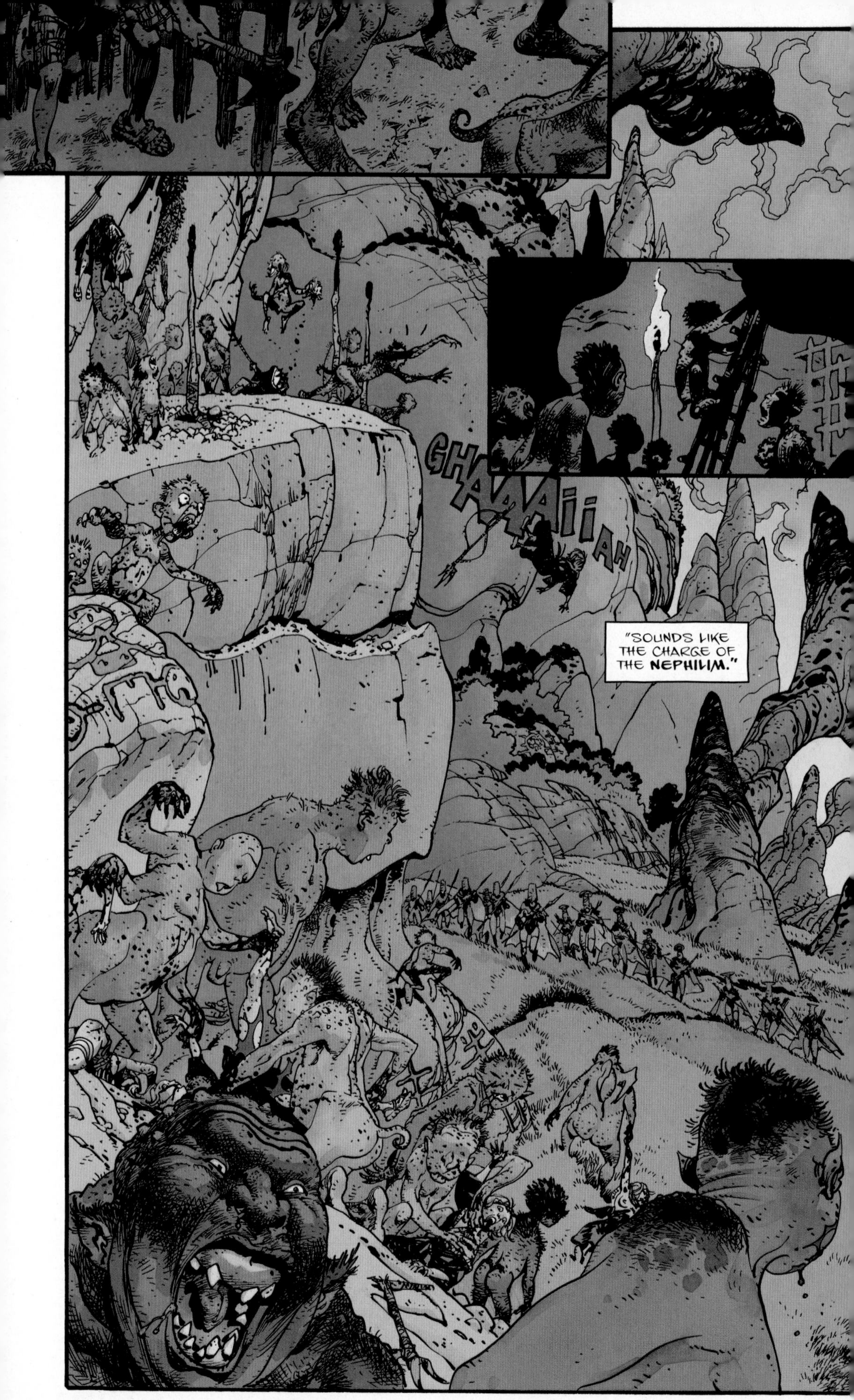
GHAAAAIIIAH
"SOUNDS LIKE THE CHARGE OF THE **NEPHILIM.**"

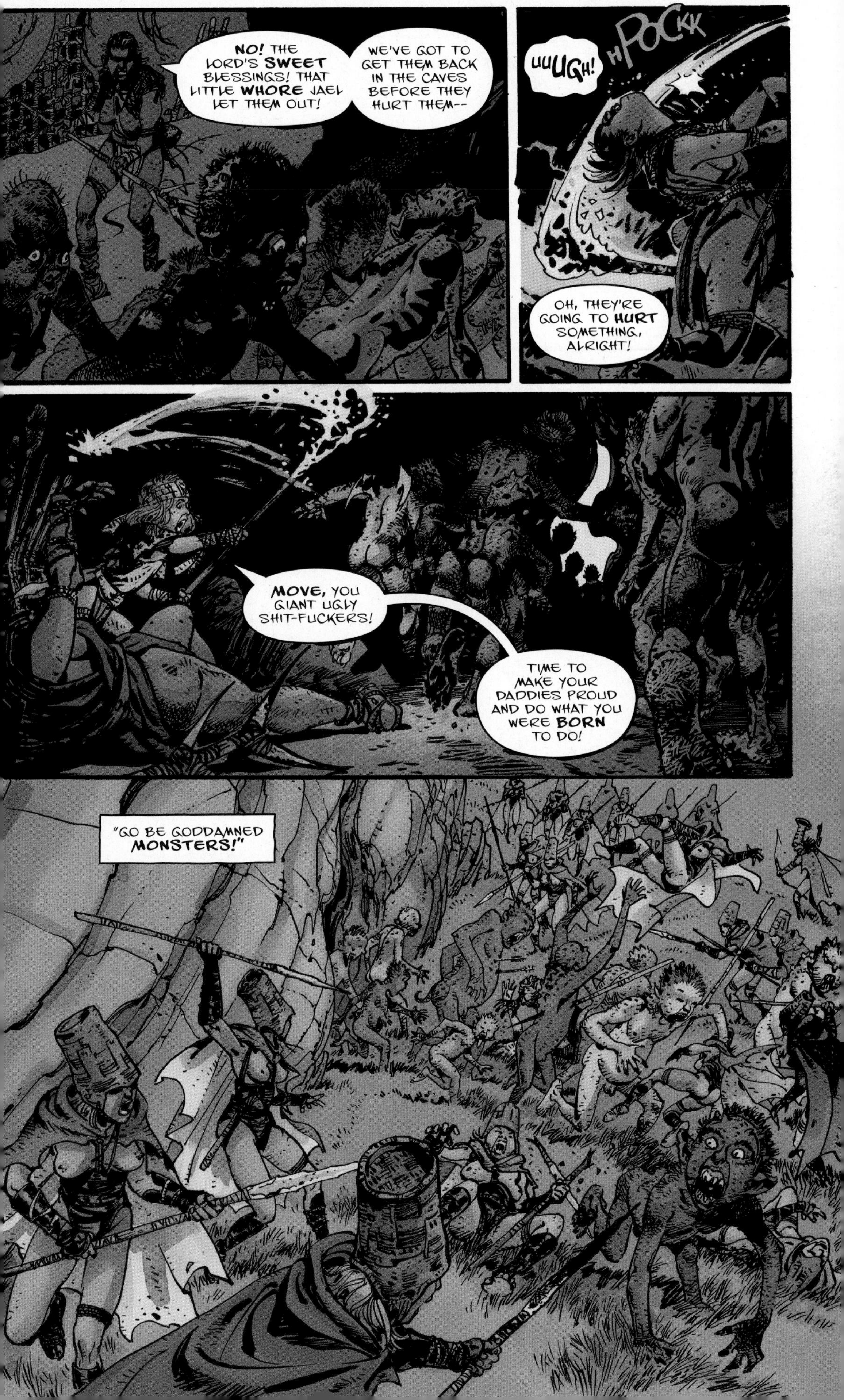
NO! THE LORD'S SWEET BLESSINGS! THAT LITTLE WHORE JAEL LET THEM OUT!
WE'VE GOT TO GET THEM BACK IN THE CAVES BEFORE THEY HURT THEM--
UUUGH!
HPOCKK
OH, THEY'RE GOING TO HURT SOMETHING, ALRIGHT!
MOVE, YOU GIANT UGLY SHIT-FUCKERS!
TIME TO MAKE YOUR DADDIES PROUD AND DO WHAT YOU WERE BORN TO DO!
"GO BE GODDAMNED MONSTERS!"

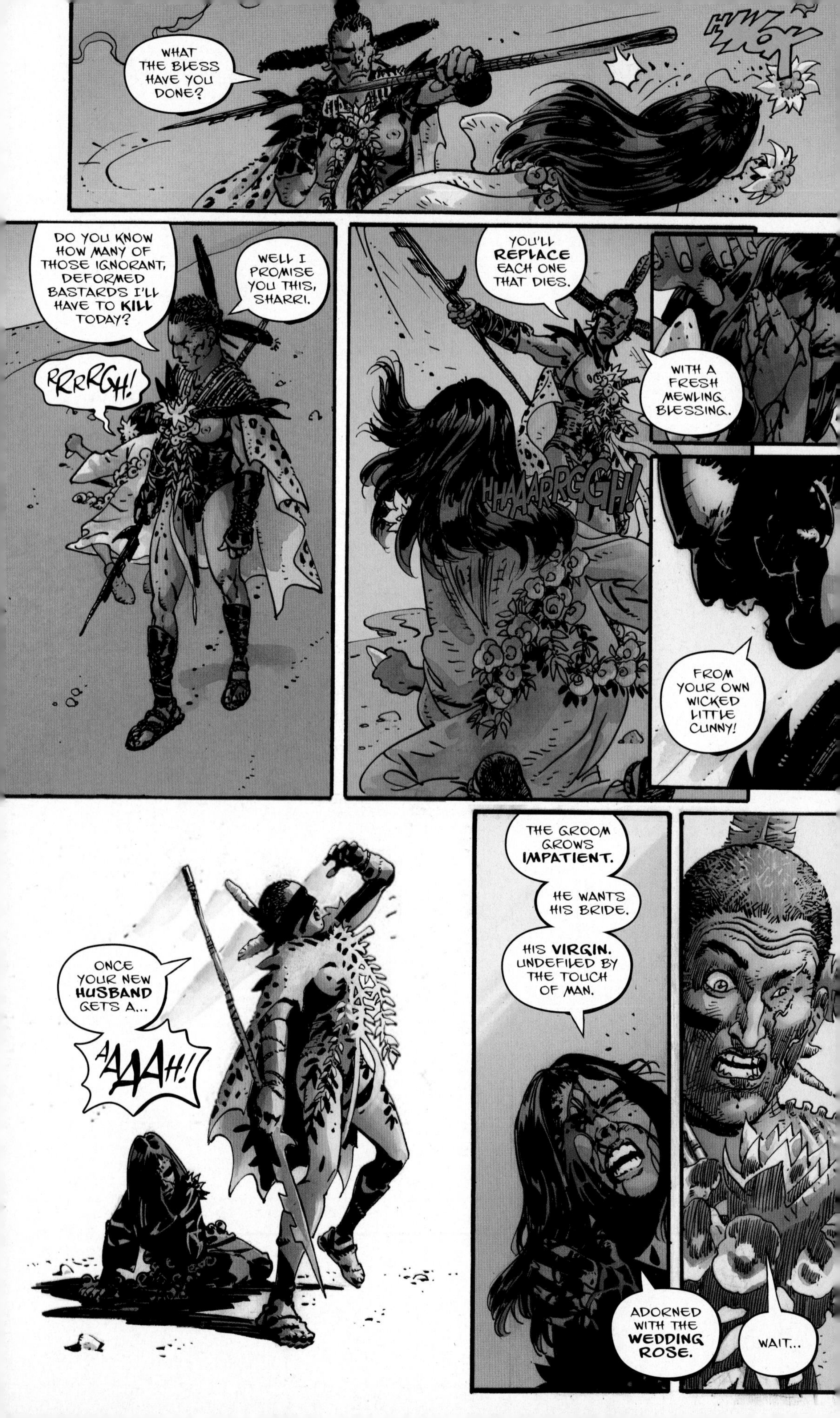
HWZOK
WHAT THE BLESS HAVE YOU DONE?
DO YOU KNOW HOW MANY OF THOSE IGNORANT, DEFORMED BASTARDS I'LL HAVE TO KILL TODAY?
WELL I PROMISE YOU THIS, SHARRI.
RRRRGH!
YOU'LL REPLACE EACH ONE THAT DIES.
WITH A FRESH MEWLING BLESSING.
HHAAARRGGH!
FROM YOUR OWN WICKED LITTLE CUNNY!
ONCE YOUR NEW HUSBAND GETS A...
AAAAH!
THE GROOM GROWS IMPATIENT.
HE WANTS HIS BRIDE.
HIS VIRGIN. UNDEFILED BY THE TOUCH OF MAN.
ADORNED WITH THE WEDDING ROSE.
WAIT...

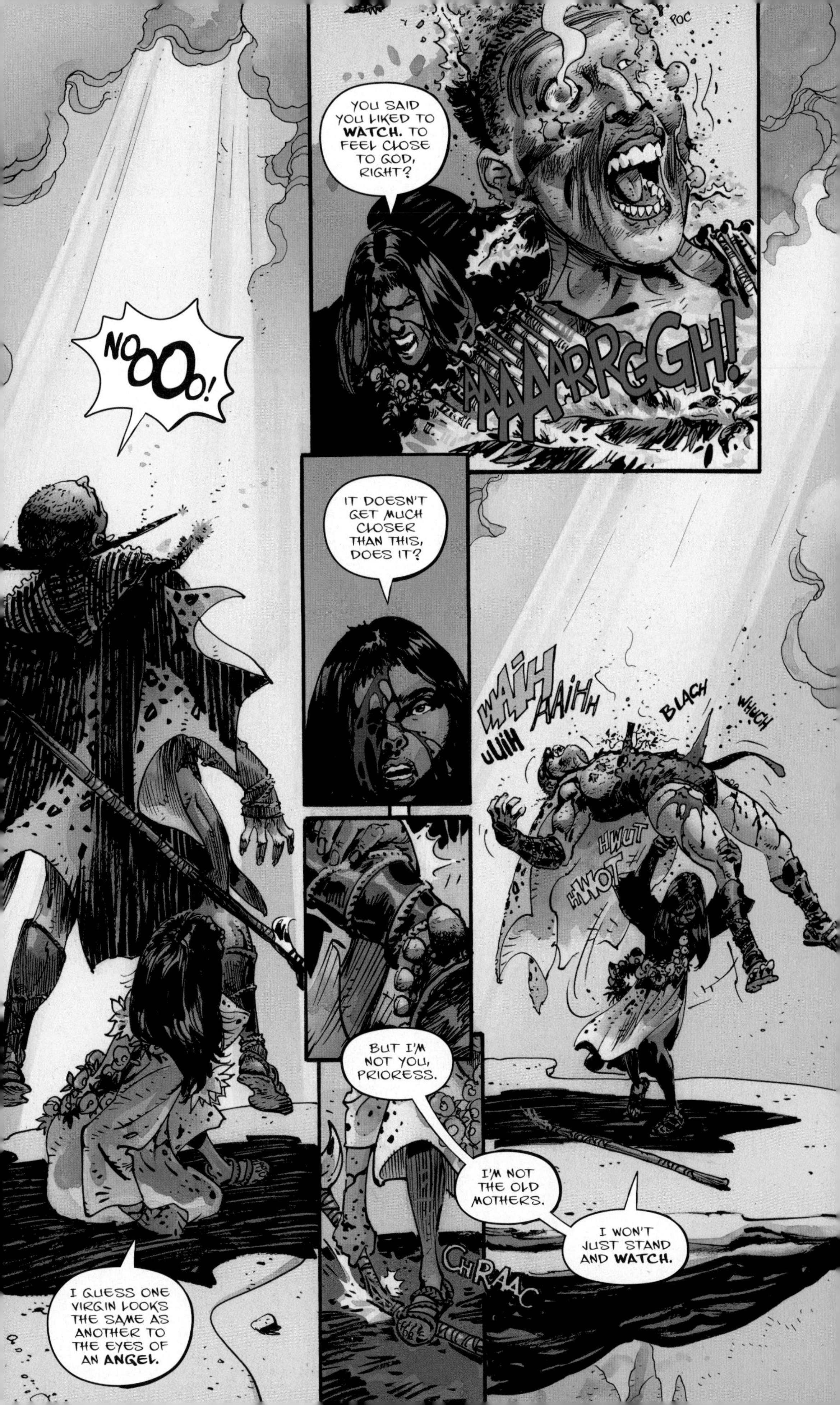
POC
YOU SAID YOU LIKED TO WATCH. TO FEEL CLOSE TO GOD, RIGHT?
AAAAARRGGH!
NOOOO!
IT DOESN'T GET MUCH CLOSER THAN THIS, DOES IT?
WAIH
AAIHH
UUIH
BLACH
WHUCH
HWUT
HWOT
I GUESS ONE VIRGIN LOOKS THE SAME AS ANOTHER TO THE EYES OF AN ANGEL.
BUT I'M NOT YOU, PRIORESS.
I'M NOT THE OLD MOTHERS.
I WON'T JUST STAND AND WATCH.
CHRAAC

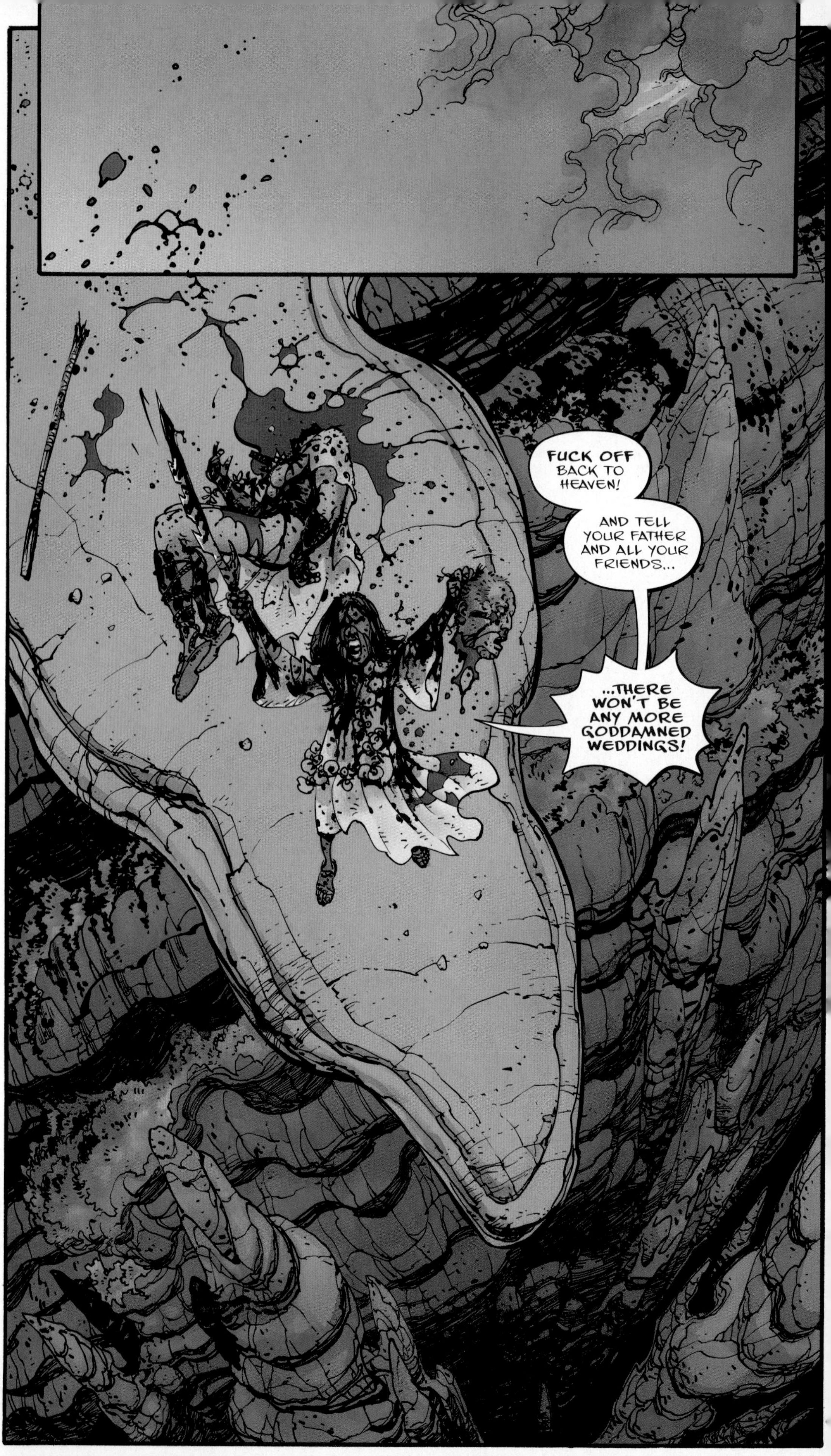
FUCK OFF BACK TO HEAVEN!
AND TELL YOUR FATHER AND ALL YOUR FRIENDS...
...THERE WON'T BE ANY MORE GODDAMNED WEDDINGS!

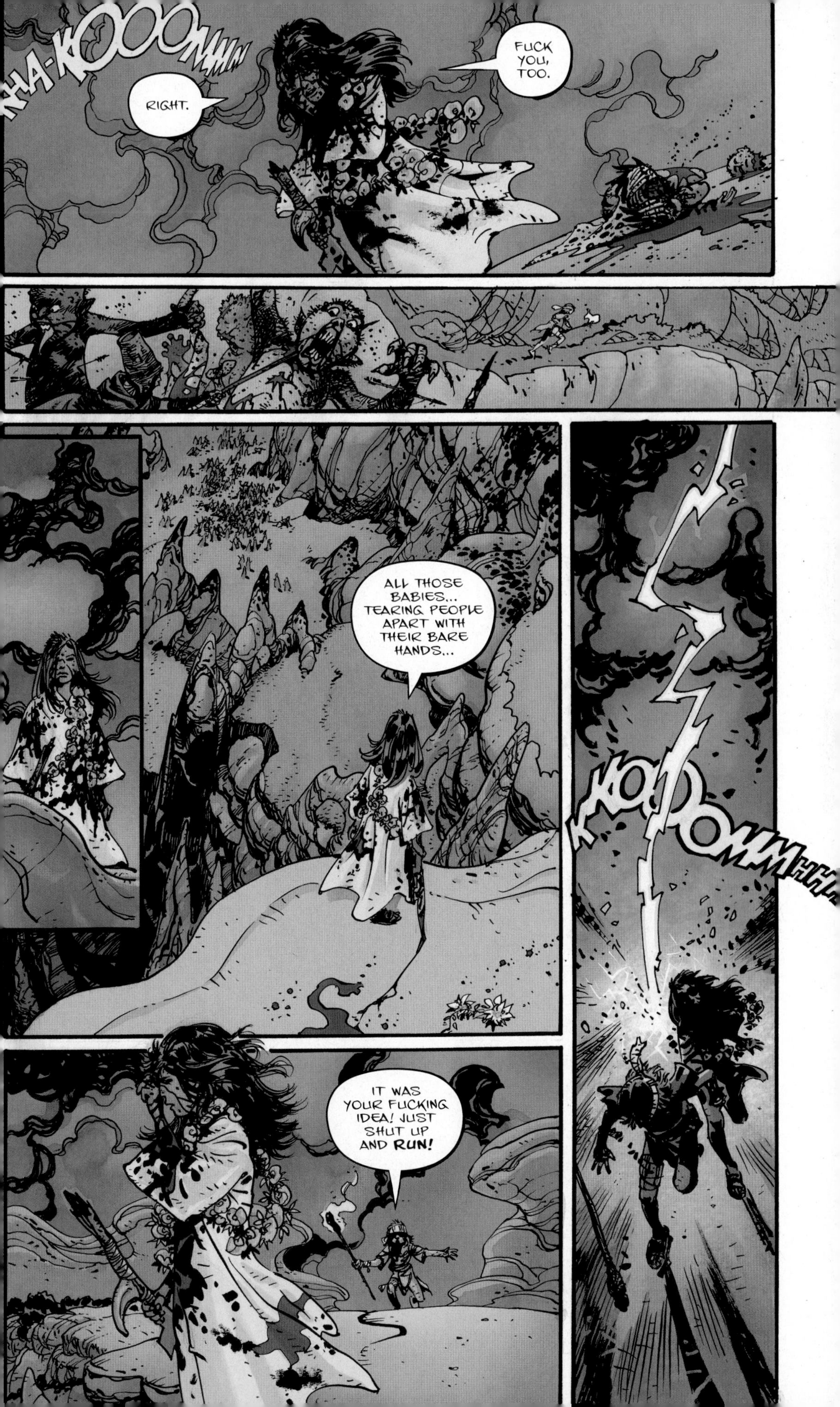

HA-KOOOMMM
RIGHT.
FUCK YOU, TOO.
ALL THOSE BABIES... TEARING PEOPLE APART WITH THEIR BARE HANDS...
IT WAS YOUR FUCKING IDEA! JUST SHUT UP AND **RUN!**
KOOOMMHH

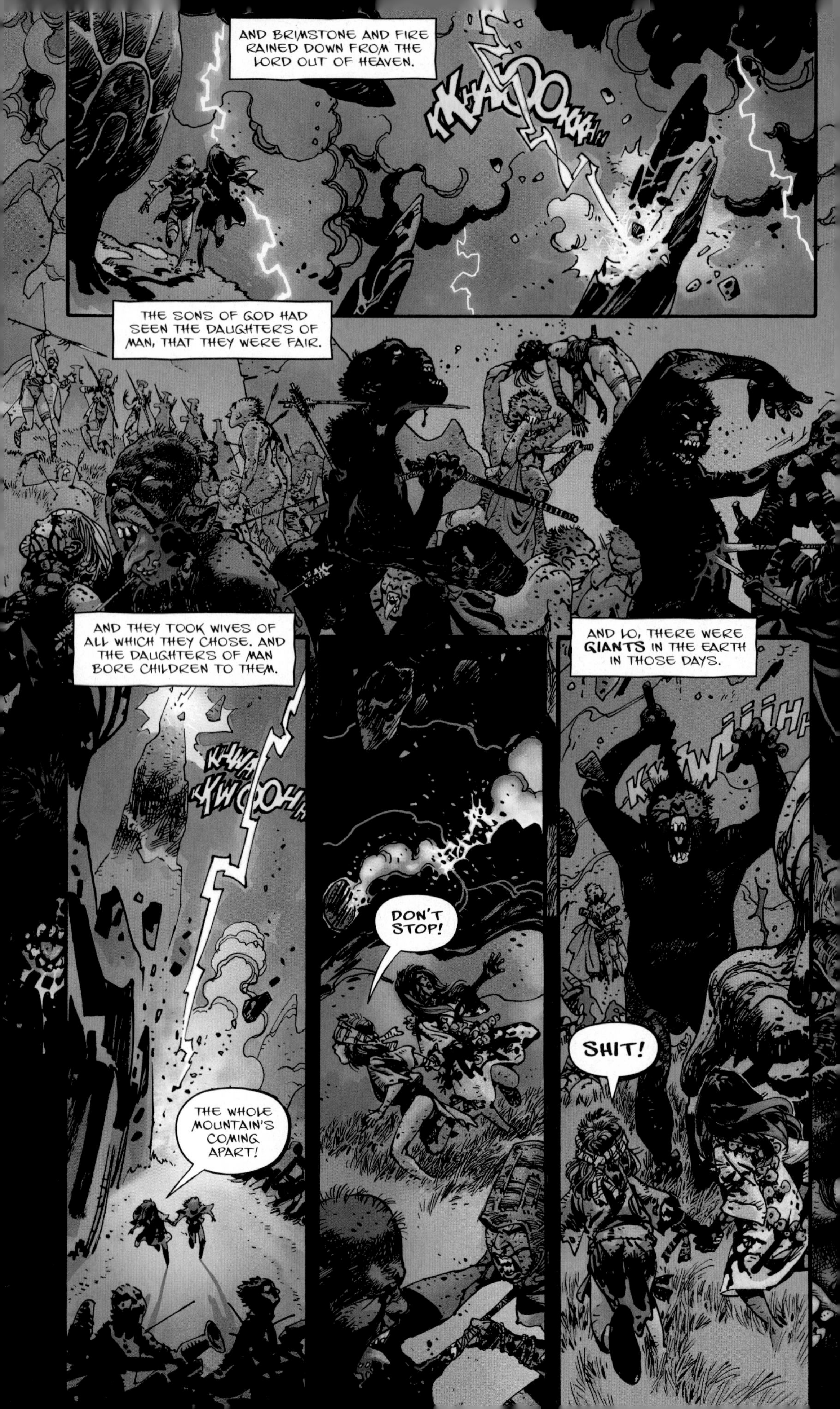
AND BRIMSTONE AND FIRE RAINED DOWN FROM THE LORD OUT OF HEAVEN.
KKWADOOKKHH
THE SONS OF GOD HAD SEEN THE DAUGHTERS OF MAN, THAT THEY WERE FAIR.
AND THEY TOOK WIVES OF ALL WHICH THEY CHOSE. AND THE DAUGHTERS OF MAN BORE CHILDREN TO THEM.
KKWA
KKWOOOHH
THE WHOLE MOUNTAIN'S COMING APART!
DON'T STOP!
AND LO, THERE WERE GIANTS IN THE EARTH IN THOSE DAYS.
KKWIIIIHH
SHIT!

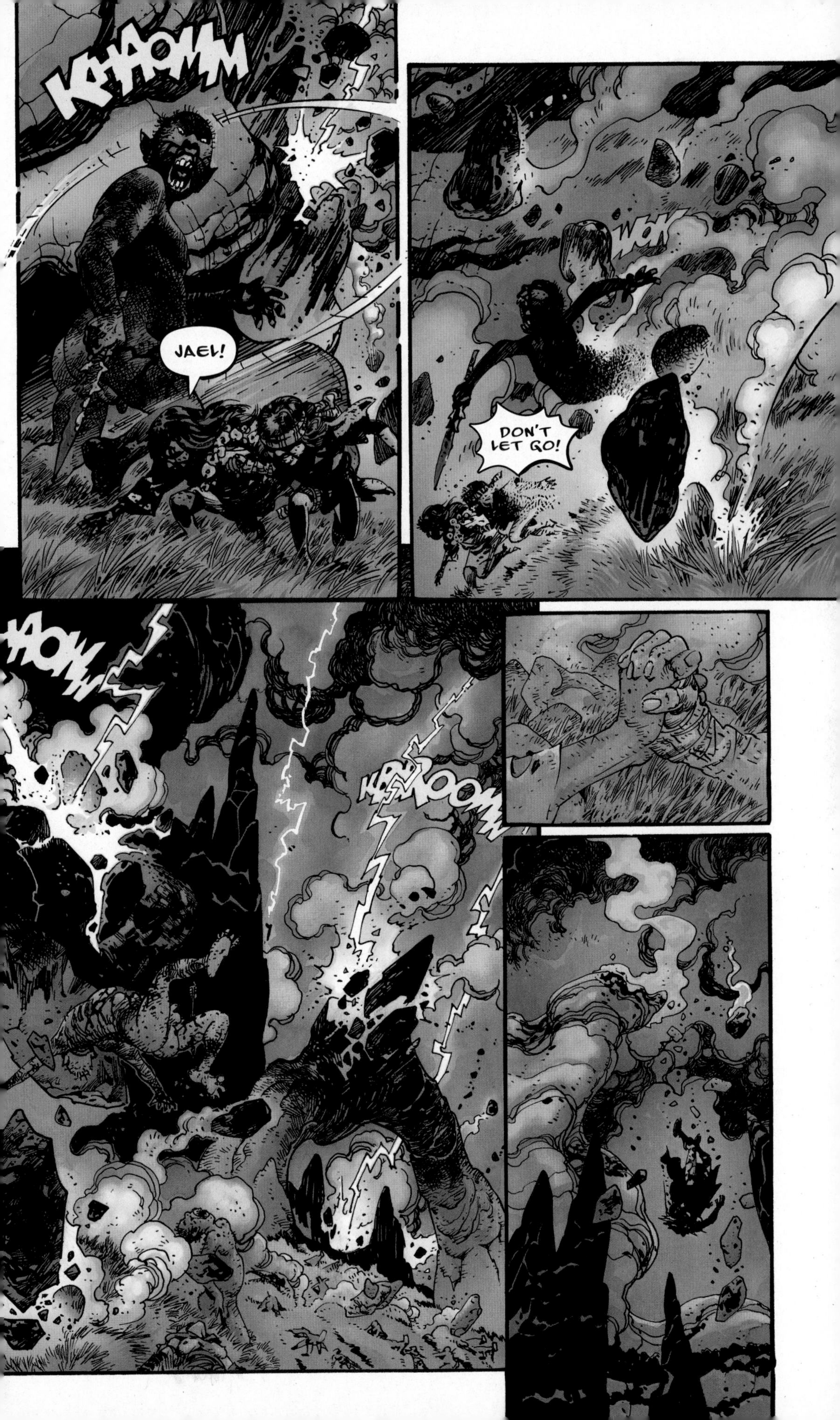
KHAOMM
JAEL!
WOK
DON'T LET GO!
KAOW
KRROOMM

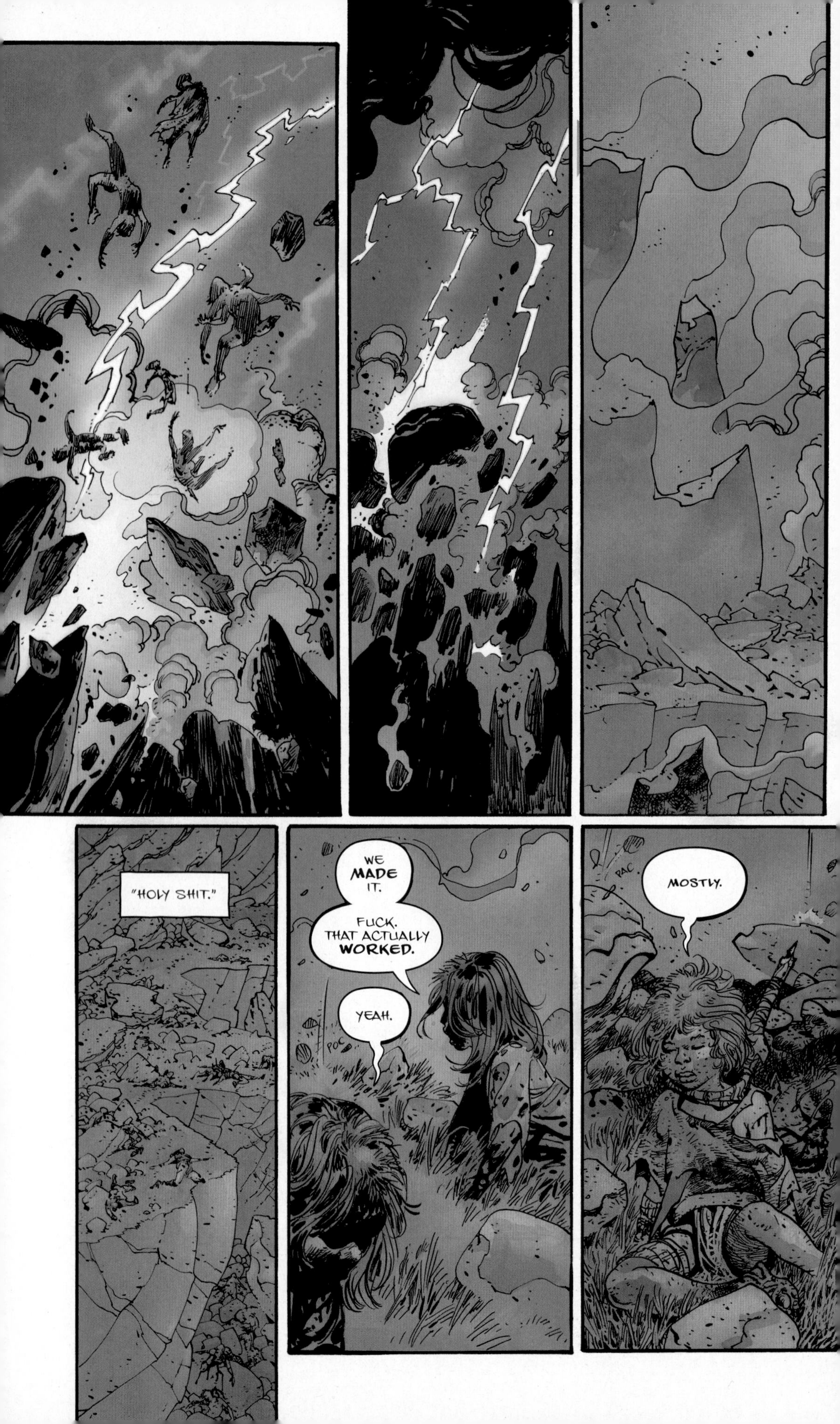
"HOLY SHIT."
WE MADE IT.
FUCK. THAT ACTUALLY WORKED.
YEAH.
POC
PAC
MOSTLY.

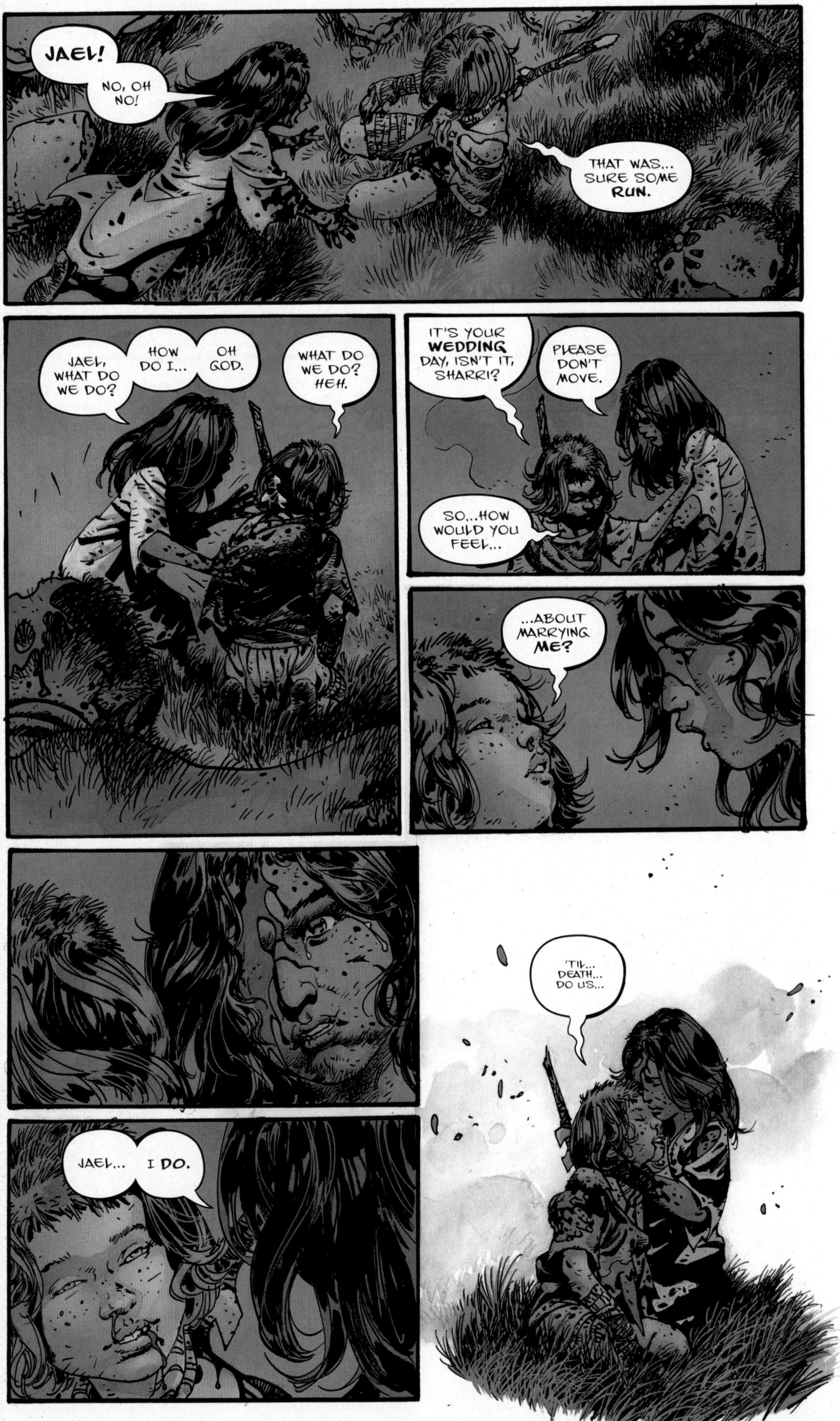
JAEL!
NO, OH NO!
THAT WAS... SURE SOME RUN.
JAEL, WHAT DO WE DO?
HOW DO I...
OH GOD.
WHAT DO WE DO? HEH.
IT'S YOUR WEDDING DAY, ISN'T IT, SHARRI?
PLEASE DON'T MOVE.
SO...HOW WOULD YOU FEEL...
...ABOUT MARRYING ME?
JAEL...
I DO.
'TIL... DEATH... DO US...

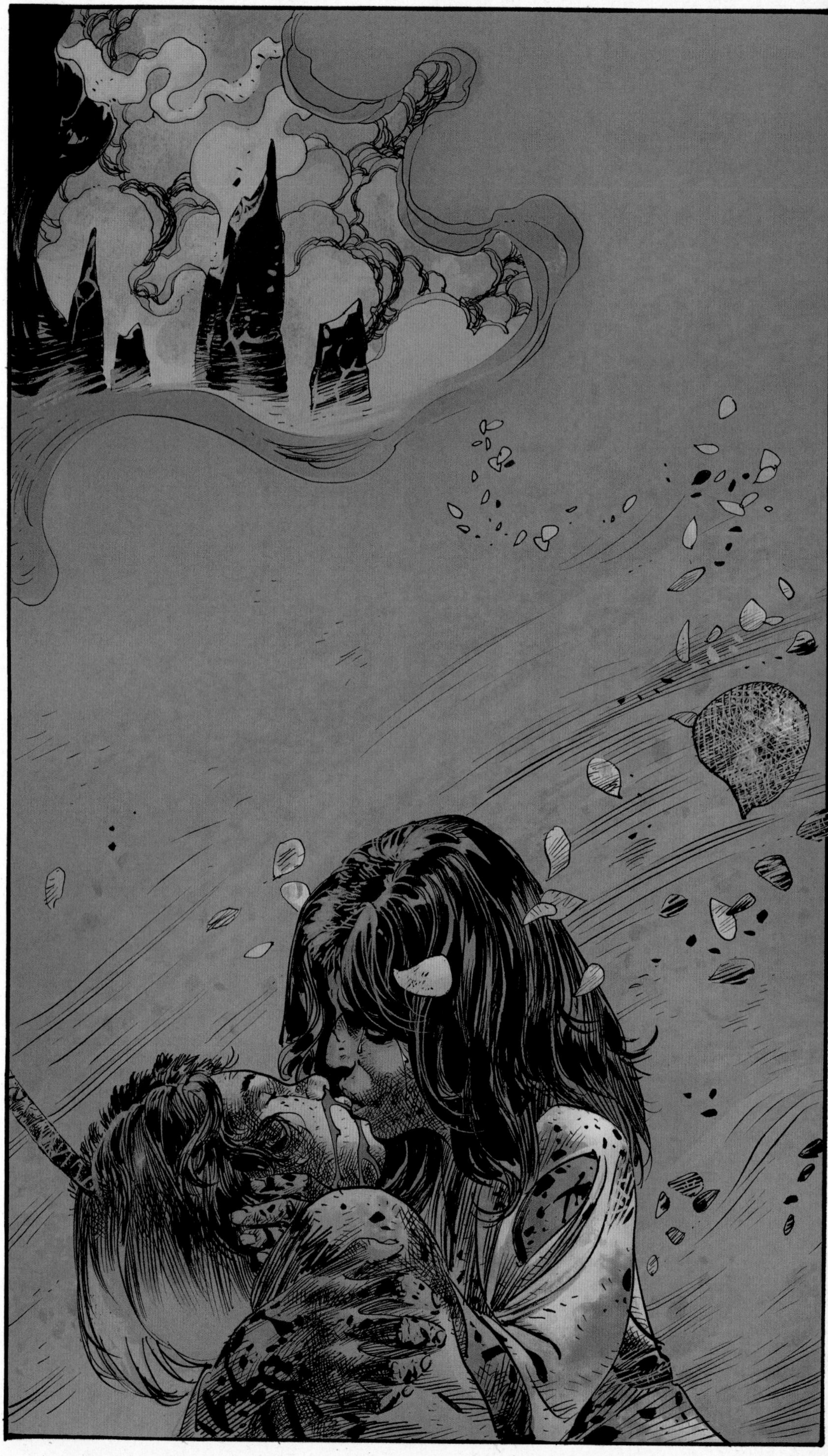

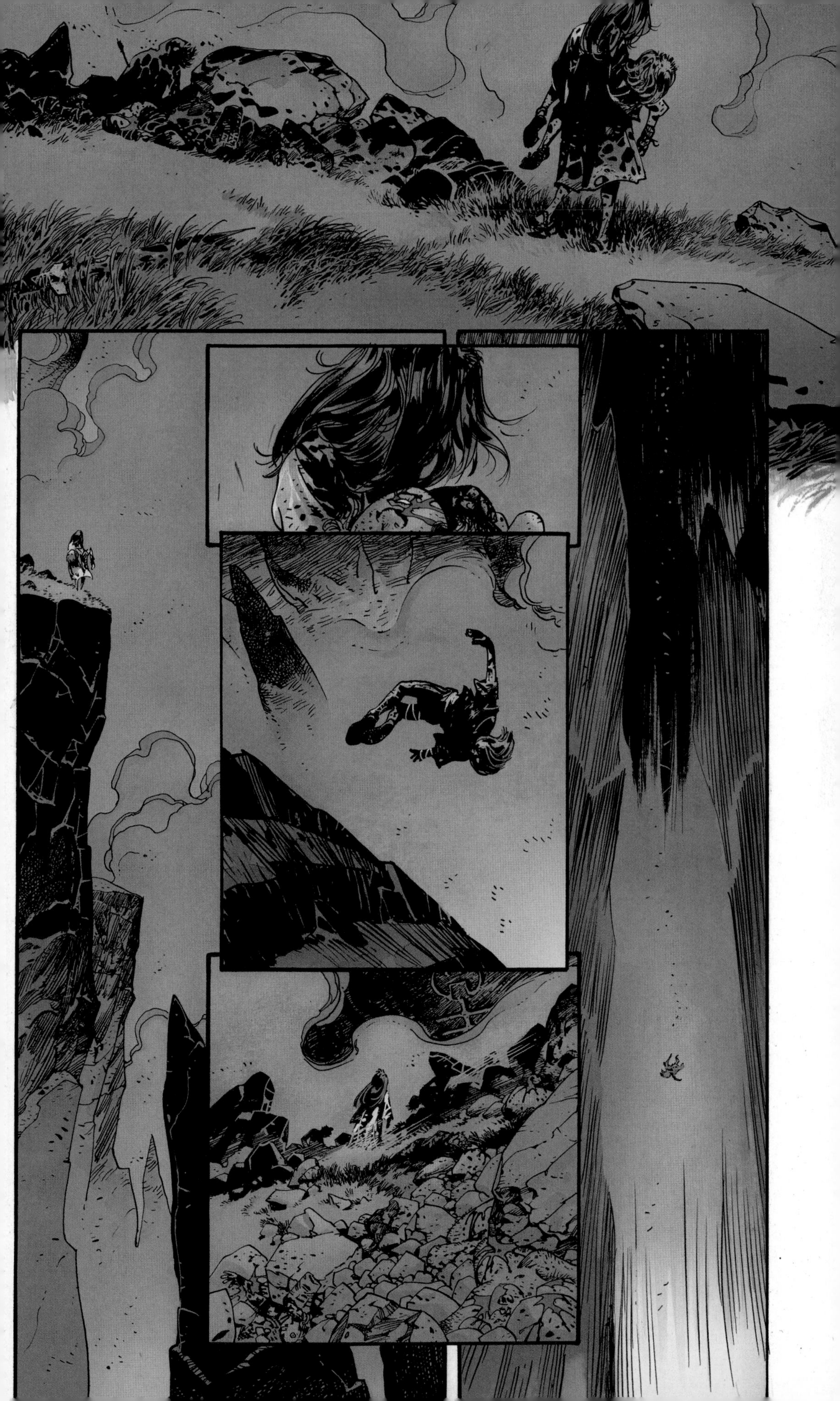

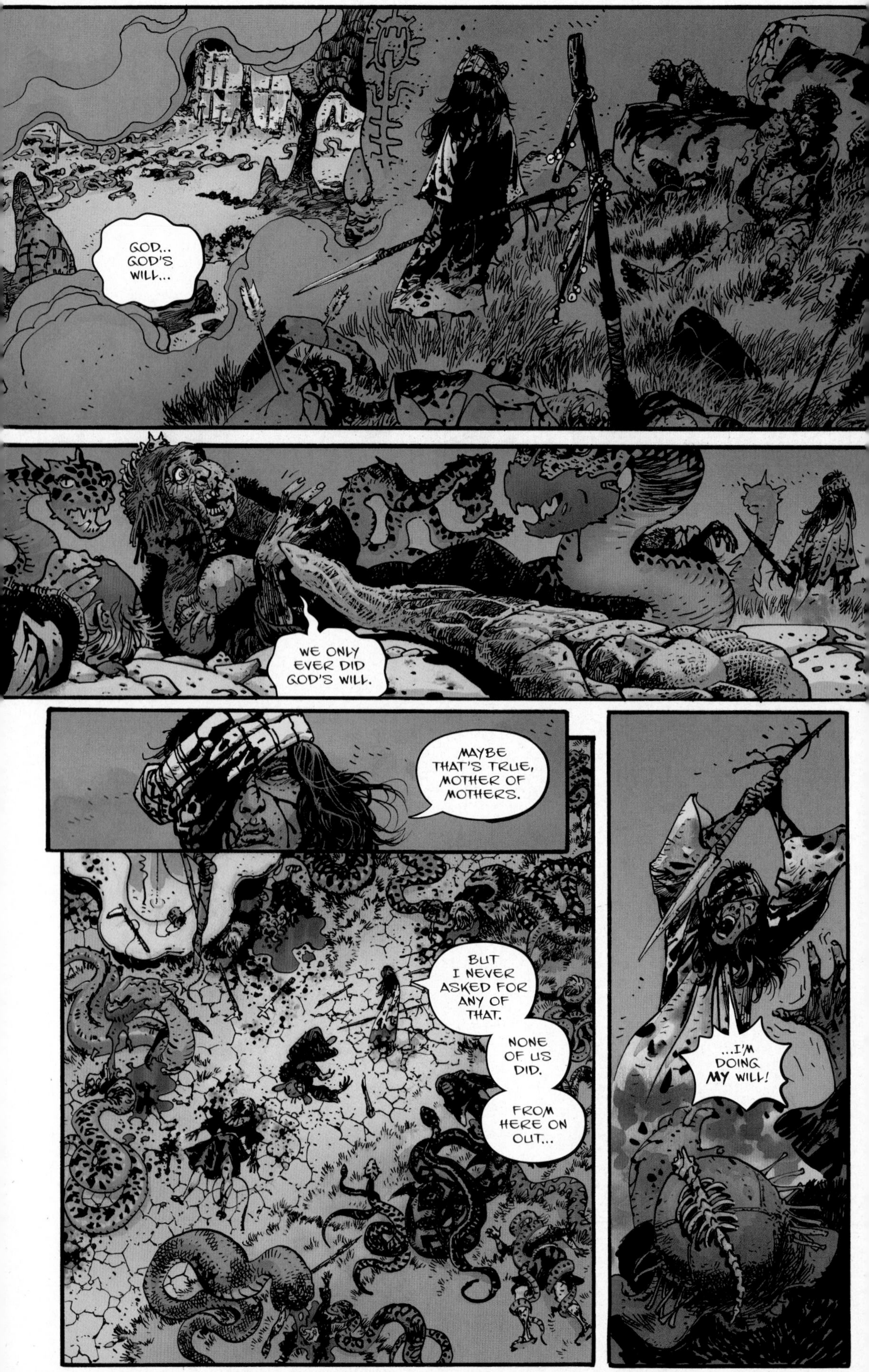
GOD... GOD'S WILL...
WE ONLY EVER DID GOD'S WILL.
MAYBE THAT'S TRUE, MOTHER OF MOTHERS.
BUT I NEVER ASKED FOR ANY OF THAT.
NONE OF US DID.
FROM HERE ON OUT...
...I'M DOING MY WILL!

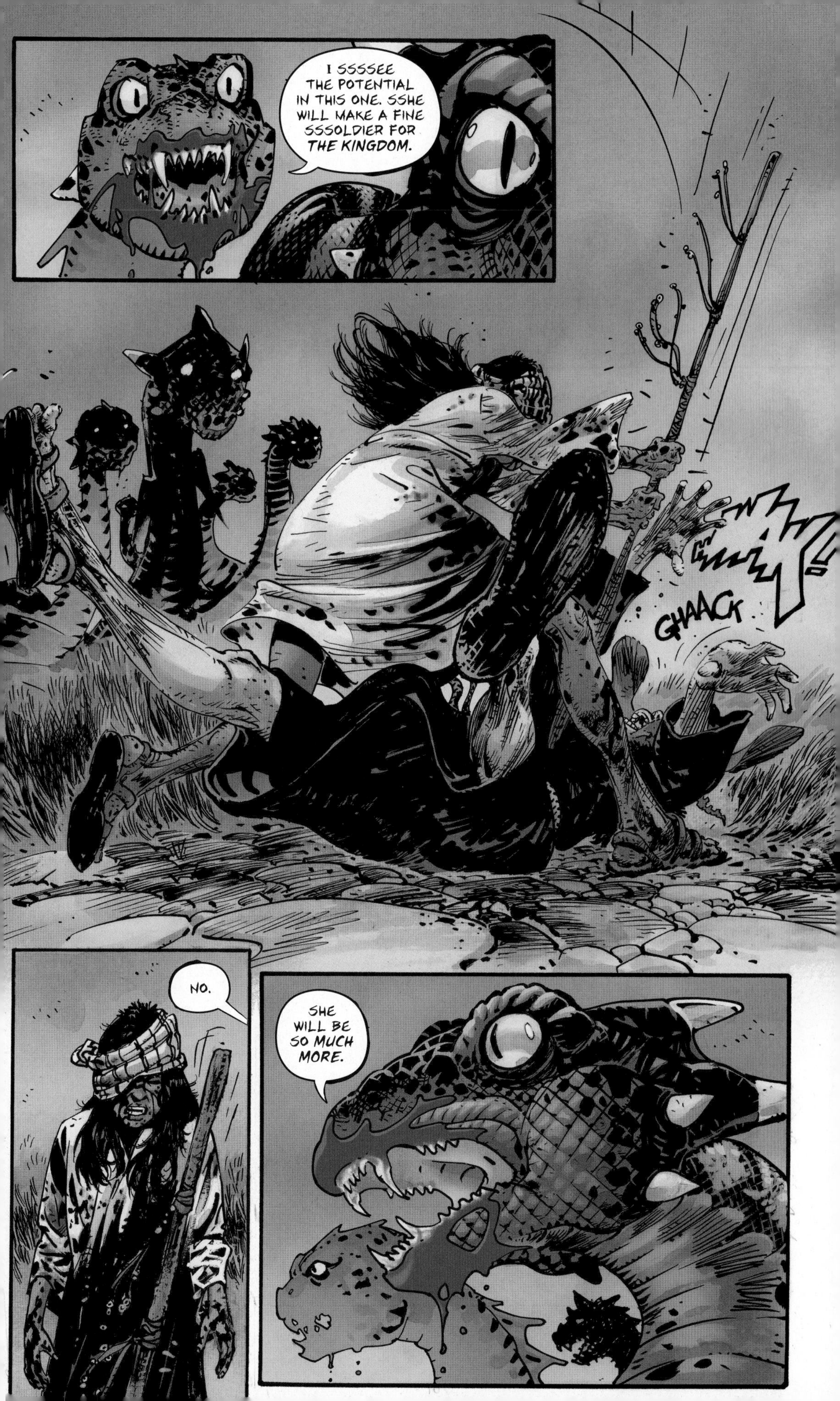

I SSSSEE THE POTENTIAL IN THIS ONE. SSHE WILL MAKE A FINE SSSOLDIER FOR THE KINGDOM.
GHAACK
NO.
SHE WILL BE SO MUCH MORE.

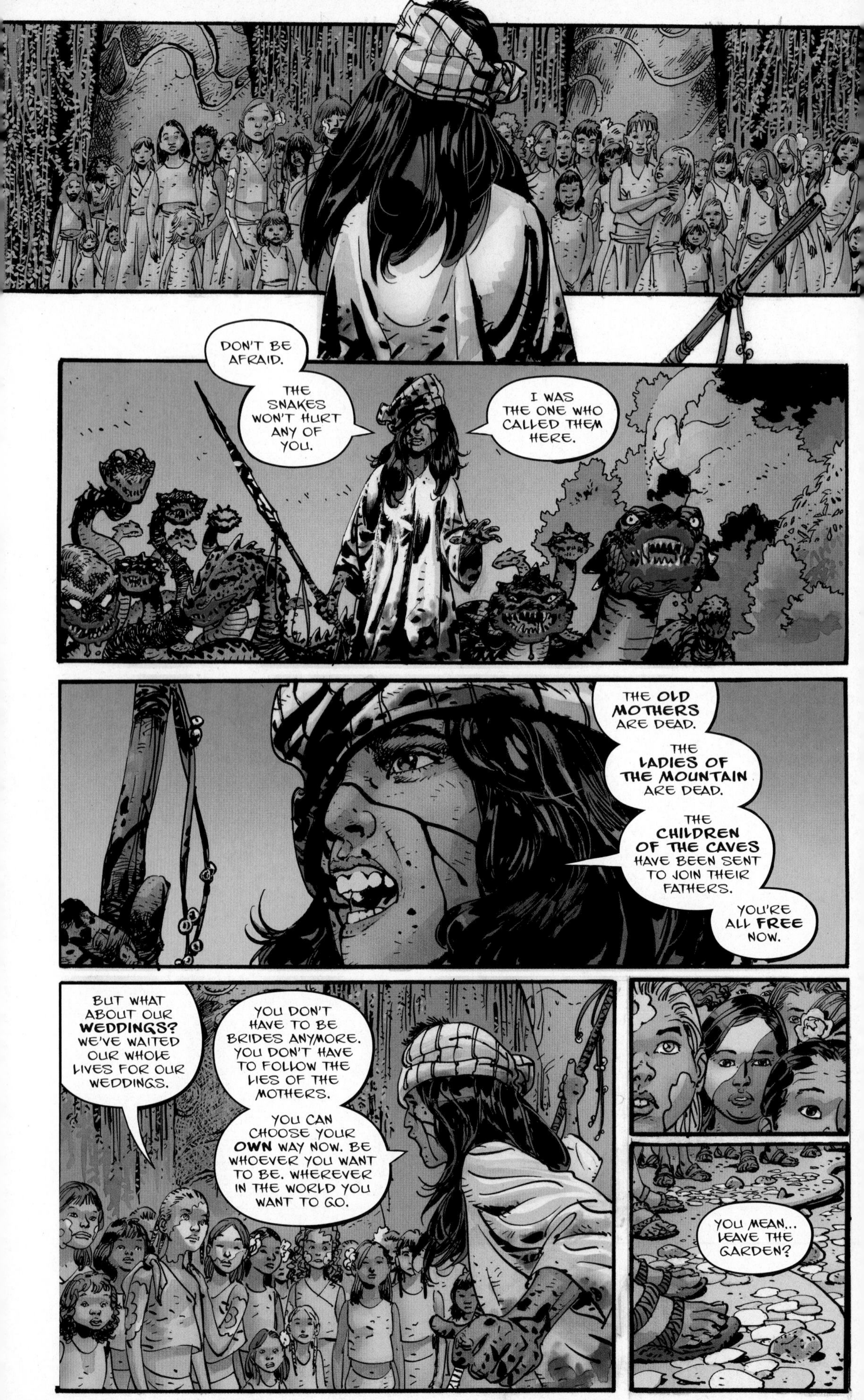
DON'T BE AFRAID.
THE SNAKES WON'T HURT ANY OF YOU.
I WAS THE ONE WHO CALLED THEM HERE.
THE OLD MOTHERS ARE DEAD.
THE LADIES OF THE MOUNTAIN ARE DEAD.
THE CHILDREN OF THE CAVES HAVE BEEN SENT TO JOIN THEIR FATHERS.
YOU'RE ALL FREE NOW.
BUT WHAT ABOUT OUR WEDDINGS? WE'VE WAITED OUR WHOLE LIVES FOR OUR WEDDINGS.
YOU DON'T HAVE TO BE BRIDES ANYMORE. YOU DON'T HAVE TO FOLLOW THE LIES OF THE MOTHERS.
YOU CAN CHOOSE YOUR OWN WAY NOW. BE WHOEVER YOU WANT TO BE. WHEREVER IN THE WORLD YOU WANT TO GO.
YOU MEAN... LEAVE THE GARDEN?

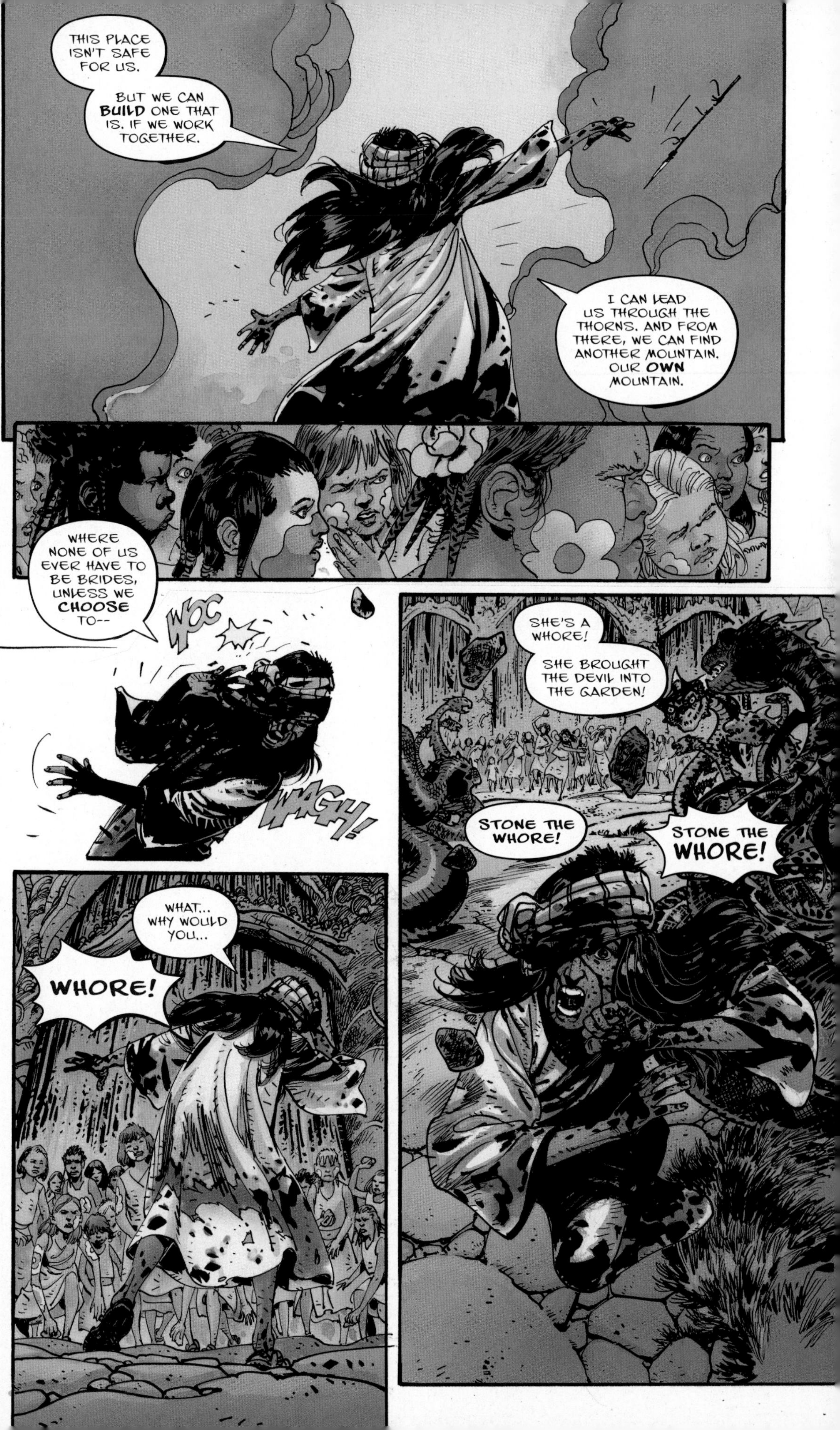
THIS PLACE ISN'T SAFE FOR US.
BUT WE CAN **BUILD** ONE THAT IS. IF WE WORK TOGETHER.
I CAN LEAD US THROUGH THE THORNS. AND FROM THERE, WE CAN FIND ANOTHER MOUNTAIN. OUR **OWN** MOUNTAIN.
WHERE NONE OF US EVER HAVE TO BE BRIDES, UNLESS WE **CHOOSE** TO--
WOC
WAGH!
SHE'S A WHORE!
SHE BROUGHT THE DEVIL INTO THE GARDEN!
STONE THE WHORE!
STONE THE **WHORE!**
WHAT... WHY WOULD YOU...
WHORE!

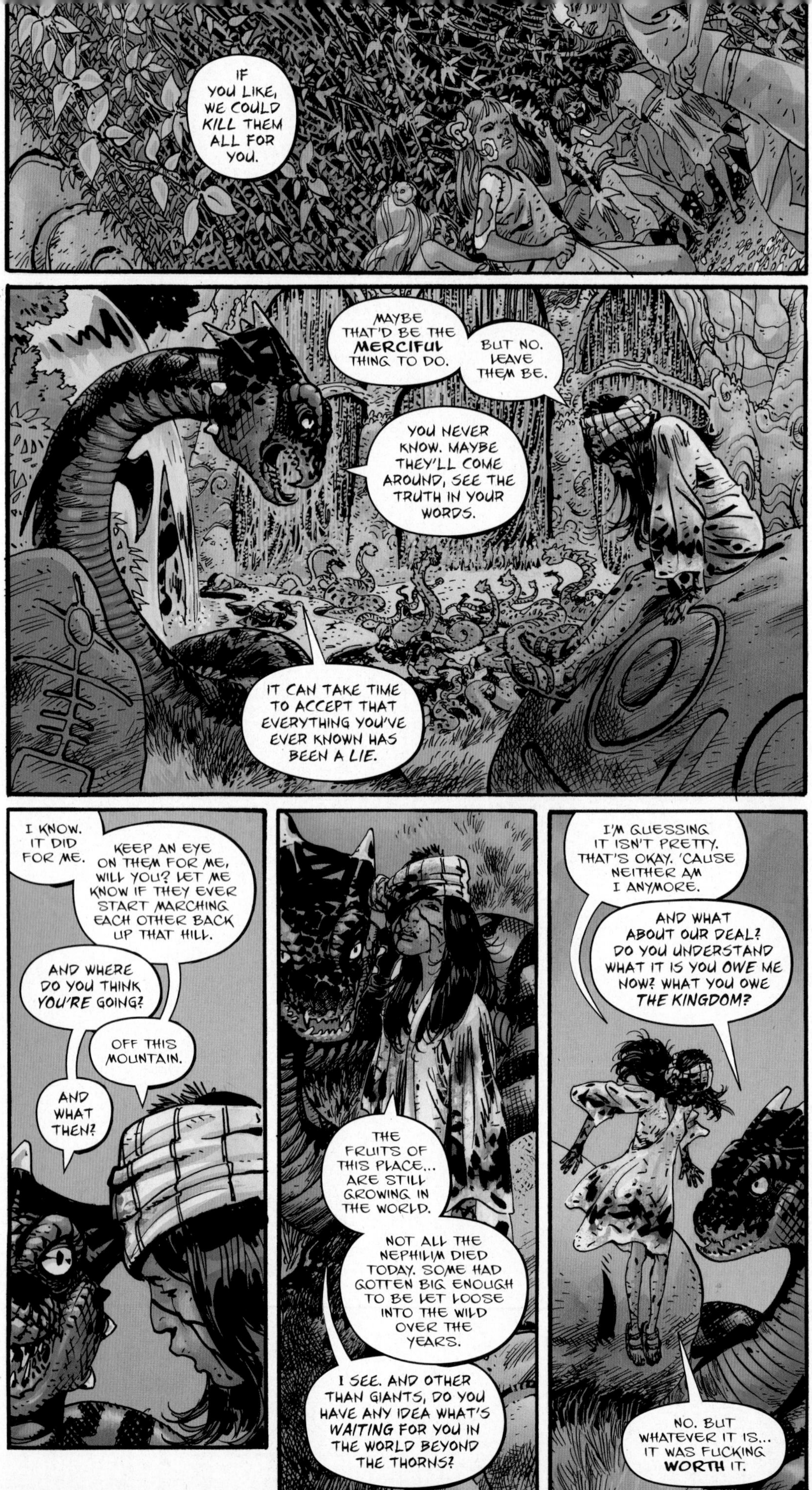
IF YOU LIKE, WE COULD KILL THEM ALL FOR YOU.
MAYBE THAT'D BE THE MERCIFUL THING TO DO.
BUT NO. LEAVE THEM BE.
YOU NEVER KNOW. MAYBE THEY'LL COME AROUND, SEE THE TRUTH IN YOUR WORDS.
IT CAN TAKE TIME TO ACCEPT THAT EVERYTHING YOU'VE EVER KNOWN HAS BEEN A LIE.
I KNOW. IT DID FOR ME.
KEEP AN EYE ON THEM FOR ME, WILL YOU? LET ME KNOW IF THEY EVER START MARCHING EACH OTHER BACK UP THAT HILL.
AND WHERE DO YOU THINK YOU'RE GOING?
OFF THIS MOUNTAIN.
AND WHAT THEN?
THE FRUITS OF THIS PLACE... ARE STILL GROWING IN THE WORLD.
NOT ALL THE NEPHILIM DIED TODAY. SOME HAD GOTTEN BIG ENOUGH TO BE LET LOOSE INTO THE WILD OVER THE YEARS.
I SEE. AND OTHER THAN GIANTS, DO YOU HAVE ANY IDEA WHAT'S WAITING FOR YOU IN THE WORLD BEYOND THE THORNS?
I'M GUESSING IT ISN'T PRETTY. THAT'S OKAY. 'CAUSE NEITHER AM I ANYMORE.
AND WHAT ABOUT OUR DEAL? DO YOU UNDERSTAND WHAT IT IS YOU OWE ME NOW? WHAT YOU OWE THE KINGDOM?
NO. BUT WHATEVER IT IS... IT WAS FUCKING WORTH IT.

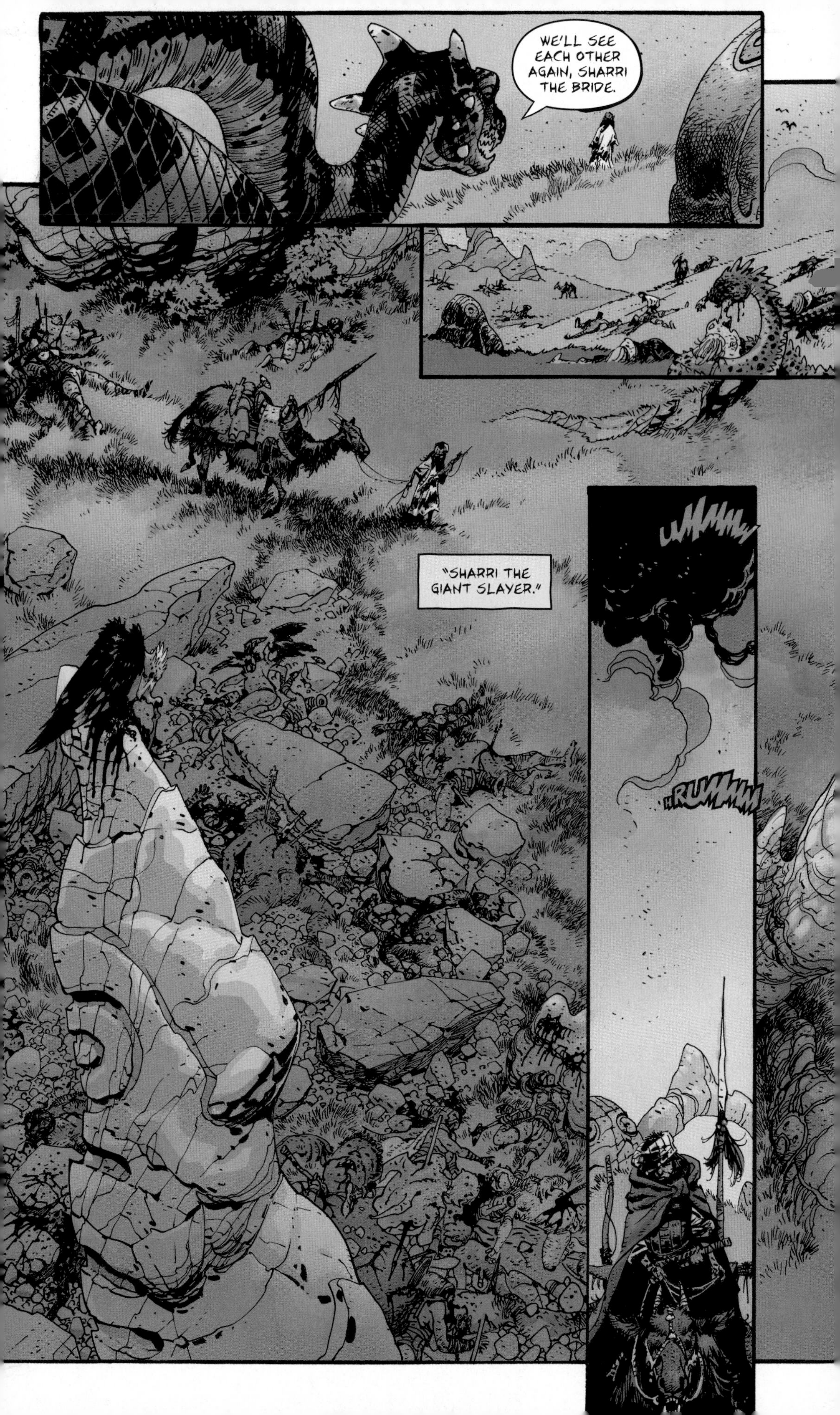
WE'LL SEE EACH OTHER AGAIN, SHARRI THE BRIDE.
"SHARRI THE GIANT SLAYER."
UMMMM
RUMMMM

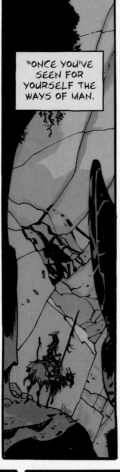

"ONCE YOU'VE SEEN FOR YOURSELF THE WAYS OF MAN.

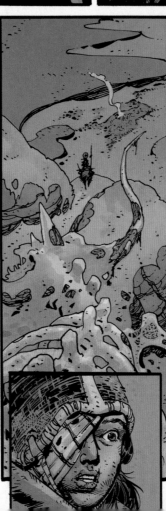

"AND THE TRUE CRIMES OF GOD."

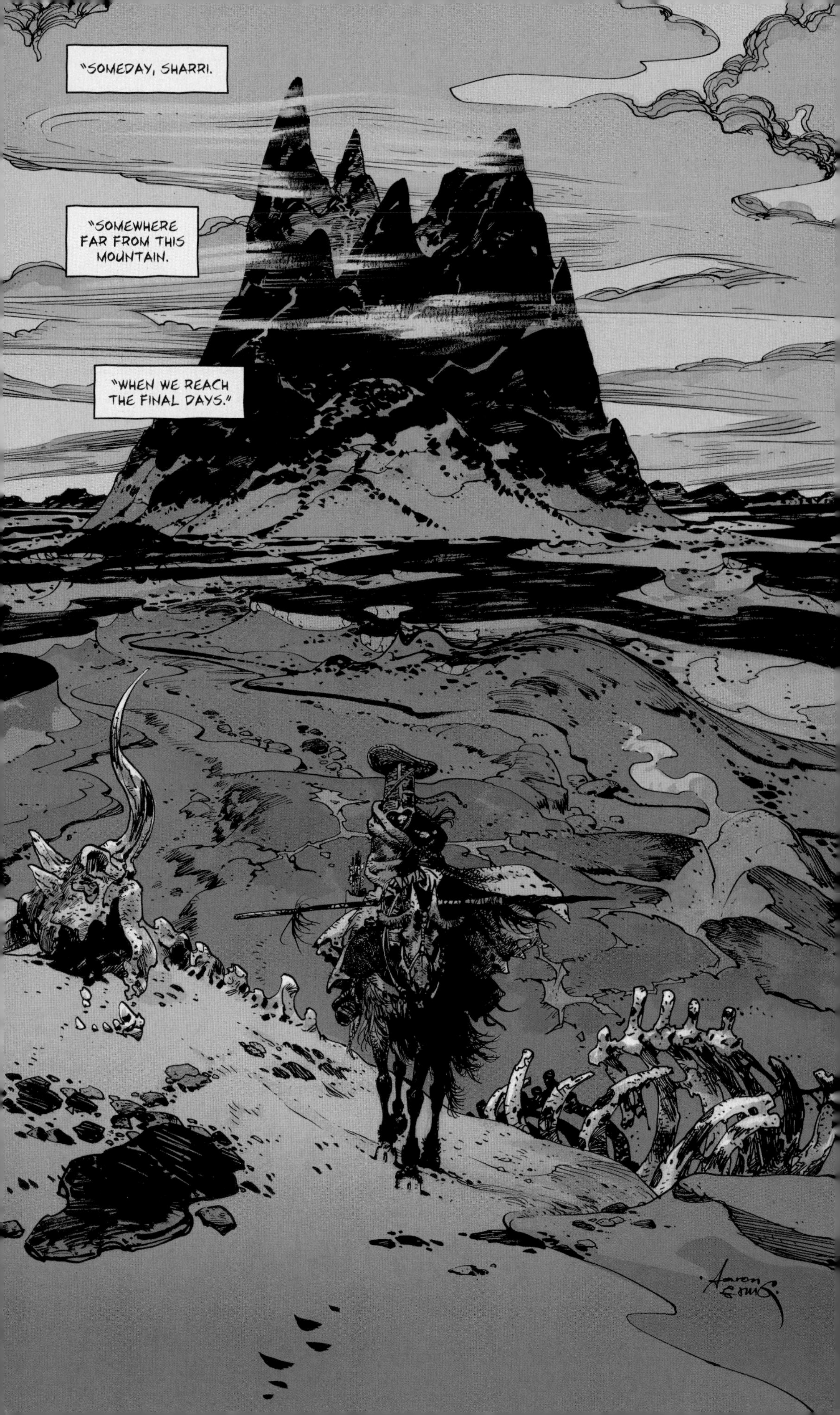
"SOMEDAY, SHARRI.
"SOMEWHERE FAR FROM THIS MOUNTAIN.
"WHEN WE REACH THE FINAL DAYS."
Aaron Gang

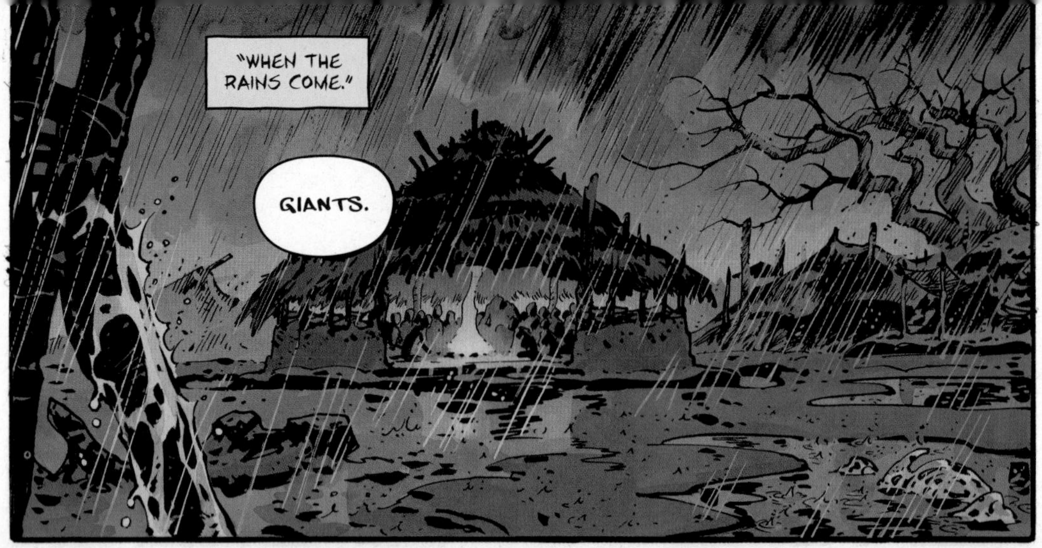
"WHEN THE RAINS COME."
GIANTS.

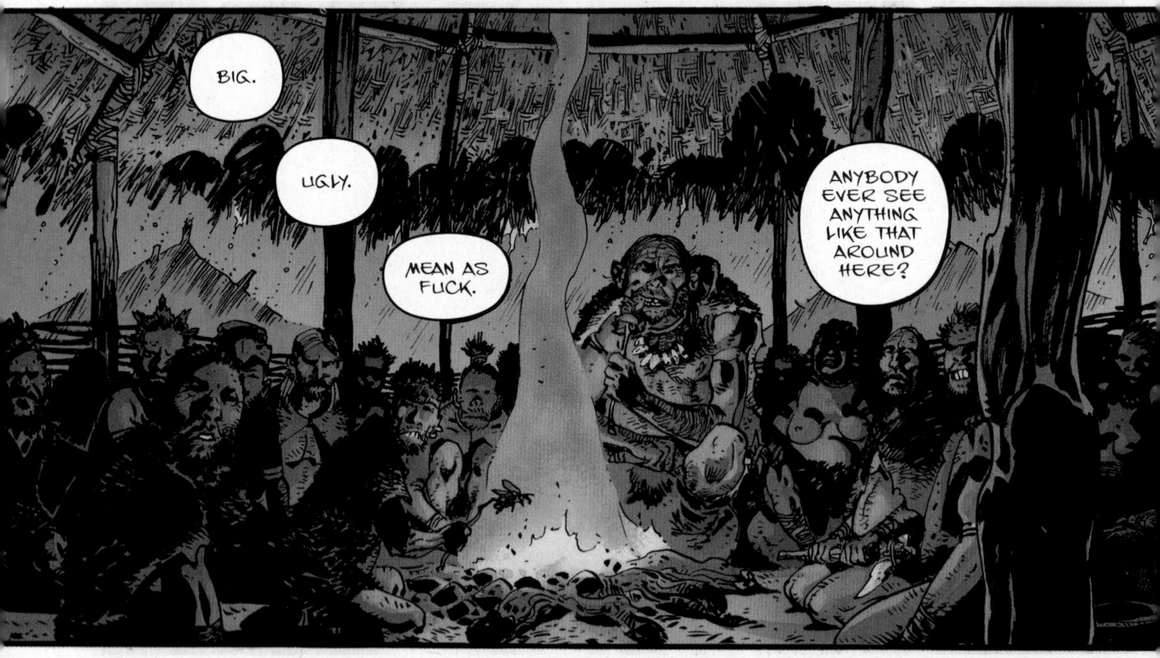
BIG.
UGLY.
MEAN AS FUCK.
ANYBODY EVER SEE ANYTHING LIKE THAT AROUND HERE?

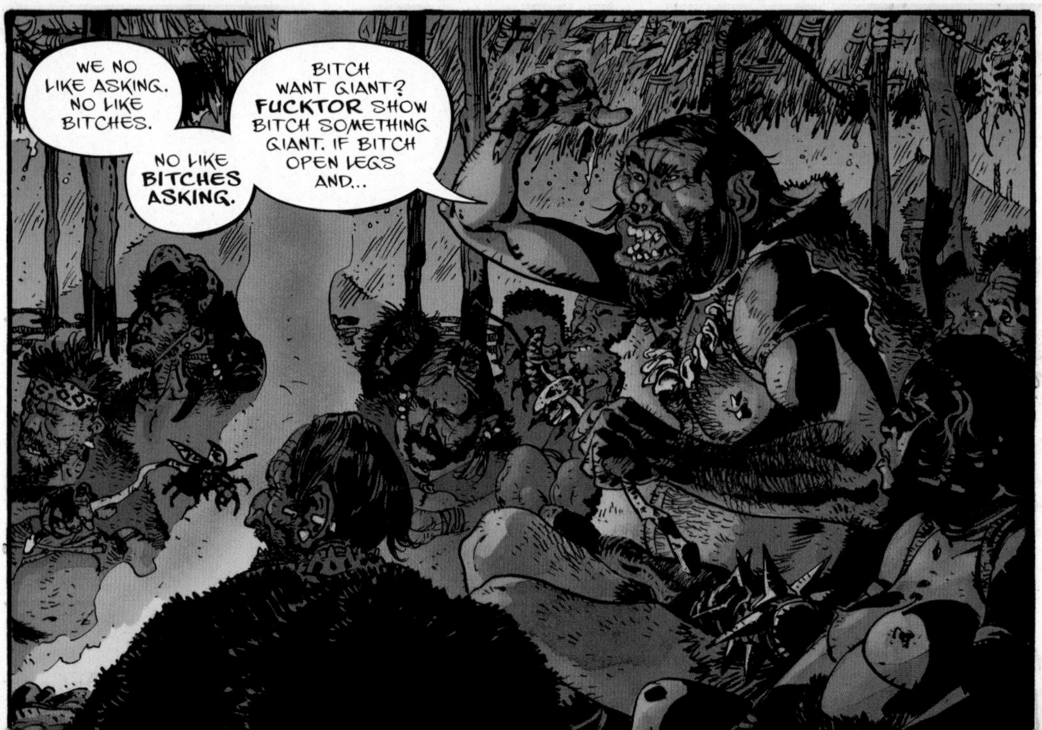
WE NO LIKE ASKING. NO LIKE BITCHES.
NO LIKE BITCHES ASKING.
BITCH WANT GIANT? FUCKTOR SHOW BITCH SOMETHING GIANT. IF BITCH OPEN LEGS AND...

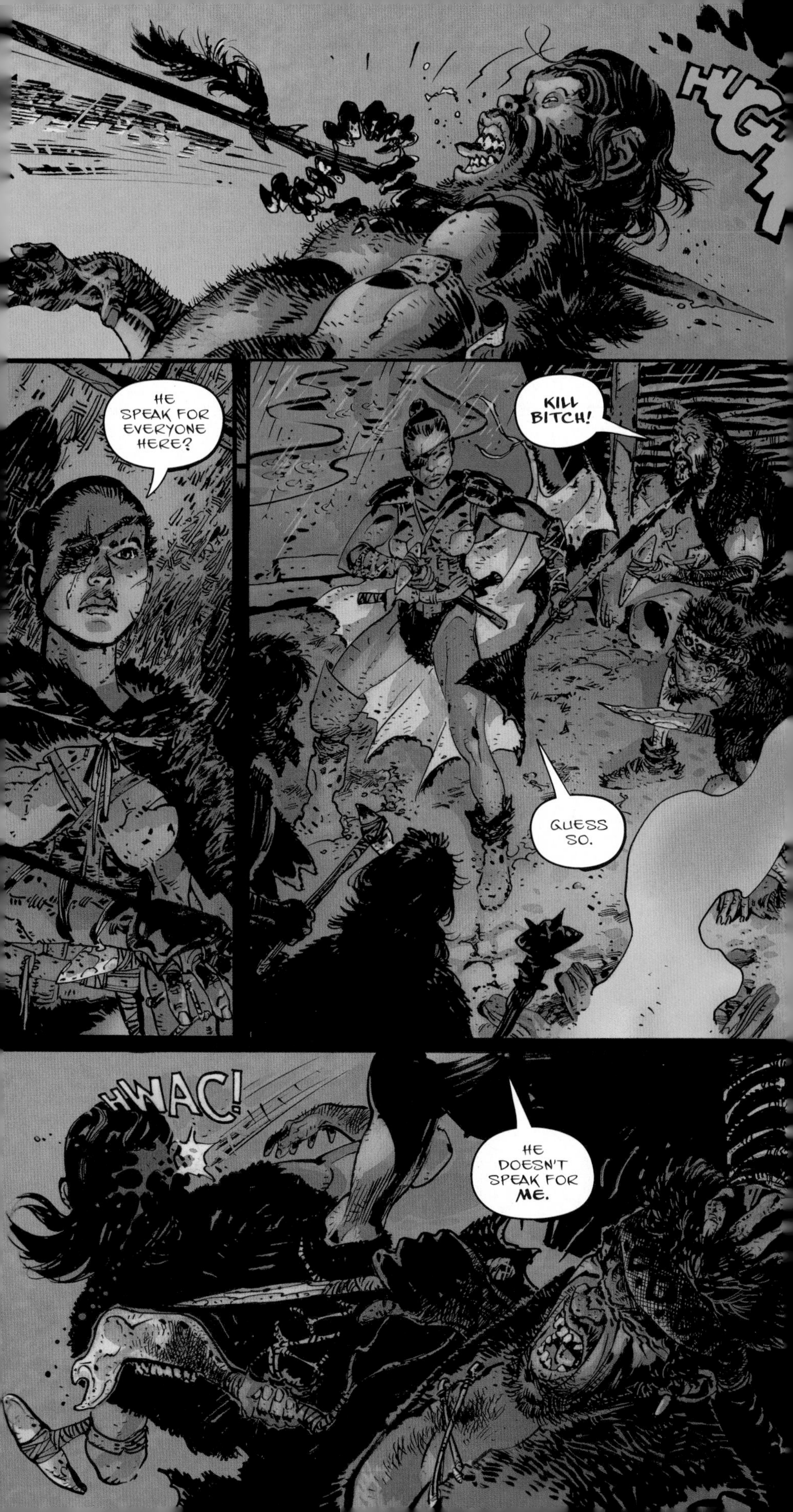
HUG
HE SPEAK FOR EVERYONE HERE?
KILL BITCH!
GUESS SO.
HWAC!
HE DOESN'T SPEAK FOR ME.

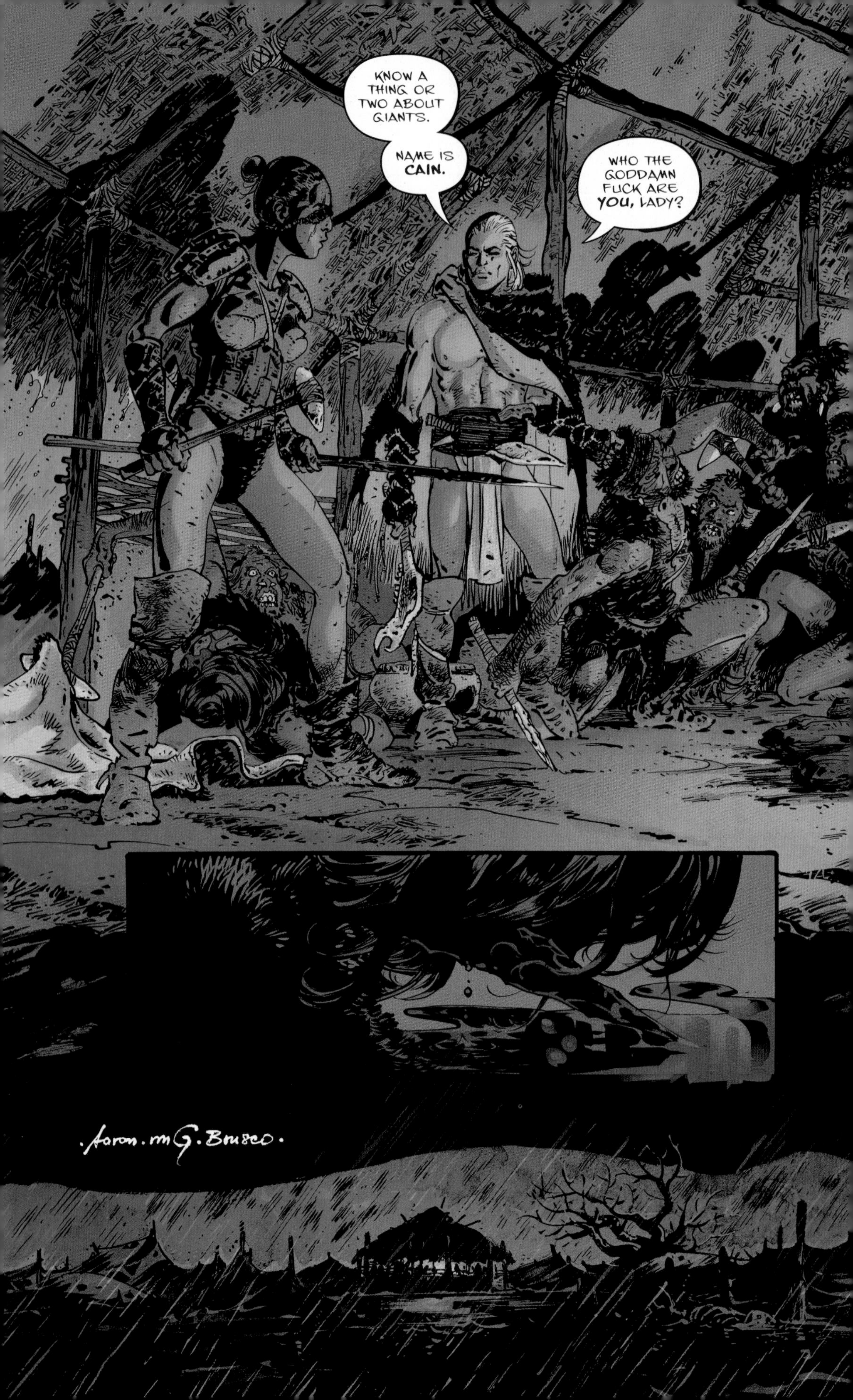
KNOW A THING OR TWO ABOUT GIANTS.
NAME IS CAIN.
WHO THE GODDAMN FUCK ARE YOU, LADY?
·Aaron·mG·Brusco·

Jason Aaron is a comic book writer best known for his work on the *New York Times*-bestselling crime series *Scalped* for Vertigo Comics and the Eisner Award-winning *Southern Bastards* from Image Comics, as well as for various projects with Marvel Comics. Aaron's work for Marvel includes the creation of the headline-grabbing female version of *Thor* and the launch of an all-new *Star Wars* series, the first issue of which sold over one million copies to become the bestselling American comic book in more than 20 years. Aaron was born in Alabama but currently resides in Kansas City.

Rajko Milosevic, known as r.m.Guéra is a Serbi... artist, living in Spain. He reached early fame a... academic awards during the 80s in former Yugoslav... After moving to Barcelona, and after a decade of worki... in publicity and animation through works for museu... and theaters, he published his first comic albums in Fran... through publishers Glénat and Delcourt. His worldwi... breakthrough came with the crime series *Scalped,* al... written by Jason Aaron and published by Vertigo, D... Comics, which garnered worldwide critical acclaim.

Guéra has worked with Quentin Tarantino on a com... book version of *Django Unchained.* He continues to publi... in France for Jour J, in the UK for *Judge Dredd,* as we... as for all US mainstream publishers including Marvel, D... and Dark Horse on many one-shots, promotional poste... and covers.

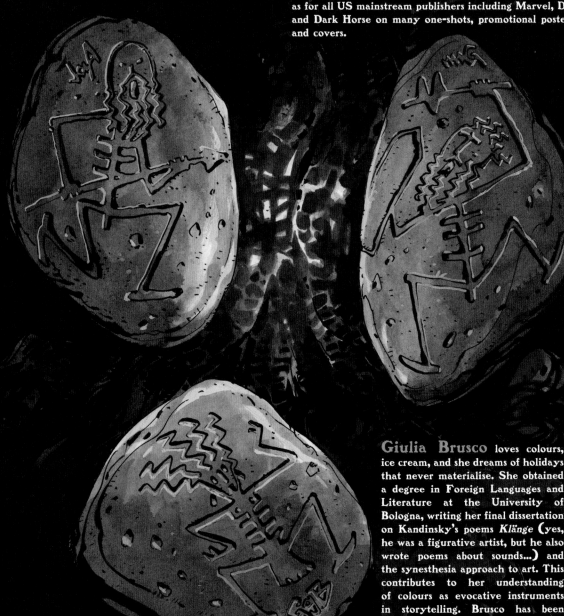

Giulia Brusco loves colours, ice cream, and she dreams of holidays that never materialise. She obtained a degree in Foreign Languages and Literature at the University of Bologna, writing her final dissertation on Kandinsky's poems *Klänge* (yes, he was a figurative artist, but he also wrote poems about sounds...) and the synesthesia approach to art. This contributes to her understanding of colours as evocative instruments in storytelling. Brusco has been colouring comic books since 2001, working on numerous titles and for various companies. She's best known for her years-long collaboration with r.m.Guéra and for her heavy Italian accent while speaking English despite 23 years of life in London, England.

# Cover + sketch Gallery

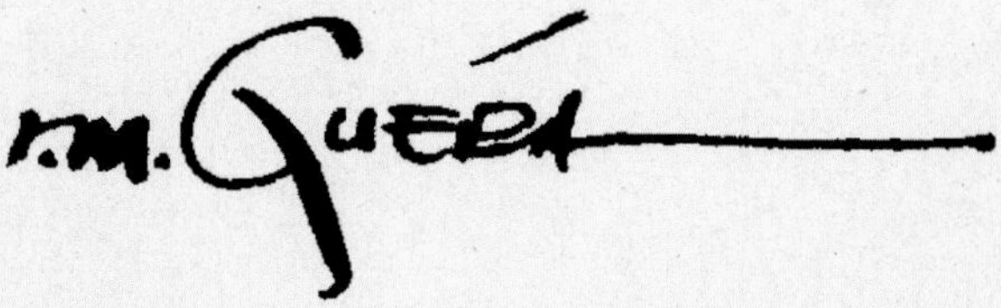

R.M. GUÉRA

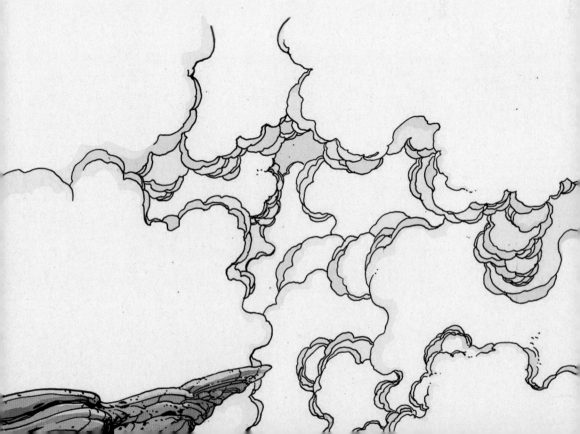

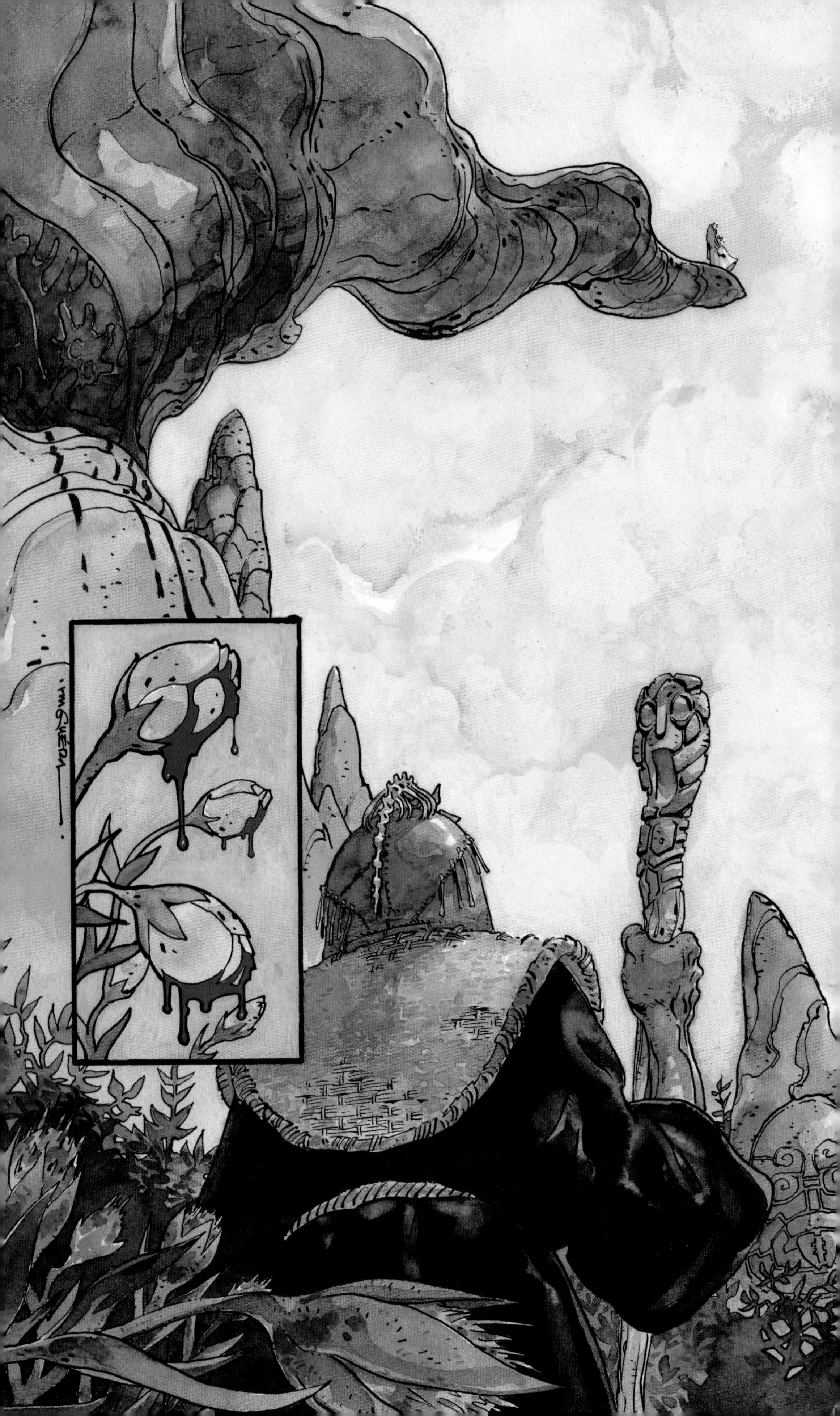

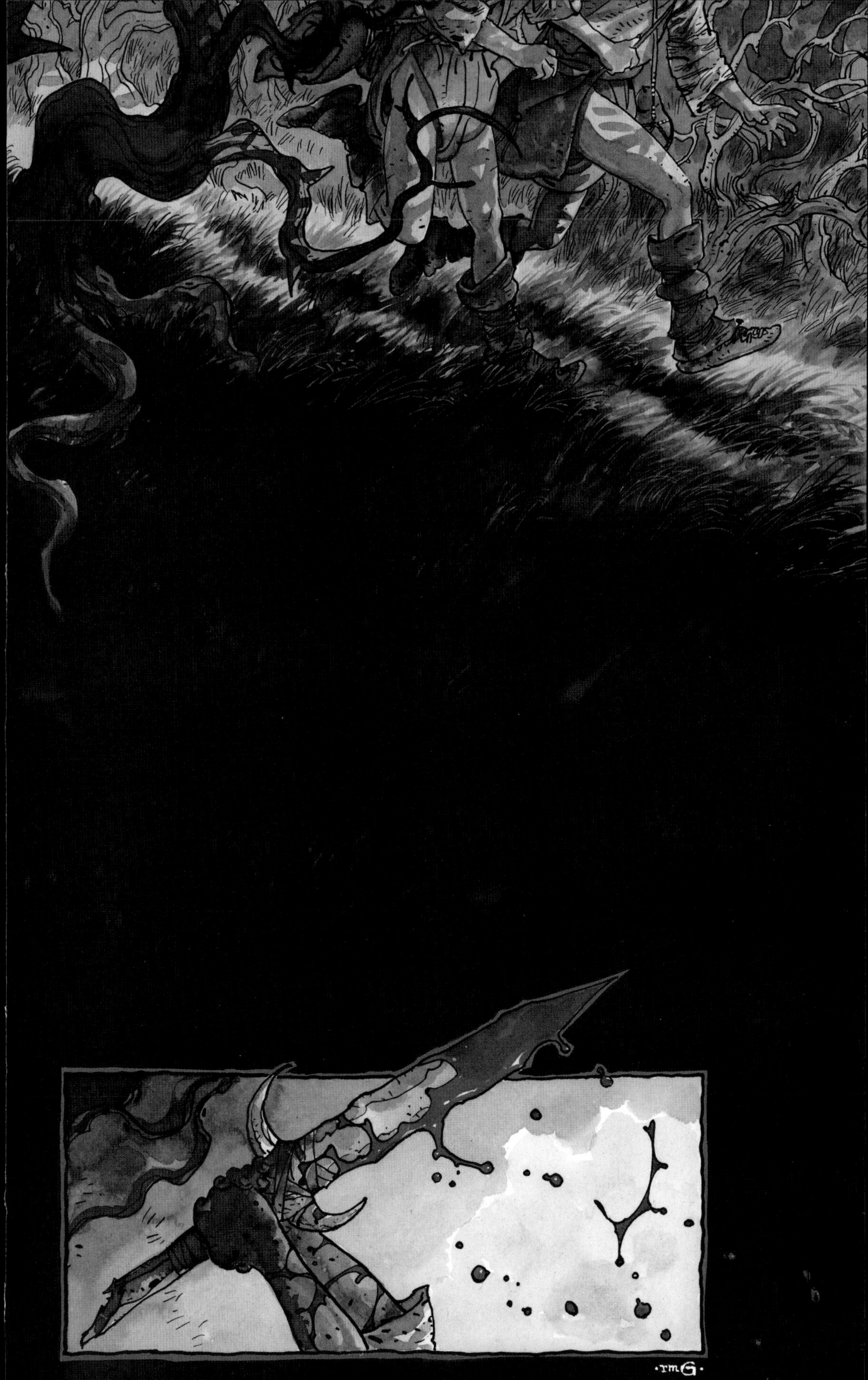

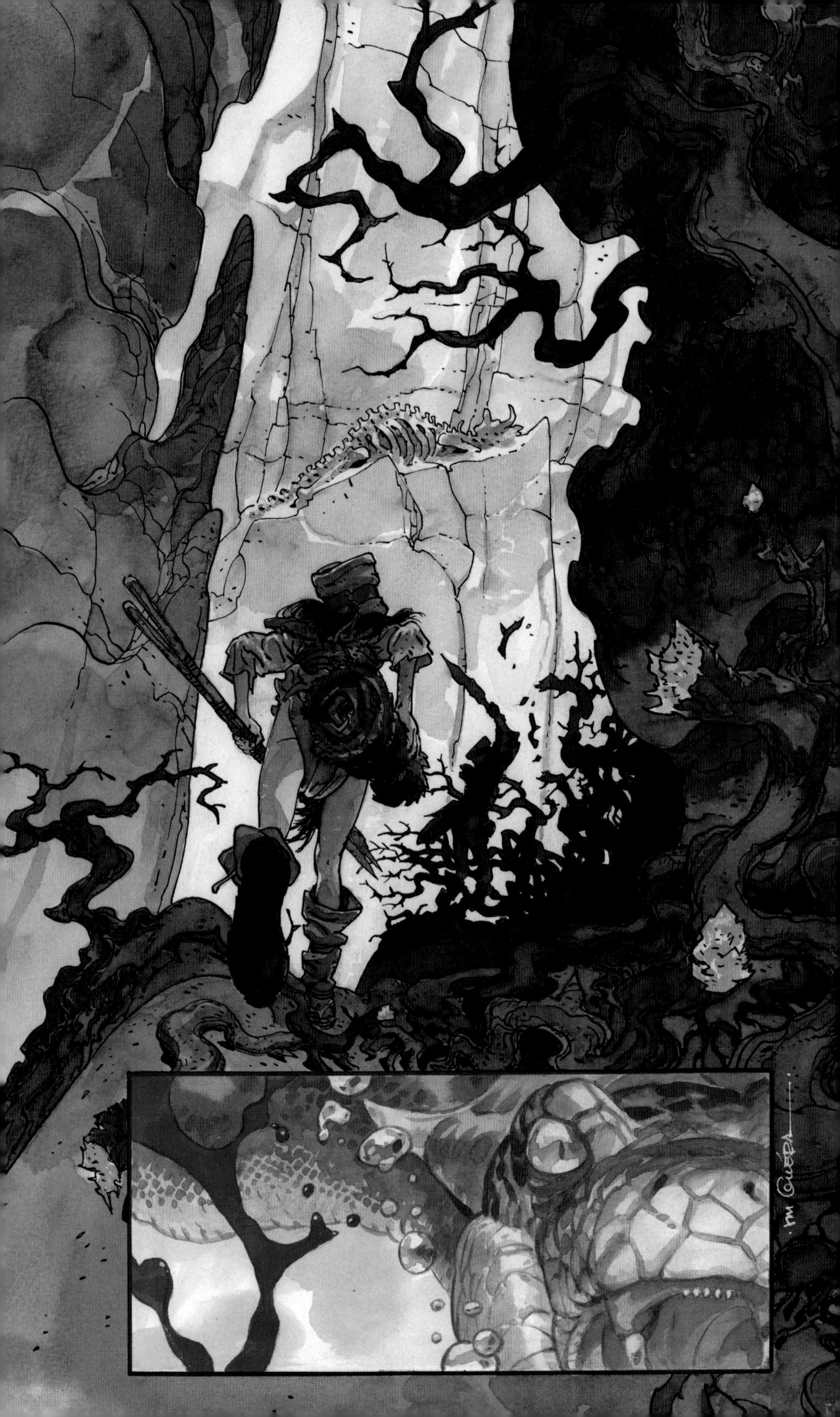

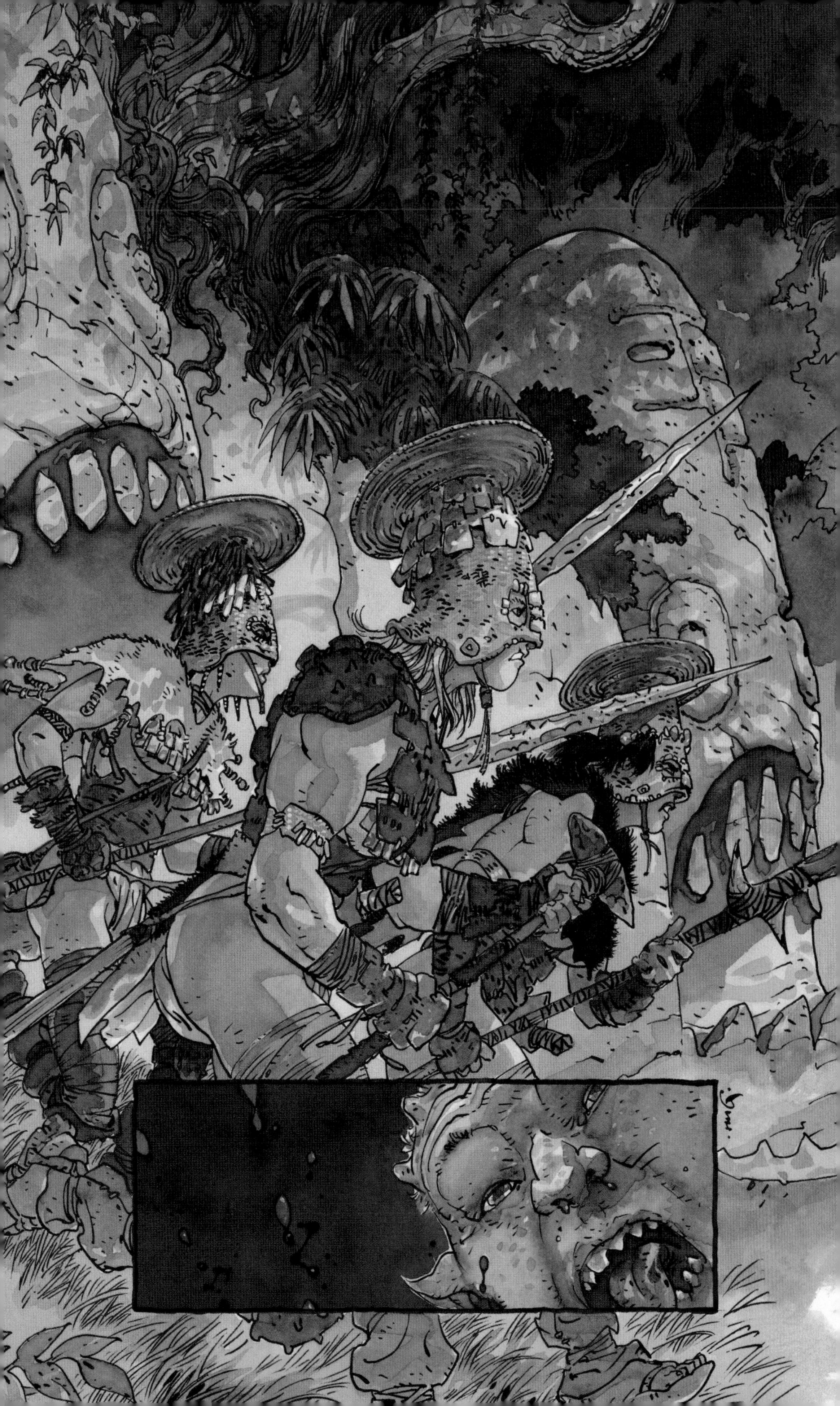

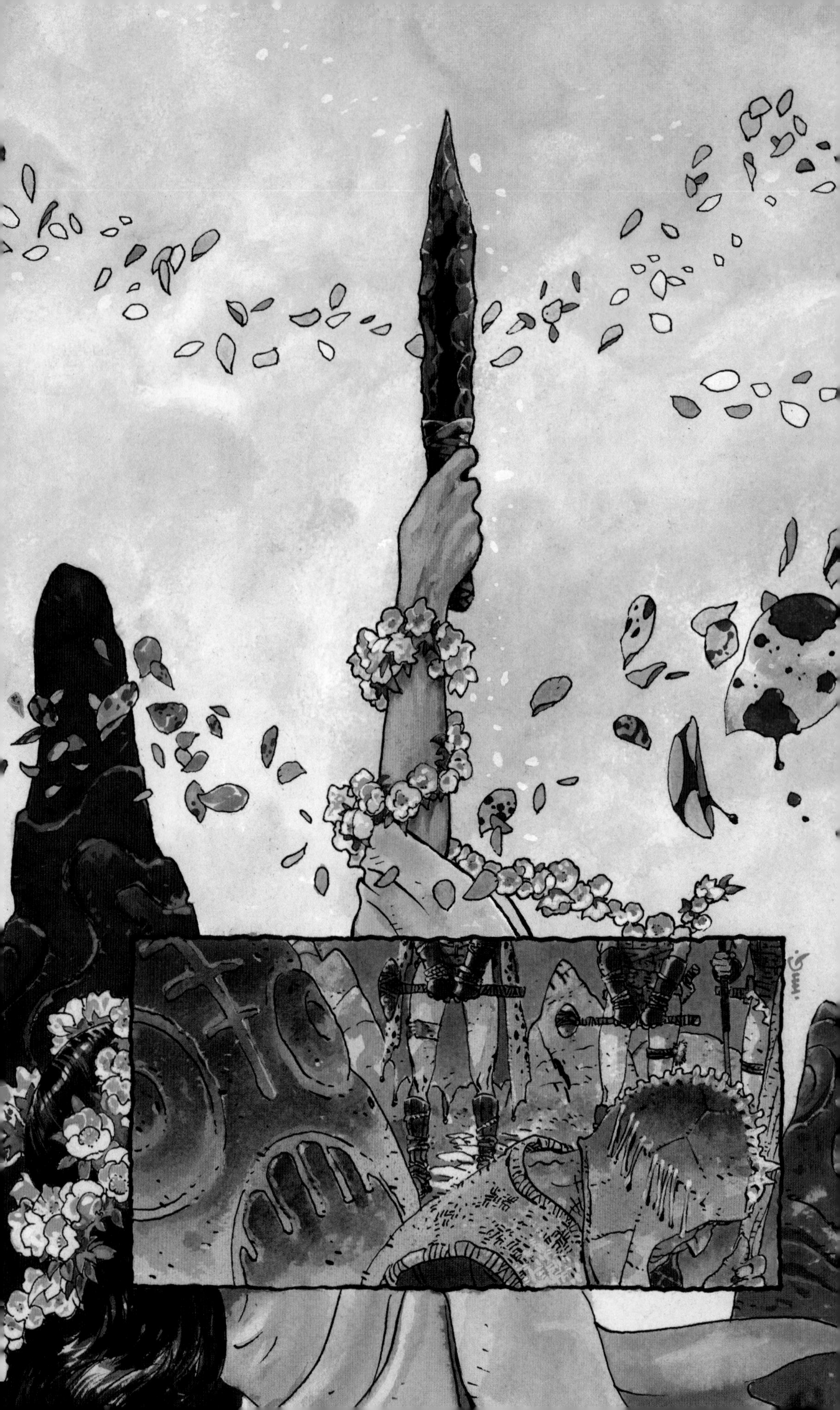

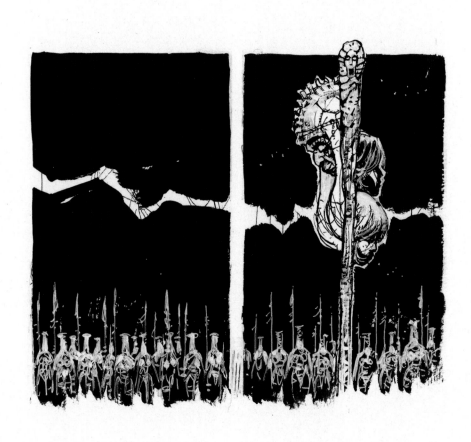

# THE GODDAMNED

## *will return*

Jason Aaron

r.m.Guéra

Giulia Brusco

*I* WILL CAUSE IT TO RAIN UPON THE EARTH FORTY DAYS AND FORTY NIGHTS; AND EVERY LIVING SUBSTANCE THAT I HAVE MADE WILL I DESTROY FROM OFF THE FACE OF THE EARTH.

GENESIS 7:4